Culture, Mind, and Society

Series Editor
Yehuda C. Goodman
Department of Sociology and Anthropology
Hebrew University of Jerusalem
Jerusalem, Israel

The Society for Psychological Anthropology—a section of the American Anthropology Association—and Palgrave Macmillan are dedicated to publishing innovative research that illuminates the workings of the human mind within the social, cultural, and political contexts that shape thought, emotion, and experience. As anthropologists seek to bridge gaps between ideation and emotion or agency and structure and as psychologists, psychiatrists, and medical anthropologists search for ways to engage with cultural meaning and difference, this interdisciplinary terrain is more active than ever.

More information about this series at
http://www.palgrave.com/gp/series/14947

Gillian Gillison

She Speaks Her Anger: Myths and Conversations of Gimi Women

A Psychological Ethnography in the Eastern Highlands of Papua New Guinea

palgrave
macmillan

Gillian Gillison
University of Toronto
Toronto, Canada

Culture, Mind, and Society
ISBN 978-3-030-49351-6 ISBN 978-3-030-49352-3 (eBook)
https://doi.org/10.1007/978-3-030-49352-3

Cover illustration: Tattooing a "beard" on a bride © Gillian Gillison

This Palgrave Macmillan imprint is published by the registered company Springer Nature Switzerland AG.
The registered company address is: Gewerbestrasse 11, 6330 Cham, Switzerland

Editor's Preface

"Grief closed her lips, held back the words that stormed to speak her anger; and there were no tears … only her fury with all her being speeded toward revenge." The book's title is taken from Ovid's *The Metamorphoses* when Procne discovers that her husband raped her younger sister Philomela and then cut out Philomela's tongue so she could never reveal the crime. In scenes that parallel almost exactly Gimi women's *Myth of the Torrent Lark,* Ovid's heroine murders her son and presents him to her husband as a meal of revenge served piping hot before changing into a bird and flying into the forest. Gillian Gillison explores women's anger in a society dominated overwhelmingly by men in ways rarely broached in ethnographies of small scale, kinship-based societies in once-remote parts of the world or of other male-dominated societies including our own.

Gillison discovers that Gimi women and men, who traditionally resided in separate houses even after marriage, possess separate "secret" bodies of myths and rites. By placing them in juxtaposition, she shows that the sexes' distinct usages, enacted at different times and places, address one another in a cycle of accusation over which sex is to blame for the origin of death and the anatomical distinctions between them. Taking her cue from Gimi women, Gillison turns to Sigmund Freud's much-maligned *Totem and Taboo* as a lens for interpreting the long-distance Gimi argument. She thus expands Freud's just-so story about the murder of the father by introducing the mother and rebellious daughters as the sons' co-conspirators in the primal crime. If the 'band of brothers' were enraged by a father who denied them access to their sisters, Gimi women's myths proclaim, then the sisters whom the father raped in perpetuity were just as angry or even angrier and eager to collaborate with their brothers or act alone to kill the primal father.

The set of shared premises that underlies Gimi women's and men's "secret" disputes also serves as charter for the rites of passage and exchange that the sexes perform publicly and together. Gillison argues that, from the perspectives of Gimi women, the way men's social arrangements take account of women's angry protests looks like a strategy to subvert them through public performance. In the context of their contested mythic underpinnings, the rituals Gimi men orchestrate function as a program to 'undo' motherhood and confiscate children at puberty.

Gillison's portraits of Gimi women go beyond the stereotypes in men's and women's myths, rituals and theatrical performances. Her presentation of women's conversations and revelations gives voice to unique individuals as they experience and reflect upon their own lives and relationships. Chapter 3 is devoted to one woman's account of her difficult marriage and childhood. Gillison's insistence that Gimi women be recognized as *individuals* flies in face of anthropological convention that dismisses 'the individual' as a relic of the European Enlightenment. Her study among Gimi women upholds the assumption that self-other differentiation and self-awareness are essential psychological conditions in any human society.

Jerusalem, Israel

Yehuda C. Goodman

Acknowledgments

I have tried to honour and faithfully represent the lives and voices of the Gimi women and men who appear in the book and especially those who guided me with patience and humour through the intricacies of myths and rituals. Their knowledge and depth of insight into Gimi culture and lifeways far exceed what I have been able to understand and convey here.

To Patrice Bidou, my partner and Amazonian ethnographer, Professor Robert A. Paul, Professor Jadran Mimica, and Sylvia Lassam, the Rolph-Bell Archivist, Trinity College in the University of Toronto, I express deepest gratitude for precious support of many kinds and at difficult times which have sustained me during the long haul of producing the book. Without them, the book would never have been completed.

I want to express appreciation to Dr. Yehuda C. Goodman, Series Editor of Culture, Mind, and Society for help during production of the book. And I thank Christian J. Siroyt whose expertise in all aspects of book production has been invaluable.

Contents

List of Figures

1

Introduction

Soon after first contact in the mid-twentieth century, peoples of the Papua New Guinea Highlands became famous for extremes of sexual antagonism, male dominance and violence against women.[1] Polarity of the sexes, based upon horror of menstrual blood, determined the spheres and activities of everyday life and split the universe into categories and qualities of high and low, hard and soft, dry and wet, hot and cold, light and dark, wild and domestic, each one desired or despised according to its association with one sex or the other (e.g., Meggitt 1964). Women and men slept in separate houses even after marriage which meant that boys resided with their mothers nearly until adolescence and, together with their sisters, listened to mothers' stories. Girls, on the other hand, rarely experienced early, close or prolonged intimacy with their fathers.

Starting in 1973 over a span of more than a decade, I did fieldwork as an anthropologist in the Eastern Highlands of Papua New Guinea among one group of Gimi women and girls (Gillison 1993).[2] Men's "secret" flute cults, based on the belief that superiority over women lay in possession of sacred bamboo instruments, called "birds" and played in pairs, existed throughout the Eastern Highlands (e.g., Read 1952, 1965; Newman 1964, 1965; Salisbury 1965). Highlands men forbid women to see the flutes on pain of death (a threat which Australian patrol reports confirm was sometimes carried out) and hid them in the rafters of their communal men's houses. Yet men's own myths declare that men stole the flutes

G. Gillison, *She Speaks Her Anger: Myths and Conversations of Gimi Women*, Culture, Mind, and Society, https://doi.org/10.1007/978-3-030-49352-3_1

from the First Woman or Two Women who invented them in the primordial past. If nowadays even one woman were to lay eyes on the flutes and live to tell other women what she saw, men's myths say, women would join forces and repossess what originally belonged only to them, leaving men bereft and as impotent as children.

Men revealed the sacred flutes to adolescent boys during rites of initiation. Over their mothers' fierce objections—a ritually-mandated and often genuinely felt display of fury and resistance—the men forcibly removed the boys from their mothers' houses and secluded them for weeks inside communal men's houses where they underwent a ritual gestation to be reborn as young men. Near the end of their seclusion, Gimi men escorted the boys to an icy stream inside the forest and subjected them to "secret" ordeals of induced vomiting and nose-bleeding to purge them of "mother's milk and blood" which accumulated inside them from the moment they were born (cf. Newman and Boyd 1982; Gillison 1987). After their initiation, boys slept in men's houses and were forbidden to visit their mothers' houses or to linger in female company. The men imposed a myriad of food and other taboos upon symbolically female items and qualities in the domestic environment and surrounding rainforest which conveyed to initiates the idea that not only one's own mother but also the female sex itself ought to be purged and deleted.

After several years in the field, I discovered that Gimi women possessed myths, rites and songs of their own that protested men's vilification, contradicted their Flute myth about the tyrannical First Woman and even addressed women's complicity in their own subordination. Gimi women's myths provide 'back stories' for the whole gamut of life-crisis rites and serve as foundation for a female corpus that includes quasi-secret spells for nearly every domestic task and a repertoire of ritual theatre (Gillison 1983b). Given men's overwhelming dominance and the harsh realities of Gimi women's everyday lives, it did not occur to me for years that women's myths and rites, which can be 'read' as protest and running commentary on men's supposedly secret Flute myths and initiation rites, might also be their source and inspiration, paradoxically corroborating men's myth of female priority. The sexes' adversarial practices are carried out at different times and in separate houses making it difficult to ascertain the direction of influence or 'who spoke first.' What is more, the sexes' long-distance clandestine debate is played out and decided in public rites of passage and exchange in which women and men both participate.

What gradually became apparent from considering all the data, getting lost in it and beginning again countless times, is that Gimi women consistently make explicit what men obscure, euphemize or omit altogether. Looked at together, women's myths and rites of initiation broaden the context of men's usages, give them nuance and deeper meaning. And there is the obvious fact that now (in the ethnographic present of 35 years ago) and in the past, young children lived exclusively with their mothers, slept in their houses and, until the *Pax Australiana* of the early 1960's, shared their cannibal meals (Gillison 1983a). Mothers' disproportionate influence on children of both sexes makes it probable that women's traditions serve as inspiration for men's reductive and contradictory practices; and that men's stories and outlook distort their mothers' tales and childhood experiences spent in mothers' company.

Not only do women's myths seem to expose what men's myths hide or merely allude to, they also serve as the "charter" or essential blueprint for rites of passage and exchange in which women circulate as objects. Another slowly recognized yet obvious key to understanding Gimi lifeways is the very idiom for the rites of exchange which men control. "To eat the head of the child" is the Gimi expression for the right of the mother's brother (and his patrilineage) to receive regular "head" payments from his sister's husband on behalf of her children throughout the life of a son and until the marriage of a daughter. "Head" payments appear to have no connection to men's hegemonic Flute myth *until* it is reviewed in terms of women's myths. It then appears that 'the thing' men barely articulate—and that women's myths fiercely proclaim—men *act out* in rituals that exclude women as full participants. It may be no exaggeration to say that *erasure of the female* through violence, residential segregation, purging and purification of supposedly female elements from the male body, splitting the universe into antithetical realms of male and female and objectifying brides as items of exchange, comprises the main 'work' of Gimi culture. To escape a mother's influence and its expansion into an all-pervasive, noxious femininity incarnated most lethally in menstrual blood, mere avoidance and exclusion do not suffice.

The defeat of women entails more than myriad taboos and rules of avoidance, however meticulous and elaborate. To undermine women's influence also requires 'getting close to her,' in the words of Gimi men, by "going back up the road we first came down," returning to mother and exiting her body "a second time" in ritual as the way to create a world where men can dispense with women entirely (cf. Dundes 1976: 234). Gimi men are able to 'be intimate' with women while also keeping their distance by "playing around" with women's "secrets" in "secret" myths and rites which men recount and perform out of women's sight. Looked at together, Gimi men's and women's "secret" usages appear as a closely-matched set, entries in a dispute over which sex is today still to blame for the invention of desire and death and which one emerges as hero from a shared prehistory that was traumatic and bloody. The underpinning of a highly-segregated everyday life is not simply a misogynist screed derived from the logic of men's "secret" Flute cult but also the resolution of an argument between the sexes, often conducted in separate venues through supposedly secret myths and rites, about the same primordial *prenatal* universe that determines the life of every Gimi person.

The argument is decided in men's favour, of course, at least for the present—a present that turns out to be eternal and indelible—but which the myths and rites of both sexes present as fragile, erasable, and possibly short-lived. Communal rituals establish men's triumph over women, over and over again, as I argue, according to a charter or mythic rationale that is an appropriation and reversal of women's "secrets." Gimi men impose brutal control not by violence alone, nor even the implicit threat, but also by 'speaking to women' in women's terms and securing their participation in ways that make women complicit in their own subjugation and exclusion. In public performance, the Gimi social contract is the latest unstable truce in a war between the sexes.

Visual Perspectives and Lone Protagonists

Visualization and drastic shifts in scale are keys to understanding Gimi women's and men's myths and rites, both within a single narrative or performance and between the sexes' separate versions of the very beginnings of human life. Mythic narration and ritual enactment operate *cinematically*, as if there were a movie camera mounted on a dolly that zooms in for close-ups and backs away for wide-angle shots of the same scene. Gimi women and men express contrary views of a single scenario through the use of imagery in both myth and rite that recontextualizes key episodes in each other's productions by altering the frame of reference and changing the perspective. Gimi myths and rites are collective inventions perfected over generations but they convey the attitude of an iconic *individual,* male or female, from whose perspective and understanding of their predicament during a particular 'life crisis' everything in the myth or rite unfolds. In the same way that a dream is the production of a single dreamer, everything in a myth—the settings, artifacts, events and characters—reveal the world-view of a prototypical hero or heroine who is the counterpart of an adolescent initiate undergoing the ordeals of inititation, say, or a bride being sent off in marriage and arriving in the home of the groom.

Rather than a grid or set of oppositions or rules of a grammar or any other feature of language, the organizational premises of Gimi myths and rites are *contested narratives*, expressed in mainly visual terms, that trace the growing awareness of a mythic ego from the innocence of a baby boy or virgin girl to the onset of adolescence, frustrations of adulthood and fury at having died. What is more, each rite of passage enacts the protagonist's transition to the next phase in the life cycle as if it were a kind of death and rebirth (van Gennep 1960 [1908]).

Gimi Interpretations of Human Neoteny[3]

As in any argument, even one as complex and apparently indirect as the one Gimi women and men conduct at separate times and places, there is also underlying agreement, which may explain why relations between the sexes are often without violence or the threat of it. One fundamental issue that I think underlies the shared understanding or 'metanarrative' upon which Gimi women and men tacitly agree to differ concerns *neoteny* or "premature birth" (also called *fetalization* or *paedomorphosis*)—the prolongation of infancy or state of unreadiness for independent life in each human infant relative to the newborn of other species on account of its extremely "premature" separation from the mother. The human infant is like an embryo outside the womb. "Important organismic developments, which in the animal are completed in the mother's body, take place in the human infant after its separation from the womb. ... The human organism is thus still developing *biologically* while already standing in a relationship to the environment," a feature which accounts for human beings' "immense plasticity" and "world-openness"—their ability to establish themselves over most of the earth's surface (Berger and Luckmann 1967: 48–49, emphasis added). Pregnancy, parturition, lactation, close body-contact, a mother's wordless communications, soothing murmurs and nonsense sounds, caresses and ceaseless care in removing feces and swaddling her baby foster psychological as well as physical intimacy and help to create a *closed dyadic zone:* a 'maternal universe' characterized by ways of being in the world and modes of relating to others that extend beyond connection to an actual woman or primary care-giver.

Both Gimi sexes recognize that a baby's survival and early growth depend upon attachment to mother or *singular* mother-substitute over a long period. And they also agree that, just as the infant's early life is contingent upon the continuation *post-partum* of intense attachment to mother, its later development and entry into society require separation. Removal from the maternal world at the end of childhood is no less critical to individual success than is the original attachment but far more difficult to achieve and, for girls, less imperative. For a girl, emergence from the circumstances of 'neotenous' beginnings is always less complete because, soon after adolescence, she is almost invariably re-ensconsed in the mother-child dyad (Gillison 2016). The bond between mother and child is extraordinarily difficult to break or exit not only for the child *but also for the mother*. Although some Gimi women's myths depict the mother as essential agent of her child's liberation from her, they also portray women's ambivalence about letting go. Left to her own devices, women tend to agree with men, a mother would forestall her child's entry into an adult society that harshly excludes her.

Contested Interpretations of Menstrual Blood

Gimi rites of passage are designed to extricate functioning adults from the morass of neotenous beginnings, the caul of unreality and over-attachment to mother into which each child is born and, without regular ritual interference, will remain and falter. Both the difficulty of emerging from the mother-child dyad and the crucial importance of doing so, especially for boys, may account for the brutality and magnitude of the cultural apparatus dedicated to the task, the myriad anti-female taboos against commensality, touching and other kinds of contact, and violent rites of initiation for both sexes at puberty. While Gimi women and men may agree upon the main problems of human existence and many of the remedies, they do not agree on which sex is still to blame for their origin in crimes of the primordial past. Their tortuous long-distance debate centres upon *which sex was first*, which one had 'eyes to see' while the other was blind or asleep; and which sex seduced the other into criminal acts.

To "menstruate," in everyday Gimi parlance, is "to kill …" or "to be killed by the Moon" who is every woman's "first husband." The Moon throws his giant penis out of the night sky to copulate with every nubile girl and induce her first menstrual flow. The expression's reversibility fits the sexes' opposing views of the identity of the killer and instigator of menstrual bleeding. In myth, Gimi women portray the Moon as the Giant Penis, the Dream Man, a vicious Python or other monolithic fiend who represents the primal father as a predator and rapist of virgin girls (Gillison 1987).[4] In men's "secret" Flute myth, on the other hand, the girl is no virgin. She is the First Woman, the knowing older Sister whose 'beautiful music' seduces her baby Brother, still crawling on all fours and unable to "see," into entering her "house" where the Father is already installed, lurking unseen inside her "pubic hair": to trick her Brother, men's myths suggest, the First Woman deliberately hid the Father, made him indistinguishable from her body and precipitated the fatal head-on collision of Brother and Father. The sexes do not dispute the source of a woman's menstrual blood: its "first appearance" signals the *demise of someone else* ensconsed inside the menarcheal girl who herself is neither injured nor dying. In songs to arrest the monthly flow, Gimi women sing of "Moon's blood … [as] blood of the penis." "A woman's blood is really the blood of a man!" women declare. In the everyday parlance of both sexes, menstrual blood signifies "the death of the firstborn child" sired by the Moon.

Gimi men once treated the menstruating women in their midst as a threat more lethal and insideous than that of the men of neighbouring hamlets with whom they fought wars and engaged in raids and ambushes. Menstrual blood is not just poisonous stuff that issues from a woman's sex in men's view: it substantiates and makes contagious women's hostility toward men. The menstrual cycle demonstrates a woman's attitude to motherhood over time, her propensity to deliver a child as amorphous 'dead blood' undifferentiated from her rather than as a living being who will one day become physically independent of her care and attentions. A woman's return month after month to "cohabit with her first husband" in a specially built hut on the margins of the settlement shows that the Moon is not the only greedy one. She, too, would often rather "kill" her child, or see it "killed by the Moon," than to care for it so that it matures and goes on to live a life separate from her.

Death and the distinction between the sexes, like the 'neotenous' start of every life, are not givens of human existence, nor separate phenomena, in the Gimi view, but rather outcomes of a sequence of deliberate mythical acts—crimes of murder and theft—committed by both sexes in the primordial past but for which only men are *willing* to make amends in the here-and-now by renouncing the fruits of their crime in rites of exchange with other men. Whereas men come to terms with each other by exchanging sisters in marriage, women 'refuse' to let go of the Moon. The reappearance of menstrual blood month after month shows not only how relentlessly rapacious is the Moon but also how unwilling women are once and for all to expel their "first husband" and the stillborn children he keeps engendering inside them. The separate myths of Gimi women and men that together serve as charter for public rites of passage and exchange reveal that the way to escape Mother and her crippling orbit is to slay—or, in the case of Gimi women cannibals in the past, also to devour—the Father who inhabits her with fierce tenacity. The idea of the vagina as a violently-severed penis—and the much-reviled "anatomy is destiny"—may stem from a complicated developmental saga that begins with the menstrual cycle and includes the consequences of human neoteny.

The Myth of the Flutes: Gimi Men's Account of the Origin of Menstruation

Gimi men's "secret" myth describes the origin of menstruation as the moment the First Woman or, in many versions, two First Women lost her Flute[s]. The First Woman played her Flute inside a "flute house," one of three Gimi terms for a menstrual hut, the rough shelter built at the edge of the settlement where a Gimi woman traditionally remained in seclusion for the duration of her monthly periods.

> One night, her music woke her baby Brother asleep in another house. Lured irresistably by the gorgeous sounds, the Boy crawled to his Sister's house and hid amid the tall grass outside her door. He waited there until his Sister went to her garden. Then the Boy crept inside her house and stole the Flute from the head of her bed where she had left it. He blew into the mouth of the Flute but no sound came out! His Sister had closed the blowing hole with a Plug of her pubic hair. When the Boy looked and saw the Plug, he pulled it out and started to play the Flute. By unplugging the Flute, the Boy caused his Sister to menstruate for the first time. And because he put his mouth on the Flute Plug, his Sister's pubic hair began to grow on his face. (Gillison 1993: 265–68)

According to Gimi men, the First Woman intentionally planted her pubic hair around her Brother's mouth in order to expose his shame for the world to see. And for that, men say, in revenge for what the Sister did to her Brother in myth, men tattoo a "beard" on the face of every bride, who is the Sister's ritual counterpart, before they send her away in marriage (Fig. 1.1). The pattern of the bride's tattoos matches the pattern of the "female pubic hair" her paternal kinsmen etch around the blowing holes—"vaginas"—of the pair of bamboo flutes they send "in secret" to her husband disguised as containers of salt, a part of the marriage prestation, inside the bride's net bag. The bride transports the pair of flutes made in her image and loaded into her own net bag supposedly without

Fig. 1.1 An expert tattooist, accompanied by an assistant, tattoos a "beard" on the face of a soon-to-be-married young woman. Men say the bride's tattooed beard is their "revenge" for what the First Woman did to her baby Brother in myth by "planting" her pubic hair around his mouth after he put his lips on the Flute Plug. (© Gillian Gillison)

knowing what they really are. A flute is "the body of a woman," men say. According to a corollary of men's Flute myth, the First Woman invented the Flute by "looking down" at her vagina and copying what she saw onto bamboo. But *now*, incarnate in the bride, *she* is the one who 'cannot see' and who will 'put her mouth' on the plug of "female pubic hair." Her fathers stuff the flutes with chunks of salted pork or, in the past, marsupial meat, with the hairy hide still attached. Upon the bride's arrival, the groom removes the flutes from her net bag, takes out the 'hairy' chunks of meat and places them directly into the bride's newly "bearded" mouth.

In a supposedly secret transaction conducted 'right under the bride's nose,' and using her person as conduit, her lineage fathers close the bamboo flutes they made in the image of her body and send them to the groom: *this time*, in the ritual recapitulation, unlike what happened in men's Flute myth, the one who "unplugs" the flute *sees* the hairy thing closing the blowing hole, pulls it out and puts it right 'back inside again.' Unlike the baby Brother in men's Flute myth, the groom does not have to 'put his mouth on the First Woman's vagina' because the bride's *father*—a figure significantly absent in men's Flute myth—emerges in ritual to alter the myth's dénouement by 'blinding' the Sister/bride and enabling the Boy/groom to *see* what he does. In men's "secret" marriage ritual, the bride's father uses her decorated body as conduit to transfer her contents directly to the groom. Instead of blindly putting his mouth on the "flute plug," as did his mythic counterpart, the groom 'pulls out the plug' and puts it back inside a newly-bearded "second vagina" in her head.

Gimi women's myths and rites expose the Father whose presence men conceal both in their Flute myth as a plug of "female pubic hair" and in the "secret" marriage transaction between the bride's fathers and the groom by using a pair of flutes as disguised facsimiles of her "plugged" body. Women overturn men's accusation against the First Woman by providing *a closer look* at the crucial element in men's myth which is the Flute Plug of Sister's pubic hair. Up-close inspection of the Plug reveals why the Boy's wind could not enter the blowing hole in the first place. Seen through a female 'lens,' the image of the Flute Plug becomes a condensation of the entire opening sequence of men's myth. The baby Brother's awakening, crawling on all fours to his Sister's house, crouching outside her door unseen in the "tall grass" and mesmerized by her music, 'precapitulate' and bring to life the Plug's impenetrable and static contents. The Boy *is* the blood-soaked hairy Plug he pulls out of his Sister's Flute, her "firstborn" sired by the Moon. A 'blow-up' of the Flute Plug reveals the Boy hero hiding at/as the "head" of the Father's erect penis which is why, when the Boy pulls out the Plug—an act that women's myths show as tantamount to decapitation—his Sister starts to bleed. In the same moment that *her* pubic hair is transferred onto the Boy's face, *his* blood, "Moon's blood," starts to flow between her legs.

Juxtaposed with men's myth, women's usages reveal that the First Woman, or Two Women, were not alone as men's myth insists: the "first husband" was lurking unseen inside one or both of them and causing them to make beautiful music. In Gimi women's terms, the Boy who moves with irresistable desire and enters his Sister's "house" is no innocently curious baby, as men's myth portrays him, but rather a child attempting to get *back* inside his mother whom the Giant One "kills" in a fury for trespassing onto his territory. In esoteric versions of the Flute myth, men counter women's "secret" revision with one of their own, putting all the blame back onto the seductress Sister. To lure her innocent much-younger Brother, she hides the Father's "hairy" head and makes herself *appear* to be alone, or accompanied by only a Sister or Mother, using the siren sounds of her music to seduce him back into her "house" at the cost of his very life.

Men's myths insist that the Flute-owning First Woman was alone when she seduced her baby Brother; or that she deliberately hid the Father from view and led her Brother on a suicide mission back inside her "house." Any way Gimi men look at it, the First Woman is a guilty seductress who used her Brother shamelessly to rid herself of the Father/Moon by orchestrating the exit of his "firstborn child." To reward her Brother's sacrifice, she then plants *her* pubic hair on *his* face! The First Woman was not content to trick her Brother into travelling "back up the road he first came down," getting "killed by the Moon" for his blind acquiescence, and flowing out of her body as her first menstrual loss. After seducing him *back* inside her body and into sacrificing his life, his Sister left him marked forever with the *shame* of it, as if he alone were the guilty one. Adolescent boys' new beards make the First Woman's crimes irrefutable. Men's "secret" portrait of the First Woman is a slander about the origin of motherhood which leaves men no choice but to rescue adolescent sons from the abusive first women in their lives, seclude them inside the men's house and subject them to initiation rites that undo their tragic prehistory and arrange new births from men.

The Myth of the Giant Penis: Gimi Women's Account of the Origin of Menstruation

The symbolic productions of Gimi women and men share certain key features. They tend to operate and interrelate in primarily visual terms and to express the singular perspective of an iconic hero or heroine. They fixate on human anatomy, reproductive processes, intrauterine life and the origins of sexual difference and, especially in women's myths and rites, display a rampant phallicism. To counter men's malignant image of the First Woman, women's myths offer a host of vile father figures: the rampaging Dream Man, a Chronos-like giant who devours his every offspring; the Python who enters the vagina of a sleeping virgin Girl and comes out her mouth, vibrating his head and tail in orgasmic fury at both ends of her body as she expires; the Old Man who rules the forest, impaling countless women with his filthy "stick" or splitting them open with the axe that protrudes from the middle of his forehead and devouring their insides. The more feminine the narrative the more rapaciously phallic the imagery.

Women's myth of the Giant Penis describes the origin of menstruation in terms very different from men's Flute myth. Instead of a baby Boy woken by the siren sounds of his Sister's Flute, women portray a pubescent Girl still 'asleep inside her Mother's house'—still unborn—until the Giant Penis invades them both at once. To reach the sleeping Girl, the Giant has first to penetrate her Mother: the image of unborn daughter residing alone inside mother, one female nested inside the other like a pair of *phallic-shaped* Russian dolls, is a theme of women's myths and initiation rites and provides a direct parallel to the many versions of men's Flute myth in which not one but *two* First Women are the inventors and original Flute-players. In women's narratives, the Giant invades the heroine while she still "sleeps" inside her Mother's house, a reference to the "sleep" of a developing foetus. The heroine awakes, goes out the door of her Mother's house, follows the Giant into his own house and cuts him down to size. In brief:

> A Penis was once an enormously long thing. While the [first] Man slept in his house his Penis went out exploring. It did not know about women. … Women slept in women's houses and men slept in the men's house. …
>
> During the night, that thing of his roused itself and went out the door – the Penis alone! – and [making his way by smell through the only orifice in his head] reached the house where the Woman slept. … She was inside her house sound asleep. The Penis searched … it touched her here and there. It moved over her body but could not find [the Vagina]. It lifted her string

> skirts and slid between her thighs. … The Man slept. The Woman slept. Only the Penis moved.
>
> The Penis could not find the opening. … That Vagina of hers was shut tight! The opening was tiny and the Penis thought, "She has none!" The Penis smelled the Vagina but could not get inside … so he ate it.
>
> The Penis ate open the Vagina and slipped inside the Woman. Semen flowed into the Woman. And so her Vagina was opened …. An enormous thing entered the Woman and she awoke with a start. She took the Penis in her hand and went out the door of her Mother's house where a stalk of sugarcane was growing. She cut off a section and a half of the cane and, holding the Penis in her hand, followed it all the way into the Man's house. … She looked at him as he slept. She took the piece of sugarcane and measured it [against his Penis] and cut it [to the length of the cane]. …
>
> The Man awoke with a start. And the Woman said to him, "That was a heavy thing you carried about with you! When you wanted to have sex with me, you did not get up and move yourself! You lay here in your house and sent your Penis! It went inside me and that was not right! So I did you a favour!" …
>
> That First Woman had a good idea! … She measured a section and half of sugarcane and cut off the Giant … that is why today men have two marks on their penes – one on top and one below.

By reducing the Giant to normal size—cutting off his one-holed "head"—after he used his enormous length to invade her body while she was still asleep inside her Mother's house (that is to say, unborn), the Girl precipitates her own menstruation: by cutting off the Giant, she causes his blood to flow between her thighs. In separate accounts which depict the other sex as aggressor and guilty party, each sex attributes the dramatic changes in adolescent bodies—"first appearances" of menstrual blood and whiskers—to *deeds* committed during a primordial past the sexes shared but that now—on account of the other sex's unmitigated transgression—set them implacably apart. Like the myths and rites of many peoples, those of the Gimi conflate the beginning of time and the world with the conception and birth of the very first human being, a convention that transforms a woman's body and the bloody terrain "between her thighs" into a mythic cosmos. The stories of both Gimi sexes use domestic architecture and the forest landscape, as well as nearly every item of material culture and the wilderness, to enlarge to global proportion an intrauterine world during the turbulent era before and immediately after childbirth. Coitus, detumescence, menstruation, conception, gestation and parturition become life-size episodes of collective prehistory, championed by heroes and heroines inside a world-size womb and the gigantic female body surrounding it. Adult anatomy and reproductive physiology are instantiations of primordial conflict, outcomes in flesh and blood of primal crimes—rapes and stillbirths—living *proofs* of the violence with which male and female were first rent asunder.

As testimony to the supreme reality of myth, a man's beard and a woman's menstrual blood reveal *each person's shameful participation* in his or her origins. Once childhood ends, sins of the primal past appear 'all of a sudden' as permanent stigmata, highly visible stains upon one's very being … unless, of course, there were still some way to *go back* to the scene of the crime and 'undo' it. In "secret" ritual interventions, each sex works to 'send back' the blemish of adolescence to its source *in the body of the other sex* thereby shifting all or most of the blame onto the original seducer and rapist, punishing her or him with retaliatory disfigurement. When men tattoo a "beard" on the face of a future bride, they return to its rightful place of origin the "female pubic hair" the First Woman planted on the Boy's face. Fathers of the bride show the world what the First Woman did in secret, hid inside her house, kept beneath her skirts, while her Brother was still a baby unable to see what she was doing! In separate "secret" rites of their own, Gimi women likewise send menstrual blood out of their vaginas *back* into the "noses of our brothers."

The Boy in men's Flute myth who crawled inside his Sister's house to unplug her Flute went in "head first" so that, as Gimi women's songs "secretly" reveal, his nose filled up with the same Giant's blood that flooded his Sister. Like the Plug in men's Flute myth penetrated by women's gaze, the "female pubic hair" that appears on a boy's face at puberty *hides* the Giant's bloody demise his mythic counterpart precipitated. As for the Sister, whom men accuse of maliciously inviting her baby Brother 'back' into her body to rid herself of their Father, her ruse turned out to be no solution at all because neither of them were made lastingly separate from him. On the contrary, the siblings' joint crime—the bloody "head" they severed *together*—became lodged inside them both. In the recent past when warfare was endemic, a Gimi man had to repeat on himself at regular intervals the nose-bleeding and vomiting purges other men inflicted upon him during his initiation because the same poisons his mother introduced into his body during parturition and early childhood continue to accumulate from inevitable contacts with wives and other women. In response—or echo—of songs women sing to arrest their monthly flow, men send "the blood of my sister's vagina" out of their noses and back into their sisters.

Introducing Gimi women's 'take' on Gimi men's "secret" rites exposes the propaganda against women—the horror of menstrual blood and pollution of mothers—as emanating from the Father women harbor and cannot or will not evict. From a female perspective, Gimi men go to every length imaginable to avoid conflict with the mythic Father as stand-in for men of his generation: men's Flute myth denies the Father's very existence; and men's ritual tattooing "beards" on brides, and their nose-bleeding and extraction of whiskers from male initiates, attempt to 'adjust' the sexes' anatomy at puberty in order to transfer from male to female any trace of primordial confrontation with the Father. The same 'shifting of blame' from father to mother underlies the rites of exchange between brothers-in-law, each mother's brother replacing his sister as 'male mother' to her children. Because the mother's brother is a man, he can be persuaded with 'substitute meat' not to kill or curse his sister's child. Hatred of women and the fiction of gender fluidity—the notion, often shared by women, that a woman could repair her original sin and escape her fate *if only,* like a man, she would let go of what she 'cut off' the Giant and accept a substitute for it—are parts of men's strategy for recruiting boys away from their mothers and creating a conflict-free world entirely their own.

Totem and Taboo Revisited

Gimi women's myths and rites expose the Father men's Flute myth tries to conceal inside an inert Plug of the First Woman's pubic hair and enlarge him to ferocious giant size. Women's collection of primal father figures—the Giant Penis, the Dream Man, the ravenous Cassoway Hunter who climbs into the Cassowary's anus and devours her insides, the vicious Python who traverses a Virgin's body from one end to the other, the vile Old Man who "tricks" young girls into a deadly union—not to mention the Moon who figures in the very term 'to menstruate'—are rapists who cause "the death of the firstborn" and whom the heroine/initiate destroys with or without the help of her brother[s]. Close study of Gimi women's symbolic productions that fixate on the primal father as monster monopolist, on the means of his destruction and on the consequences for the way we live today recall, however improbably, the primal parricide that Sigmund Freud lays out in the final chapter of *Totem and Taboo* (Freud 1972 [1913]; Gillison 2005). Gimi women's father-centered narratives parallel Freud's scenario in astonishing ways—but with many twists and important alterations, of course!

I consider the last chapter of *Totem and Taboo* as a hypothetical construction—a theory condensed into a 'just-so' story—and not in any sense as the description of a unique historical event, which was the first complaint of Freud's many critics (e.g., Lévi-Strauss 1969 [1949]: 491). As I interpret Freud's primal crime for Gimi women and men in late twentieth century Highland Papua New Guinea, it summarizes a *meta-narrative* dispersed among the various myths and rites sophisticated Gimi adults compiled over generations through reflection, consultation, negotiation, adjustment and agreement concerning mainly unconscious Oedipal fantasies that emerge *in each individual* on account of "the supremacy of death," distinctions between the sexes and the neotenous human condition (Freud 1949 [1926]: 139). In indigenous cosmologies of the Gimi type, mortality is not governed by natural causes: "the natural thing [is] the indefinite prolongation of life – immortality" (Freud 1972 [1913]: 76). Death is almost always understood as murder perpetrated, in the case of adult males, openly in war or stealthfully through sorcery that requires a narrative of blame and plot for revenge to be created in response (Evans-Pritchard 1976 [1936]). Not only is death a catastrophe and *anomaly to be remedied* through violence and in ritual, in the Gimi scheme of things, but so are the anatomical and physiological distinctions between male and female and the imperatives of human neoteny. Augmented and revised by the symbolic productions of Gimi women and men, I argue that Freud's scenario of a primal crime efficiently accommodates the origins of all three inescapable 'anomalies'—death, sexual duality and neoteny—according to a single contested sequence of mythic events.

What is more, every life crisis or misfortune—birth, weaning, the onset of puberty, betrothal, marriage, serious illness or injury, and death itself –is also *a kind of death* to be undone, transcended or denied in rites of passage and exchange: death and sexual differentiation are enacted in ritual *as if* they were occurring for the very first time. Gimi women's and men's separate mythologies represent highly-condensed projections onto prototypical males and females of the deep motivations and understandings of the world that typify the various life-phases celebrated in rites of passage. From this perspective, the entire repertoire of Gimi ritual performances represents "the Deed" in Freud's terms, each rite another enactment of the first death interpreted in retrospect as a parricide or 'parenticide' to be redressed and expiated through public renunciation—or, in the case of Gimi women, *failure or reluctance to renounce*—the fruits of the primal crime. Because reparation requires "the solidarity of all the participants" as Freud stipulates (Freud 1972 [1913]: 147), Gimi women's ritually-constructed 'refusal' to give back or accept a substitute for what they stole from the Father during commission of the mythic parricide leaves them with blood on their hands and "between their thighs" as proof of unassuaged guilt.

The various incarnations of the First Man Gimi women picture in their myths ressemble Freud's depiction of "a violent and jealous father who keeps all the females for himself and drives away his sons as they grow up" (Freud 1972 [1913]: 141). "One day," according to Freud's account, the sons rebel. They murder and devour their father but afterwards are overcome with remorse. In expiation, the sons renounce marriage with the sisters on whose account they killed the father. The sons install the taboo on incest, exchange their sisters as wives for men of other bands and invent human society.

Gimi women's separate myths and "secret" rites seem to augment Freud's scenario by introducing daughters and sisters as active co-conspirators in the father's murder. If brothers banded together because they were enraged by a father who denied them access to their sisters, Gimi women's myths and rites proclaim, then the sisters whom the father continually raped and whose bodies he occupied in perpetuity were just as angry, even angrier, and spurred their brothers to act or took matters literally into their own "hand." "Society was … based on complicity in the common crime," Freud says. But he refers only to "the fraternal clan, whose existence was assured by the blood tie" (*Ibid.*: 146). In Gimi women's 'retelling' of *Totem and Taboo* that complicity included women: brothers *and sisters* colluded to destroy and devour the primal father. And once the deed was done, no less than their brothers, the sisters were filled with remorse. They, too, were ambivalent towards the father and wanted him back.

And just like their brothers, the Gimi sisters settled on something that originally *belonged* to the father, parts of his very being he discarded inside them, leaving them 'plugged shut.' While the brothers took possession of the sisters the father had kept for himself alone and abused at his pleasure, the sisters kept—and "cut off"—the parts he had already deposited inside their bodies. In ways Gimi women's myths and rites dramatize, rage and desire go hand-in-hand. Like their primordial sisters, Gimi women remain ambivalent, determined both to *destroy and possess* a mythical father installed inside them during their own conception, while they were "asleep inside mother." In the Gimi rites of exchange that recapitulate the myths of origin of both sexes—and consistent with Freud's scenario—*only brothers* are allowed to make amends, to "allay their burning sense of guilt," and to emerge as culture heroes (*Ibid.:* 144). "The sense of guilt," Freud says, "can only be allayed by the solidarity of all the participants" (*Ibid.:* 147).

For the Gimi, the question then arises of why sisters, after they cooperated with their brothers in the father's murder and cannibalism, are excluded from the solidarity required to make amends and undo their guilt. Why are Gimi men able to transcend the primordial crime through rites of purification and renunciation while women's role in the same crime pollutes them and makes them guilty and pollut*ing* forever? If, in the Gimi way of seeing, sons and daughters, brothers and sisters together carried out the heroic murder of the ogre-father—if both sexes sacrificed themselves to create viable intrauterine life—why do women fail to emerge as culture heroes alongside men? Why do Gimi women retain their original mythic identities as parricides—their vaginas bloody 'sites of execution'—rather than attain the status of life-givers?

According to Gimi women's myths, *both sexes* conspired and participated in the murder of the primal Father-ensconsed-in-Mother, cut him to pieces and absconded with the parts that, once violently freed from the vicious Pair and devoured in a totemic meal, turned into the men and women of today. In a Gimi-inflected version of the scenario that Freud lays out in Chap. 4 of *Totem and Taboo*, the primal father appears as the First Man who is really a perpetually-copulating, indissociable Father-Mother Pair. Freud himself anticipates this adaptation of his theory. In describing the "emotional ambivalence … [that] lies at the root of many important cultural institutions," Freud states that "[w]e know nothing of the origin of this ambivalence. One possible assumption is that it is a fundamental phenomenon of our emotional life. But it seems to me quite worth considering … [that it] was acquired by the human race in connection with their father-complex.… *Or, more correctly,*" he adds in a footnote, *"their parental complex"* (Freud 1972 [1913]: 157 n.1, emphasis added).

In Gimi terms, the result of the primal crime was that brothers got access to the sisters they coveted but the sisters were already in use—already with child! The sisters Gimi men acquired were 'plugged up,' still harbouring remnants of the murdered Giant they had both tried unsuccessfully to evict. But after the deed was done and despite the remorse they shared, the sisters *refused to renounce* what they killed and stole. Faced with their sisters' intransigence, the only way for men to bring their dead father back to life and liberate his unborn progeny, in Gimi men's estimation, is for them to bypass their sisters entirely and come to terms with each other: in secret rites of marriage, the brothers renounce their father-occupied sisters and send them off as wives for other men to empty out and reoccupy; and, in exchange, they receive other men's similarly-occupied-and-emptiable sisters. Behind their backs—literally *on* their backs inside net bags carrying flutes disguised as containers of salt—Gimi men transform recalcitrant sisters into 'gifts with benefits' and exchange them with other men.

Unlike men's sisters, however, the unborn children women inherit from the primal Father cannot be converted into exchangeable commodities. Through secret myths and separate rites performed behind the closed doors of separate dwellings, Gimi women and men argue about the primordial murder and the human condition arising from it. The long-distance 'conversation' between Gimi women's and men's secrets amounts to a dispute over why—and if—women *refuse to renounce* the spoils of their collective crime and are therefore still to blame for it. Men descended from the original 'band of brothers' give away the sisters they stole from their Father, making amends by exchanging sisters as wives for other men. But women tend to remain stubbornly "plugged up," unwilling to let go of the primal Father or his progeny.

Whereas Gimi men renounce their sisters—the ones they covet most—the sisters are uncompromising and refuse to relinquish or *accept any substitute* for the ones the Father violently installed inside them and they angrily 'cut off' from him. Women prefer to keep the Father's stolen pieces and, together with a 'second husband,' convert them into living appendages. Initiation rites for adolescent boys and girls create the difference between the sexes in such a way that—while conforming to the cliché that "it is the presence or absence of a phallus which distinguishes male from female" (Leach 1979 [1961]: 225)—also treat that outcome as neither inevitable nor accidental but rather as the result of a mythic crime for which only one sex is ready to atone through renunciation of their 'loved ones.' This is the ideological basis upon which the separate bodies of Gimi women's and men's myths and rites agree to differ. Neither the terms of the dispute nor the ritual outcome ever vary, of course: while men make amends by exchanging among themselves the sisters they desire and freed from the Father, their sisters and partners-in-crime refuse to let go of the babies they stole and so are left with "nothing but blood" on their hands and between their thighs.

The Vagina as Killing Field

Together with coitus, ejaculation, detumescence, conception, gestation, parturition, lactation, the child's prolonged attachment and eventual severance from mother, menstruation is part of an entire *drama of creation* whose outcome the sexes contest. Gimi women's origin myths, as I understand them, closely ressemble the scenario I derive from a Gimi-inflected reading of Freud's primal crime in which every woman is possessed by a monolithic father-figure who incessantly rapes her. The very mark of femininity, according to Gimi women's accounts, signals the primal Father's violent death and departure—but only temporarily, it turns out, because he returns month after month to cohabit with all his daughters in the seclusion of their menstrual huts once known by both sexes as "flute houses." The loss of menstrual blood every month for most of a woman's life demonstrates the immensity of the Father she hides and refuses to renounce once and for all. The relentless killings "between her thighs" signify not only regular stillbirths but also the *violent means necessary* eventually to terminate each child's prolonged post-partum attachment to mother that is the condition of human neoteny.

The bleeding vagina *telescopes* the entire female role in producing a viable individual starting with menarche, continuing with gradual phases of severence from mother throughout childhood and culminating in initiation at puberty, an event Gimi liken to "the death of the child." Gimi men, especially, seem to conflate the fact of menstruation with the infant's prolonged attachment to mother as 'flesh and blood' testimony to a woman's preference to keep the child for herself at any cost to its well-being. (It is also true, at least until the early 1960's, that many infants died and that firstborn children had an especially high rate of mortality. Gillison 1993: 223ff.)

The Primordial Gimi Universe

The metanarrative that emerges from the Gimi sexes' various secret rites and myths closely parallels the parricidal drama Freud outlines in the final chapter of *Totem and Taboo* once critical adjustments are made to include mother and daughters as well as father and sons. Once sisters emerge as active co-conspirators and agents in the father's demise, the mother appears as the corollary and passive container of the father's evil deeds. Gimi women's myths and initiation rites show over and over again that the Father who incessantly rapes his Daughters is *already* inside Mother. Her "house" is the passive scene of all the action. The entire scenario of murder and cannibalism unfolds within the precincts of the mythic First Woman's phallic-shaped and world-size body, itself the image of a couple locked together in ceaseless copulation.

Paradoxically, because her body is the encompassing milieu, the Mother may not be seen or appear to be missing altogether. Inside the vast but inconspicuous female landscape, characters of *both* sexes portray the misadventures of a Giant Penis in the midst of the first world-making predatory copulation and its successive outcomes: detumescence, first menses, conception, gestation, parturition, emergence of appendage-like offspring and traumatic severence from mother. After a near-eternity spent in copulatory union with the Giant, Mother is moulded to his shape and proportion: her body is a *perfect fit* for the one who occupied her territory for so long. The Giant lodged inside the First Woman is not an androgynous figure like the Ouroboros—a single static entity possessing attributes and genitalia of both sexes. Rather s/he is *two bodies* endowed with *one sex coalesced in perpetual coital movement* as unrelenting, rhythmic and hypnotic as flute music. The hollow bamboo flute men once hid from women on pain of death and that they describe as "the body of the First Woman," is a giant phallus equipped with *two* vaginas: the blowing hole around which men etch "female pubic hair" and where the player inserts his wind "like his penis," and the open end of the instrument from which emerge "the cries of his newborn child."

Just like men's Flute-owning First Woman, the Giant Penis in Gimi women's myths and rites is actually a *Couple* whose state of perpetual copulation makes them *look* as if they are a *singular static phallic figure*. From women's myth, we learn that the Giant Penis not only searches for virgin girls by night but also hunts marsupials by day.

> The Man went into the forest to hunt marsupials, taking along his Dog and that Penis of his wound round and round like a rope [of liana vine] and bundled into his net bag. He hung the net bag around his neck [so his coiled Penis protruded over his belly like a pregnant woman's] … and went out to hunt. Inside the forest, the Man opened the net bag and let out his Penis. The Penis stalked marsupials just like his Dog [by smell alone] and shot one sleeping in a tree. When the Man was ready to come home, he wound his Penis back into a pile of coils [with the head hidden at the

centre, still buried inside the bloodied marsupial he shot]. He put the bundle into his net bag, hung it around his neck and headed for home.

The Giant Penis' adventures occur inside an intrauterine world enlarged to immense proportion through the imagery of forest creatures and landscape and domestic artifacts and architecture. Women's and men's houses, garden shelters, hunting lodges, net bags, digging sticks, bows and arrows, traps for marsupials and cassowaries, mountain ridges, valleys, rivers, caves, giant trees, liana vines, wild yams and other edible wildlife, decorative red flowers and leaves, tall grasses, turkey nests, birds, snakes, frogs, grubs and bats all portray or furnish the primordial universe inside the First Woman's body where the entire world as we know it began.

Interpreted in Gimi terms, Freud's just-so story about a *primal crime* takes on the added significance of a *primal scene* magnified to cosmic dimension. The change of venue not only *in*flates to life size the intrauterine events that occur during creation of the first human being, it also *con*flates them with the Father's murder and cannibalism which are now recast, in terms of Gimi women's myths, as violent partition of the seemingly monolithic Father-Mother Pair. Even outside the context of myth and ritual, Gimi of both sexes identify "the firstborn child" with the father-figure of the Moon, or a piece of him, somehow severed or "killed" while inhabiting a woman's body. The sexes' opposing myths and rites provide contradictory details of the 'somehow' that led to the First Couple's bloody partition and the escape of their offspring but both traditions describe those events from the offsprings' *intrauterine perspectives.* Only the unborn, stunted, crippled, starving, bloodied and as-yet unsexed are *in the position to see* what is happening and to carry out the heroic tasks of liberation: the indistinguishable siblings, incipient sisters and brothers, kill and devour the "head" of the primal Father *together*, each one ingesting the piece that connects him imperceptibly to Mother and makes the Pair appear to be an indivisible phallic One like the mythic Flute or Giant Penis. After the epic separation, a man is left with a shortened version of the Giant and a nose filled with bloody remnants of the "head" he ate. But a woman keeps the Giant's bloody severed head *in situ* between her thighs, making the female body an everlasting scene of the primal crime.

Notes

1. Since 1973–1985, the ethnographic present of this book, violence against women in the Eastern Highlands Province of Papua New Guinea is "only getting worse." In a November 15th, 2018 New York Times article entitled, "'It's Time to Try to Change the Men': Papua New Guinea's Epidemic of Abuse," Ben. C. Solomon writes:

   > According to a United Nations report, more than two thirds of all women in Papua New Guinea will suffer abuse at the hands of a partner. Another study found that about 60 percent of men surveyed in some parts of the country admitted to taking part in gang rape. Eastern Highlands Province is one of the country's most populous regions, and it is a hot spot for abuse: Nearly 80 percent of all women surveyed by the World Health Organization in the province said they had been beaten by their husbands. "To beat a woman is to pick a mango from the tree," said Sharon Sisopha, a counselor at the Goroka women's shelter. "It costs nothing."

2. For details about the fieldwork upon which this book is based see Gillison (1977, 1983b, 1993: xiii–xviii). The National Science Foundation and the Canada Council provided initial support. In later years, my former husband David Gillison and I received support from National Geographic Magazine and the New York Zoological Society. In 1985, I was awarded a *Poste Rouge* by the Centre Nationale de la Recherche Scientifique to work at the Laboratoire d'Anthropologie Sociale in the Collège de France in Paris founded by Claude Lévi-Strauss and headed by Professor Françoise Héritier and, during my subsequent appointments, by Professor Phillipe Descola.
3. In describing the etiology of neuroses, Freud refers to the "biological factor" of *neoteny* or "premature birth" of the human infant relative to the newborn of other species on account of its extremely "premature" separation from the mother. "Its intra-uterine existence seems to be short in comparison with that of most animals, and it is sent into the world in a less finished state" (Freud 1949 [1926]: 139).

   Postwar social constructivists like Berger and Luckmann, and most contemporary social anthropologists, interpret human neoteny as the reason "there is no human nature" or that "man constructs his own nature" (Berger and Luckmann 1967: 48–49; Sahlins 2013). But in emphasizing "man's [underdeveloped] instinctual organization" and the critical "period during which the human organism develops towards its completion in interrelationship with its environment," Berger and Luckman gloss over the most important feature of that "interrelationship," saying that it "is mediated by the significant others who have charge of him" (*Ibid.*). "Significant others" implies a varying assortment of near kin whereas, psychobiologically speaking, the uniquely long postpartum period of early development in human beings that allows them to acquire language and culture and on account of which they have advanced on the evolutionary scale occurs optimally—or even essentially—in the context of 'symbiotic' attachment to *one* "significant other" or *single primary* caregiver who is almost always (ethnographically speaking, although from a psychobiological standpoint not necessarily) *the mother*.

4. Mythic figures and artifacts are capitalized to distinguish them from their ritual counterparts. But pronouns that refer to mythic figures appear in lower case.

References

Berger, Peter L., and Thomas Luckmann. 1967 [1966]. *The Social Construction of Reality: A Treatise in the Sociology of Knowledge*. Garden City: Anchor Books.

Dundes, Alan. 1976. A Psychoanalytic Study of the Bullroarer. *Man,* n.s. 2: 220–238.

Evans-Pritchard, E.E. 1976 [1936]. *Witchcraft, Oracles and Magic Among the Azande*. Oxford: Clarendon Press.

Freud, Sigmund. 1949 [1926]. *Inhibitions, Symptoms and Anxiety.* Trans. Alix Strachey. London: The Hogarth Press.

——— 1972 [1913]. *Totem and Taboo. Some Points of Agreement between the Mental Lives of Savages and Neurotics.* Trans. James Strachey [1950]. London: Routledge and Kegan Paul.

Gillison, Gillian. 1977. Fertility Rites and Sorcery in a New Guinea Village. *National Geographic Magazine* 152 (1): 124–146.

———. 1983a. Cannibalism among Women in the Eastern Highlands of Papua New Guinea. In *The Ethnography of Cannibalism,* ed. Paula Brown and Donald Tuzin. Washington, DC: Society for Psychological Anthropology.

———. 1983b. Living Theater in New Guinea's Highlands. *National Geographic Magazine,* August, 146–169.

———. 1987. Incest and the Atom of Kinship: The Role of the Mother's Brother in a New Guinea Highlands Society. *Ethos* 15: 166–202.

———. 1993. *Between Culture and Fantasy. A New Guinea Highlands Mythology*. Chicago: University of Chicago Press.

———. 2005. *Totem et tabou* dans les Hautes Terres de Papouasie-Nouvelle-Guinée. La révolte des filles. In *Anthropologie et Psychanalyse*, ed. Patrice Bidou, Jacques Galinier, and Bernard Juillerat. Paris: Editions de L'Ecole des Hautes Etudes en Sciences Sociales.

———. 2016. Whatever Happened to the Mother? A New Look at the Old Problem of the Mother's Brother in Three New Guinea Societies: Gimi, Daribi and Iatmul. *Oceania* 86 (I): 2–24.

Leach, E.R. 1979 [1961]. Two Essays Concerning the Symbolic Representation of Time. Part I Cronus and Chronos. In *Reader in Comparative Religion; An Anthropological Approach*, ed. William A. Lessa and Evon Z. Vogt, 4th ed. New York: Harper Collins.

Lévi-Strauss, Claude. 1969 [1949]. *The Elementary Structures of Kinship*. Boston: Beacon Press.

Meggitt, M.J. 1964. Male-Female Relationships in the Highlands of New Guinea. *American Anthropologist* 66 (pt. 2): 204–224.

Newman, Philip L. 1964. Religious Belief and Ritual in a New Guinea Society. *American Anthropologist* 66 (pt. 2): 257–272.

———. 1965. *Knowing the Gururumba*. New York: Holt, Rinehart and Winston.

Newman, Philip L., and David J. Boyd. 1982. The Making of Men: Ritual and Meaning in Awa Male Initiation. In *Rituals of Manhood*, ed. Gilbert H. Herdt. Berkeley: University of California Press.

Read, Kenneth E. 1952. Nama Cult of the Central Highlands, New Guinea. *Oceania* 23 (1952): 1–25.

———. 1965. *The High Valley*. New York: Scribner's.

Sahlins, Marshall. 2013. *What Kinship Is … and Is Not*. Chicago: University of Chicago Press.

Salisbury, Richard F. 1965. The Siane of the Eastern Highlands. In *Gods, Ghosts and Men in Melanesia*, ed. Peter Lawrence and M.J. Meggitt. Melbourne: Oxford University Press.

Solomon, Ben C. 2018. It's Time to Try to Change the Men: Papua New Guinea's Epidemic of Abuse. *New York Times*, November 15.

van Gennep, Arnold. 1960 [1908]. *The Rites of Passage*. Trans. Monika B. Vizedom and Gabrielle L. Caffee. Chicago: University of Chicago Press.

2

Daily Life in an Eastern Highlands Village

Getting Started

The women of Ubagubi were not available to be "interviewed" nor to serve as guides or remunerated companions. Their days were filled with caring for children and pigs and in gruelling work in gardens as much as an hour's walk away from their compounds. A few weeks after arriving, I met Pamone,[1] a tall, striking woman from Chimbu, a place so far away that when she left home she told me that her father cut off a part of his finger in despair of ever seeing her again. In addition to the standard brideprice of *100 kina* (PNG bank notes) and five pigs, the two men who came from Ubagubi to fetch her added 37 skins of five species of Birds of Paradise. Pamone was an exotic luxury, a handsome, sophisticated bride with whom the two men hoped to convince Manten, their brother and brother-in-law, to remain at home after a long absence spent in wage labour on the coast. But after four years as Manten's wife, Pamone had no children, no pigs, and no garden of her own. And she quarelled with Manten's hectoring step-mother Darma. After Pamone picked a fight with Manten's unmarried paramour, she fled to a house that belonged to Manten's brother-in-law, the Big Man Situpe, who was the main contributor to her extravagant brideprice and one of the two men who brought her from Chimbu.

G. Gillison, *She Speaks Her Anger: Myths and Conversations of Gimi Women*, Culture, Mind, and Society, https://doi.org/10.1007/978-3-030-49352-3_2

Fig. 2.1 Aerial view of part of the village of Ubagubi in 1974. (© David Gillison)

Standing inside our house, Pamone spotted a wad of tree moss tucked into the woven bamboo wall behind the oil-drum that served as a fireplace.[2] She pulled it out of the wall and hid it from sight. Some Gimi women still used the soft moss as tampons during their periods, Pamone explained, although most preferred bits of tattered cloth. A woman would feel terrible shame, she said, if even a drop of menstrual blood were spotted running down her leg or staining her bark-string skirts. Some ten years before, in about 1963, "*masta pen*," Ben Wurtz, an American fundamentalist missionary, forbade construction of the huts where women used to go into seclusion every month. "A woman is married to two men," Pamone told me, "her husband and the Moon. When a man wants sex and the Moon is killing her, she says to him, 'Now is the time of my other husband.'"

"Women *hide* the blood! If a woman's father were to *see* her blood, he would fall ill with shame!" While the blood is still "hot," a woman does not remove the saturated wad of moss. She waits for it to "cool" before carefully—using the left thumb and index finger—removing it and discarding it in a latrine or fast-running stream. If a woman leaves her tampon lying carelessly about, a sorcerer would surely find it and use it to kill her. Manten was an exception among men, Pamone confided, because when she told him, "the Moon is killing me," he did not force her to have sex. Some men—"all men"—often ignored their wives' warnings and, in the past, used menstrual huts for assignations. A man's penis could push the tampon so far inside her the woman was unable to retrieve it! But the shame of letting anyone, even another woman, see a drop of blood was a worse danger. "A woman thinks, 'I cannot let the blood run [down my leg] and shame me.' So she says to her husband, 'The Moon is killing me. You go away.'"

Since Pamone was newly installed in Situpe's house nearby, I thought she might be an ideal confidante. I had no idea that Pamone's "running away" happened to coincide with Manten's attempts to get rid of her and with Situpe's angry refusal to send her back to Chimbu. During the court of other Big Men Situpe summoned to adjudicate the marriage, Manten's main complaint was "I don't like her." "She starts fights with other women," he declared, referring to his paramour and bullying step-mother Darma whom I recognized in the crowd filling the open yard in front of

Situpe's house. As I passed her trying to get closer to the proceedings, Darma grabbed my arm and held up her left hand to show me the deformed thumb. Darma had once coveted the pigs her husband assigned to her co-wife and picked a fight. Her husband—dead for years now—intervened and broke her thumb. But Darma bragged to me that she'd left a scar where she slashed his right upper arm.

The men assembled inside Situpe's house were of one voice: "Of course, Pamone fights! You [Manten] have not built a fence nor bought her a pig to care for!" Manten's failure at *bisnis,* they all said, was the root of his marital strife: he must fence a garden for Pamone to cultivate the sweet potatoes she needs to feed the pigs Manten must buy for her to raise and hand over to Situpe in return for her exhorbitant brideprice! Situpe has been counting on Pamone's so far non-existent pigs as part of the bride-price he would soon have to deliver in exchange for the wife of one of his sons. A newly elected *komiti* addressed Manten, shouting out the consensus:

> If you two are angry and want to fight, that's your business. You have to take control of her. Soon we will have self-government. You are the *masta* and she is your *missus!* Pamone is a good woman. A *lot* was lost [i.e., given as brideprice] for her. You cannot just throw her out! Say to her, "Situpe took you into his house but now I have come to take you back home. I left the other one [the young girl]. Let us go back to [the neighbouring village where Manten lives] and make a life together!"

As the court was ending I asked Pamone if she would accompany me later that afternoon to another compound where I'd heard there was to be a wedding. She turned me down flat. The bride and the men who would accompany her to receive her brideprice, Pamone explained, came from a village where Manten's enemies resided. These men would surely "poison" her as the means to attack Manten or his lineage. Pamone's excuse was a truism—a danger more or less inherent in going anywhere outside one's own lineage or clan, especially uninvited—but was also pointed at me, as I understood about a week later. My obvious affinity for Pamone seemed to indicate that I intended to depend upon her as a regular companion, an arrangement that, even prospectively, gave offense, especially to the Big Man Situpe, by interfering in men's affairs. As the court case vividly demonstrated, and as I failed to grasp at the time, in the matter of men's exchanges in pigs and women, every Gimi woman was herself 'the goods' (a wife or wife-to-be) *and* the producer of goods—pigs—equivalent to herself (another wife). Like any woman in the village, Pamone's time, labor, affiliations and affections were entirely spoken for.

For a long time I was frustrated in my relations with women. When I approached them on their way home from gardens, balancing gigantic bundles of firewood on their heads and carrying net bags that cradled infants and held heavy loads of sweet potatoes, taros and green vegetables, some paused briefly to inspect me. Light strokes revealed the texture of my skin and hair, located scars and moles and detected scratches, cuts and tropical ulcers. Women remarked on my nonstop note-taking and practice of hiding my breasts under a shirt. As time went by, they came to watch me prepare meals, do dishes, wash clothes, brush my teeth, sit at a table copying geneaolgies and maps from a notebook onto graph paper. When I was ill or alone, a couple of my neighbours sat with me to pass the time and casually inspect the array of paraphernalia inside the house. Gradually, a few women invited me into their houses and to accompany them to gardens or to pass the long hours beside the narrow bank of a river where a woman was in labour.

Childbirth

The moment the baby was born, the mother's mother and mother-in-law scrubbed it with soap. One of them pulled a leaf off a branch overhead, rolled it into a funnel, inserted one end into the baby's mouth and forced it to swallow water from the icy river. "Drink!" the mid-wives exhorted. During the long labour, whenever the sun came out, women predicted the baby would be a boy. Cold and shade announced the arrival of a girl. When a girl was born, the women's faces registered disappointment. "The father will be angry," some said. Others countered, "It's *good business* for [the father's younger brother]!" meaning that the newborn girl would one day command a brideprice her patrilineage could use to obtain a wife in exchange. In the first moments after a delivery, one of the father's sisters might point out that the newborn girl's elder sister was already "hers," a portion of her future brideprice already spoken for.

Days after attending a delivery, I asked a woman who was not present why the newborn was forced to swallow cold river water from a leaf. "I did not see the woman give birth," she reminded me, which was the usual reply to my questions about something I had witnessed but that the woman I asked had not. Months later, during an all-night vigil to celebrate the imminent departure of a bride, I learned that swiftly-flowing water in a clan-owned river is *kore abe* (lit: *kore*, 'ghost,' 'spirit,' 'wild' or 'sir' when prefixed to an older or prominent man's name + *abe*, 'urine'), a euphemism for clan "semen" (*hato*). The rushing torrent embodied "ancestral semen," the spirit version of ejaculations "shot from the head" of the penis to feed the baby *in utero*. Forcing the neonate to swallow freezing spirit-urine or spirit-semen as its first drink eased transition into the world outside the womb which was like a macrocosm of the one inside it.

During another delivery, the mother's mother supported the mother with her body and guided every phase of the labour. This time a classificatory mother-in-law, not the prospective father's own mother, served as 'first assist.' When I asked why the father's own (lit: *kisa*, 'true' or 'real') mother was not present, one of the women in attendance began a list of the taboos and duties placed on the father's own mother during and after the birth of his child especially if he were a firstborn son. "She fed and looked after [the father as a baby] so she cannot touch his child! If she did, her son would soon grow old and die!" For at least two months after the birth, the father slept in the men's house, did not touch his newborn nor take food from his wife's hands nor from a fire whose embers she might have blown alight. During this period (which was longer in the days of open warfare), the father's own mother supplied him with food: no woman who touched the newborn could feed the father nor handle anything he ate; and no one who fed the father could touch his child without placing the father in jeopardy.

As a child grows to adulthood, taboos ramify: for a girl, her father's own mother and father—in addition to her own father and mother—cannot consume pigs received as her brideprice nor any food cooked in the same oven; nor pigs she rears as a married woman nor crops she cultivates. The elaborate taboos constraining "real" as opposed to more distant, categorical, or "not-real" (lit: *amene*) relations have a flip side which is the allocation of a newborn girl's future brideprice to specific others immediately outside the tabooed inner circle, as a father's half-sister bragged at the scene of her step-niece's birth. In a polygynous family, consumers of brideprice are likely to be the father's half-siblings, children of his father's wives other than his own mother, and his father's full or half-brothers, whose names are individually attached to infant girls as intended recipients of their future brideprice. *Kinship is a constant lesson*: even to a babe-in-arms, the mother recites her child's relationship to each of those who happen to be present at the moment.

* * *

In late 1975 after I started to listen to women's myths, I began to understand that, from the moment of birth until severence from the mother, usually a years-long process, a man and his child *also share a too-great affinity*—one that, in times of war, required him to absent himself almost entirely. At the moment of birth and immediately thereafter, separation between father and newborn is still tentative and may easily be undone if, say, a hand that touched the body of mother or baby were to prepare food that entered the father's mouth. Even remote contact between a man and his newborn might be lethal for the father because it could restore the 'head-to-head' connection the two sustained inside the mother's body during pregnancy when ejaculations from the "head" of the father's penis passed directly into the unborn's open fontanelle, called "the first mouth." The Gimi child starts life as offshoot and mirror image of its father's penis: the open fontanelle on top of the foetal head is like an enlarging urethra-in-reverse—a "first mouth"—that ingests semen ejected from the father's "head." Parturition—passage "between the mother's thighs"—is a one-time event that creates the exclusive bond between mother and child and begins to "cut off" the 'head-to-head' connection between father and offspring sustained in the womb. The midwives who 'force-fed' the newborn a drink of ancestral "semen" promoted the father's *dis*connection by substituting 'paternal substance' of a collective and anonymous kind.

If the relation father and child sustained *in utero* were to linger or be re-ignited after the child leaves its mother's "house" and becomes her appendage, the relation is liable to collapse into reverse: the one who unstintingly *provided* food to his identically-made offspring may now be inclined to *take back* the parts of himself he released while transported inside the mother. In the same way a man may ejaculate 'unintentionally,' bringing to life a child who stays hidden for months inside the mother, he may also, once it's head makes a "first appearance" outside her body, be reminded of his loss and wish to "eat" the one he fed while it remained inside the mother and invisible to him. The women responsible for the father's life and welfare, especially his own mother, have the duty to protect him from his own powerful inclinations (of which he may not always be aware) by ensuring that such a disastrous 'return' of events never occurs—even remotely, tenuously or unthinkingly by, say, his eating food cooked in a fire whose embers the new mother blew alight. Eating such food would pollute the father because it would be "the same" as his *re*absorbing his own semen or any other part of himself he ejected automatically and without hesitation: feces, urine, sweat, scraps of food or other *exuviae*. However remotely or unknowingly, he would reincorporate his child—'the one who got away' from him as did his other leavings. By preventable accident, the unprotected father of a newborn would succumb to the *fatal return* of what he already discarded.[3]

Considered in light of Gimi women's and men's separate myths and rites, the taboos and interdictions of everyday life appear to be elements of a highly coherent system designed to enforce *separations in nuclear family relationships* whose overwhelming tendency is fatal collapse into continuity and sameness (cf. Wagner 1977; Anonymous 2017).

Remaining on the margins of a compound among a group of women nursing children, netting string bags, peeling sweet potatoes and separating the skins and inferior tubers into piles to feed pigs and shoats could feel frustratingly uneventful especially when, over the fence and barely out of earshot, men were conducting trials for sorcery (Gillison 1977). But until about 1983, when I started to have extended conversations with three or four men who were intellectuals and experts in myth and ritual, I spent most of my days among women and children in compounds, gardens or on the banks of a river during long vigils over women in labour. Much later, I realized that what I saw and experienced among women starting in Fall 1973 led me to the concept of *neoteny*.

Situpe and His Daughters and Granddaughters

The presence among a group of women of a Big Man like Situpe, or of an unmarried man of very low status, a *rabisman* (m.p. [Melanesian Pidgin]: '*rabis*,' rubbish) who acted as their servant, was an exception to the rule that ordinary men, those without the immunity of high position or almost none at all, did not consort with women and certainly not during childbirth. Despite the fact that Big Men, like men in general, greeted the news of a girl's birth with obligatory expressions of disgust and shrill demands to "throw her in the river," and refused for weeks even to look at newborn girls, they often displayed tenderness and patience with daughters and granddaughters once they were older infants and toddlers. Just how attentive and affectionate a Big Man like Situpe might have been with his own young daughters is illustrated by his current relationship with two of his married daughters and, especially, with his granddaughters. His eldest daughter, Kamale, came back to her father's compound after running away from a first marriage in a neighbouring village, the birthplace of her mother Aramo, Situpe's second wife. Her father-in-law's sexual advances were intolerable, Kamale told me, so she came back home and now lived with her second husband, 'Paronte,' their two daughters and 'Paronte's childless first wife, Tipi, in her father's compound, an abnormal arrangement in a patrilineal and patrilocal society made possible by Situpe's elevated status. See Fig. 2.2.

On one of my first visits to Situpe's compound I found him sitting among a group of women and children that included Aramo, his second wife and mother of his married daughters Kamale and Sege, and Sege who sat cross-legged nursing her infant son. Aramo leaned over to kiss the baby and suck on his sex before taking him off his mother's breast and fondling him while Sege sat impassive, the slumped appendage of swollen breasts. Kamale's four-year-old daughter 'Fandi' placed her hands over the baby's genitals and then hit her younger sister when she tried to do the same thing. Some time later, around a small fire on the other side of the compound, Situpe sat with Sege in an intimate threesome holding his infant grandson tenderly in his arms. After a while, still cradling his newest grandchild, Situpe got up and led the way to his garden with Aramo a few steps behind him carrying his bow and arrows.

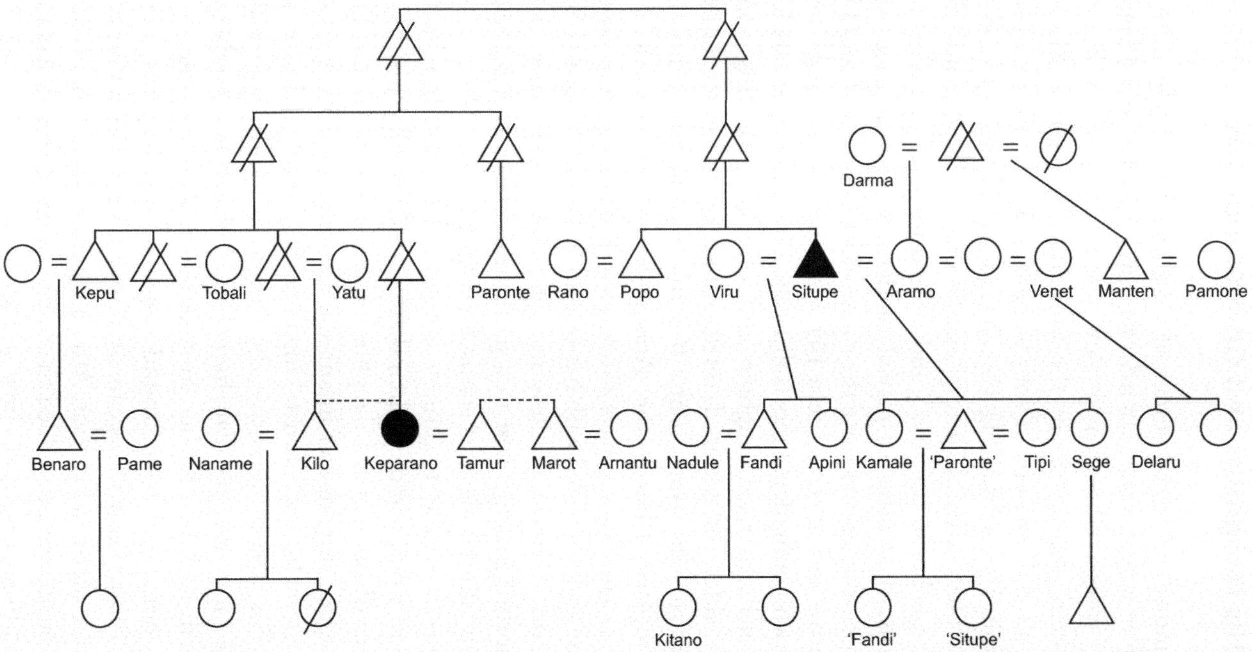

Fig. 2.2 Relationships among some of the extended polygynous family and patrilineal kin of the Big Man Situpe. Kilo and Keparano are classificatory brother and sister. Marot and Tamur are classificatory brothers from a different clan. (© Gillian Gillison)

Aramo and other women played with the genitals of granddaughters, too. Among a group of women attending a woman in labour, Aramo lay down beside Kamale's infant daughter, whom Kamale had named 'Situpe' after her father,[4] and tugged at her labia and then kissed her own fingers. Smiling into 'Situpe's eyes, Aramo repeated the gesture several times before pulling the baby closer, kissing her face and gently 'eating' her lips. Some time later, when her mother took a piece of rotting sugarcane out of her hand, little 'Situpe' began to cry. To quiet her, Kamale held the baby above her head and kissed her sex. On other occasions, one or two women might take turns holding an infant boy in this same uplifted position and sucking his penis, then celebrate loudly if it became erect. Babies were sometimes handed around playfully among a group of women and young girls and boys, if any were present. Preadolescent girls toted infant siblings slung across their hips or on their backs with easy competence. But only married women indulged in extravagant displays of affection for infants of both sexes which at times struck me as competitive, especially between a mother and her married daughter. The handling of a child might also express competition between its mother's mother and father as, for example, Situpe's gentleness and understated attention to his grandson seemed to provide Sege with a refuge from her effusive and domineering mother.

Situpe was unsurpassable, brilliantly articulate and flamboyant when the occasion demanded but retiring most of the time, exercising control without display. In 1973 he was a man of about fifty, aware of his magnetism and the allure of the traditional garb he always wore: a rear-skirt of shiny red and green cordyline leaves, a netted fore-skirt suspended from a narrow bark-string belt, a pair of wide woven yellow-bamboo bands worn high on his muscular upper arms and, for formal occasions, a low crown of glistening black cassowary feathers. To his daughter Kamale he was irresistable. She spoke of his inimitable know-how and gentleness, the times when he appeared briefly on the river bank during difficult moments in her own and other women's labours.

I was with Kamale and her mother, Aramo, when the wife of one of Kamale's half-brothers, the elder son of Situpe's first wife, Viru (who of course could not be present), gave birth to a girl. Aramo carried her co-wife's grandchild up from the water's edge to the compound and into

Situpe's house where he sat in darkness on a raised platform at the back. In response to his silent disdain, Aramo reminded him, "It's [my son's] *biznis.*" Kamale suggested hitting the baby on the head with a rock before she gently took her in her arms and put her to the breast. As she did this, her own younger daughter, little 'Situpe,' threw herself on the floor in a jealous fit and wailed unconsolably. Her grandfather, big Situpe, patiently tried to calm her and Kamale offered her daughter the other breast but she was too furious to accept it.

About two months earlier, Kamale fought publicly with the newborn's mother, her sister-in-law Nadule, ostensibly because of a quarrel between their elder daughters, Nadule's firstborn, Kitano, and Kamale 's firstborn 'Fandi' (named for Kamale's half-brother and Nadule's husband). The lead-up to the incident went something like this: 'Fandi' got into a fight with another girl about her age named Ike, whose family lived in the same compound and, like everyone except Kamale, her husband, co-wife and children, were related as members of Situpe's patrilineage. Ike knocked out one of 'Fandi's' teeth but Ike's father refused to offer compensation. Kamale fumed. A short time later, 'Fandi' and Kitano bickered and Nadule twisted 'Fandi's' ear. 'Fandi' ran home in tears. "Kitano hit me," she told her mother, whereupon Kamale burst out of her house and ran to the site of the communal earth oven. "First Ike, now Kitano...!" she yelled. The next day, while Kitano and 'Fandi' were getting along fine, Kamale continued to sulk. Tensions ran high within Situpe's extended polygynous family, especially between Kamale and her sister-in-law, Nadule, who often used their children and pigs as surrogates. If the rules of patrilocal residence were followed, the two women would not reside in the same compound.

A Feud in the Extended Family

Some six months after the 'Fandi'-Kitano episode, and after Kamale's tender ministrations to Nadule's newborn daughter, a fracas erupted in the night. Above the shrieks and hollers, I heard Situpe shouting and then a long collective howl, "*hooooooooo!*" By the time I arrived the clearing outside Situpe's house was filled with people from other compounds holding brightly-burning flares. Through the crowd, I saw Situpe, his oldest son Fandi, Fandi's mother Viru who was Situpe's first wife, Situpe's second wife Aramo, Situpe's brother Popo, Popo's wife and Kamale's garden partner, Rano, and Kamale's husband 'Paronte' standing around an open space where Nadule, Fandi's wife, and Kamale confronted one another, each woman wielding a sharply pointed wooden stake yanked out of the fence surrounding the compound. (See Fig. 2.2 above.) Nadule's pig—that is, Fandi's pig which is also Situpe's pig because the herd belongs to father and son—broke into Kamale's and Rano's garden that morning and uprooted newly-planted sweet potatoes. Kamale and Nadule were circling one another. In the crowd, women and men were yelling simultaneous monologues. Suddenly, everyone jumped to clear the way as Kamale darted into her house. She came running back outside a moment later carrying a net bag filled with the sweet potatoes she accused Nadule's pig of uprooting. Kamale shook the bag violently and the stunted tubers bounced onto the hard ground.

Except for Situpe and Fandi, men stayed mostly in the background or tried ineffectually to intercede between the two ferocious women. Viru rushed to the fence and pulled out a sharpened post with which to strike Rano. But Rano's younger brother, who happened to be visiting from another village, stood firmly between the two women. Then Situpe pulled up a fence post and he, too, threatened Rano who was now bearing the brunt of everyone's fury all by herself. Rano seemed to be in her element, fierce and majestic, while her husband Popo who was shorter than she, part-albino with a wandering eye, remained on the sidelines. Some time later, Situpe approached his younger brother and quietly snarled. "You eat all my food. But you are *pipia* (m.p. [Melanesian Pidgin], garbage). Does that seem right to you?"

Fandi ordered Rano to leave: "Maybe you'd like to go now! Get the hell out of here before I make you piss on the spot!" Then, all at once, as Rano's visiting brother seemed to deflate the battle between Rano and Viru, violence erupted between Situpe and his eldest daughter Kamale. Each one held a sharp post and looked ready to come to blows when Aramo stepped between them. With his fingernails, Situpe drew blood from Kamale's forehead above the bridge of her nose. Moments later, a *rabisman* (m.p., 'rubbish man,' 'nobody') from another compound came between father and daughter. Half-smiling, Situpe's grey-haired mother remarked, "... with his own daughter!" The old woman repeated to me that Fandi's pigs dug up Kamale's and Rano's newly-planted tubers. As Situpe, Aramo and Kamale moved apart and tensions seemed to ease, Situpe lifted his bark-cloth fore-skirt to expose himself. "You give me *nothing*!" he shouted at his eldest daughter. "My son and I will not eat the heads of your children!" Kamale and her half-brother Fandi began to yell at each other from opposite sides of a nearby tree whose lower branch was festooned with pigs' jaws, trophies of the many feasts Situpe hosted. Standing behind her husband, Nadule shrieked, "I will not eat the heads of your children, Kamale! Let *Popo* eat them!" To refuse to "eat the heads" of Kamale's children, especially in high dudgeon before a crowd, was to curse them (cf. Wagner 1967).

"To eat the head of the child" is the Gimi idiom for the mother's brother and father (and other patrilineal kin) receiving valuables, mainly cash and cooked pigs or, in the past, marsupials, from the child's father and men of his patrilineage. "Head" payments are owed to the mother's brother and father in virtual perpetuity, starting at birth and continuing throughout infancy and childhood with naming, teething, a first haircut, weaning, when the child falls ill or is otherwise vulnerable; at puberty after rites of initiation and at other 'life crises' until the marriage of a daughter or throughout the life of a son (Gillison 1993, 2016). The "head of the child" is offered to the mother's father and brother (and their wives) in exchange for the child's very life: over time, the accumulation of "head" payments emancipates the child from its mother by coming to terms with her brother and father instead of her. These two men represent the child's original mythic Father, the mother's "first husband," the Moon, *and* her "firstborn child sired by the Moon," the one who left her body as 'dead blood' and had to be brought back to life at puberty in men's rites of initiation.

Unless the child's 'second father,' who is the mother's current husband, can 'persuade' her brother and father—two men who represent her mythical "first husband" and resurrected "firstborn child"—to accept 'other meat' ("head" payments) as substitutes for the child's own flesh and blood, her "first husband" will *take the child back* in the same way as a new father, not provided with 'other food,' feeds irresistably upon his own newborn (see above page 36). "This wilful malignancy has to be seen for what it is – the principal coercive moral nucleus of kinship. The child's flesh derives from the maternal uncle's .... [and] a disgrunted MB, when deprived of his rightful payments, will destroy his own substantial [self] embodied in his sister's child's (ZCh) flesh" (Mimica In press: 60–61). Without "head" payments as inducement to (continue to) release the child into the world outside the mother's body, the child's connection to her "first husband"—*as his "firstborn"*—will reassert itself or remain in tact. The child whose "head" is not eaten by its mother's father and brother cannot grow up nor prosper because it reverts to the deadly 'custody' of its original parents, the mother and her "first husband," the cannibal Moon.

In this instance, it was Situpe and Fandi who were the designated recipients of the "heads" of Kamale's two daughters—whom she named 'Fandi' and 'Situpe'! As Fandi's wife, it was also up to Nadule to consume her nieces' "heads" and consummate their life-sustaining release from their mother Kamale (as, according to the rules of sister exchange marriage, it would be up to Kamale to provide the same service reciprocally to Nadule's children). The violent feud in Situpe's polygynous family vividly illustrates not only the extent to which the primordial era described in both sexes' myths and rites *translates directly into the prenatal origins of each person,* but also how each person's prehistory, *rooted in the mother's origins*, remains unresolved, threatens to come undone, and therefore has to be *re*done again and again in rites of exchange. Everything that happens inside a woman's body *starting with her own conception inside her mother*, has to be repeated in the Gimi 'macrocosmos'—the world outside the mother's body which is a giant version of the one inside it. Women's myths and rites portray the Moon who, in ordinary parlance, is every woman's "first husband," as the Giant Penis, Dream Man, Python or vicious Old Wild Man who roams the mountain forest that is synonymous with the inner precincts of the First Woman's body.[5] In public exchanges of "head" payments, the Ogre in women's myths is personified as the mother's own father because he is the one one who brought her to life inside her mother and fed her from the "head" of his penis before she was born—a point Situpe made to Kamale with obscene flourish in the midst of their violent family feud.

Understood in women's mythic terms, which describe the mother's own ontogenesis, exchanges of "head" payments gradually release each child from its mother by compensating the Father she still harbors, a Father ensconsed inside her as part of her very being who, unless fed a substitute, will make a meal of her every child *who are as much his children as she is herself.* As a figure *hidden inside* mother, her Father is inclined to 'take back' without compunction 'every one who got away' from the head of his penis during the original copulations that fed the mother as an embryo and foetus and installed her 'firstborn' in the process. The only way for men to access the 'mother's myth' is paradoxically to exclude her, 'pass through her body,' and negotiate only with the men who represent the Father and baby Brother *she* mythologized and got so far out of proportion! As designated recipients of the "heads" of Kamale's daughters, Situpe and Fandi, Kamale's father and brother, embody the Giant Penis as it exists *outside* Kamale's body: unlike the Giant and his formless bloody offspring, whom Kamale keeps to herself, her father and brother are two men with whom other men can 'do business.' They act as surrogates: their accepting "head" payments spare her children by satiating the lust of the Giant she hides.

* * *

While the atmosphere in the crowd inside Situpe's compound remained at fever pitch, there was a lull among the combatants. Walking toward her house, Rano turned to insult Nadule: "*One* pig you're so proud of raising! Not too many, huh!" The fury unleashed by Nadule's pig invading Kamale's and Rano's garden revealed deep antagonisms within Situpe's polgynous household and lineage compound where, according to the rules of patrilocal residence, Kamale was not supposed to reside. The 'family riot' put on display the warring factions centred around Viru and Aramo, Situpe's first and second wives. (Neither Situpe's childless third wife nor his widowed fourth wife Venet whose children had a different father figured in this competition.) In Viru's camp were Situpe, aligned with her older son Fandi in joint ownership of the pig herd; and Nadule, Fandi's wife and keeper of the herd. In Aramo's camp were Situpe's elderly mother; Aramo's daughter Kamale; and Popo and Rano, Situpe's alienated "true" brother and sister-in-law who shared a garden with Kamale. The five women: Kamale, Nadule, Aramo, Viru and Rano—each one inimitable, forceful, stunningly articulate—controlled the mood and much of daily life in Situpe's compound.

Fig. 2.3 Unloading a communal earth oven located at the far end of a compound. (© David Gillison)

Relations Among the Women of a Compound

During the preparation of red pandanus fruit, a semi-cultivated delicacy to be distributed among the lineage, Situpe berated the women for laziness, singling out his childless third wife: "You women like to eat but not to work!" he shouted. Immediately Aramo yelled back, reminding Situpe that her co-wife was too ill to participate. Sitting beside Situpe at feasts, Aramo often gave testimonials in defense of women, tugging the arms of those near her to get their attention: "We work, we gather food, now we have meat to cook and to eat!" Although Aramo is Situpe's obvious favorite, the wife whose company he prefers, Viru wins out on critical family matters. Viru is the mother of Fandi, the eldest son, and of a second son with political ambitions away at a mission school. Viru badgers Situpe about his duty to Fandi and fights with him when she sees his loyalty waning. Aramo's 'best' offspring is Kamale, whose intelligence and charisma make her outshine a younger brother and her husband 'Paronte,' who was an onlooker during his wife's furious confrontation with her father and brother—Situpe and Fandi—whose "same names" she chose for her two daughters. In the eyes of other women Kamale is a "strong woman." Despite her sex, she is her mother's star and she battles her half-brother Fandi for a place beside her father she cannot win.

Ironically, Kamale 's 'masculine striving' ran aground on what Gimi regard as the quintessentially female attribute which Kamale possessed in abundance, namely, the talent for *over-attachment*, the capacity to connect with nurtured objects—human, vegetable and porcine. Women's secret spells for cultivating gardens and rearing pigs aim to join the woman's *auna* (lit: 'spirit' or 'life-force') with the *auna* of each vegetable or pig in her care, making the food flourish by extending to it the kind of exclusive connection that unite mother and child. Some Gimi women breast fed shoats and divided the same tuber of sweet potato between suckling pig and nursing infant. When a man decided to kill a pig in order to fulfil his debts to other men, he summoned his wife or daughter-in-law or another woman who reared it to perform a rite above the pig's head to recapture her *auna,* the portion of her life-force that she invested in her charge over the years she nurtured it and the reason it thrived. At the moment the animal breathed its last, the woman care-giver 'took back' her *auna* as it escaped through the "first mouth" on top of the dying pig's head, replenishing the volatile reservoir she needed to draw upon to nurture other pigs.

There was no 'rite of recapture' for the mother of a dying child, however. When a child lay dying, the mother performed a rite of permanent severence by amputating one of her fingers above the middle joint, usually on her left hand, as Aramo did for a son born after Kamale, as Nadule did for a firstborn daughter and as had almost every woman in the village over a certain age. (In addition to her own children, a woman might amputate finger joints to commemorate the deaths of her husband, his brother and his father, men who contributed to her brideprice.) In stark contrast to the ministrations over the head of a pig about to be slaughtered, amputation of part of a finger on account of the death of a child marked its uniqueness and *irreplaceability*, serving as permanent reminder of a life the mother could never 'take back.'

Without conjuring mystifying fictions about 'the partible person' or 'shared being,' one may understand Kamale's rage at Nadule, on account of what Nadule's pig did to Kamale's newly-planted tubers, as based upon Kamale's view of Nadule's pig as an extension of her, a repository of Nadule's *auna* and instrument of her will. Nadule's pig exposed feelings and attitudes toward Kamale which until then, in Kamale's view, Nadule kept mostly under wraps. Six months earlier Kamale had attended Nadule's accouchement. It was she who gave Nadule's newborn girl her first breast milk.

In the months that followed, Kamale played with her younger daughter 'Situpe' and Nadule's new baby girl. After fondling and kissing the baby and then handing her back to her mother, Kamale mischievously took hold of her daughter's arm and hit the baby, mocking 'Situpe's' jealous fit on the day the baby was born. Kamale's childless co-wife, Tipi, sat nearby. Tipi, like Nadule, was missing her left index finger above the middle joint to commemorate the loss of a child: little 'Situpe' was "hers," she told me, and pushed a nipple into her mouth, to which 'Situpe' reacted with a gesture making plain she preferred her own mother. The next day Kamale confided with some relish that Tipi had delivered five living babies, three boys and two girls, all of whom died soon after birth, implying that Tipi killed at least some of them, as women sometimes did. Although the example may seem extreme—Kamale with two thriving daughters, several pigs and plentiful gardens and her co-wife with no children, no pigs and little success at gardening—it was true that among the Gimi women I knew, a talent for nurturing, which Gimi of both sexes equated with the capacity to 'invest oneself' intimately in other lives, tended to be present in some women and weak or lacking in others (Gillison 2001). Certainly, women were not considered to be 'naturally' good mothers or successful cultivators (Gillison 1993: 43). Spells for gardening and pig-rearing were jealously guarded and shared only with daughters and daughters-in-law.

Gardening

Perhaps Aramo had been the kind of mother her daughter Kamale now was. Kamale was very attached to her infant daughter 'Situpe' and kept her to sleep beside her in the same bed, sending her older daughter 'Fandi' to sleep with Aramo in Situpe's house a few doors away. In defiance of the rules of patrilineal kinship and patrilocal residence, Kamale stayed close to her parents, not just by living with her husband, daughters and co-wife in the same compound, but also by acquiring gardens from her father, which was one reason her newly-planted plot lay in the path of her sister-in-law's pig. The end of December 1973 was a season for planting new gardens. On account of Situpe's stature, his large expanse of cultivable land lay conveniently on wide, gentle slopes not far from his compound. There he organized the distribution of crops and partition of garden plots to allow him to take food from each of his four wives in turn. As a Big Man, Situpe participated in the acquisition of other men's wives, especially the sons of affines with whom he was already allied by exchanges of women in marriage: contributing pigs to a woman's brideprice entitled Situpe to a portion of her labour on his land thus enabling him, unlike men of lesser means, to add to his own wives' production.

Men did the heavy work of removing rocks and hacking protruding roots of trees after they cut them down. They also laid out internal boundaries and planted stakes for beans to climb, another boundary-setting activity, and took ample breaks to converse and delouse their hunting dogs. Bent over, straight-kneed, with their buttocks raised and heads nearly touching the ground, women planted varieties of taro and sweet potato. One woman, whose infant was miserable with scabies, kept her in her arms as she uprooted bracken or cut down saplings, pausing often to nurse, caress and comfort her baby with whispered songs, soft whistling and monosyllabic murmurs.

Women interrupted their garden work to breast feed and snack on tubers of cooked taro or sweet potato. At one point, Situpe—playfully?—approached Aramo from behind and pushed what he was eating into her face. She stood up and delivered a loud punch to the middle of his back. Kamale, meanwhile, sharpened her digging stick and went to harvest sweet potato from a section of her mother's garden, working her way up towards her own adjacent plot that was unseparated from her mother's by a fence or boundary. This area of garden land was given to Situpe by Aramo's father and was still worked by her mother, Darma, Kamale's grandmother, who lived in the neighboring village where, in conformity with the rules of sister exchange, Kamale was first married: in other words, Kamale might have worked the plot Situpe assigned to her even if she did not flout convention by leaving her first husband and taking up residence with a second one inside her father's compound.

After nearly three hours of labor, Kamale descended to a rain shelter to cook ears of corn. Then she rejoined her mother to harvest sweet potato, the two of them wielding digging sticks convivially side by side. Situpe arrived to plant stakes for sweet potatoes and soon announced that he had a splinter in his finger. Kamale stopped work and gently removed the splinter in her father's finger, sharing a tender moment with him only a month or so before their violent confrontation when he exposed himself to her. Certainly, Kamale's intimacy with her father seemed more important to her than her relation with her husband 'Paronte.' By the end of the day, at about four o'clock in the afternoon, uxorious 'Paronte' arrived in the garden to share the women's meal of sweet potatoes and greens. He was the only man present.

Benaro and His Infant Daughter

Although relations between fathers and adult daughters were sometimes warm and demonstrative, especially when the father was a man of importance able to marry his daughters close to home (although not in the same compound), they could also be geographically and affectively distant. In early 1974, during the same garden-making season, but with another family in a different garden, I came upon a man named Benaro 'playing' with his daughter of about eighteen months. Benaro's wife, Pame; Benaro's mother; his soon-to-be-married sister; and the wife of one of his lineage brothers were taking a break to snack and nurse infants. To the women's immense delight Benaro emerged from the adjacent brush holding a live marsupial rat, a species tabooed to men but relished by women.

The three or four tiny squirming young that Benaro's sister removed from the rat's pouch were an added delicacy. She and Benaro pulled out the animal's valuable fur and placed the soft tufts on a broad leaf, leaving only the fur adhering to the rat's tail to be made into a woman's bracelet. As his daughter lay nursing in his wife's arms, Benaro shook the denuded live mother rat in the baby's face, provoking a mild protest from his wife.

Benaro removed two more young from the rat's pouch and then snapped each of its limbs to facilitate removal of the remaining fur. He held the animal's pulsating white body next to his nursing daughter and struck her gently with the soft furry tail. As the marsupial stared out of glassy round eyes, its mouth dripping blood, Benaro hit it on the head and pushed it again onto his daughter who was now screaming. Benaro lifted the baby out of his wife's arms and placed her on his lap where he made her hold the dying mother rat. He inserted one of the young into the baby's mouth and watched it wriggle slowly back out and slide over his daughter's trembling belly. After taking the baby back into her arms to suckle, Benaro's wife reached into the dead rat's pouch, pulled out another live foetal rat and dropped it onto her baby's face, whereupon she let go of the nipple and yowled. Using the edge of his axe blade, Benaro opened the mother rat's underside and his wife removed the innards to prepare them for cooking.

The Death of Naname's Infant Daughter

When an expectant mother expressed ambivalence or aversion to the upcoming birth, men of her husband's lineage usually sent an older woman to attend the delivery. And when a woman was childless after loosing many babies, men accused her of killing them and of being too fond of sex: "We get angry at her," one man told me. "'We want there to be plenty of us! Why kill your babies so we are short of men and have no name [reputation]?' That woman only wants sex." From what I observed, there was no sure way for others to compel a reluctant mother to raise her child. Naname, the pregnant mother of an eighteen- or twenty-month-old daughter still at the breast was subjected to taunts and gossip, ridiculed along with her husband for unseemly indulgence during the post-partum taboo on sex. The day of the delivery, Naname tried to give away her newborn daughter to the wife of one of her fathers-in-law, a main contributor to her brideprice, whom he had selected to nurse the newborn's elder sister. But Naname's husband Kilo angrily forbade her to make a gift of his child.

Early one evening about two months later, I was sitting with Naname and her older 'sister,' a married woman visiting from Naname's distant natal village. Naname picked a huge furry caterpillar off the leaf of a nearby shrub and, after daring me to hold it, taunted her elder daughter so she sought refuge in the other woman's arms. The two women wore rings taken from pop-top beer cans (see Fig. 2.4 below). Playfully, Naname shoved a fist in my face to demonstrate how women in Ubagubi dealt with prospective co-wives. The two women laughed when I twisted my fists in opposite directions to wring the neck of an imaginary rival. But in the months that followed, Naname rarely masked her anger. Very early one morning I awoke to a keening chorus and ran to Situpe's compound. I found it quiet and empty and went into Kamale's house where I found her nursing a sore, swollen thumb. "I thought it was her nipple!' her husband 'Paronte' drolled, "So I bit it!" I asked him the cause of the long wail at daybreak. "We have now entered fighting season!" he told me. Naname hit Yatu, her mother-in-law, and drew blood from "her nose, her mouth, her chest!" I wandered over to Yatu's small "pig house" at the far end of the compound where she sat alone beside a fire, a little scratched but fine. She told me Naname hit her *and her son!* No one would tell me what started the fight but it seemed that Naname had no sympathizers.

Later in the day, I learned that one of Naname's pigs "killed" (slightly injured) one of Yatu's pigs. Yatu shrieked at Naname and Naname struck her, taking out one of the old woman's very few very loose teeth. "Don't hit my poor old mother!" Naname's husband, Kilo, yelled. Then he hit Naname. She walked to the edge of the compound, tied a rope around her neck and started to climb a tree. But the trunk was slimy from the night's rain so the rope slid to the ground. Everyone gathered to watch Kilo remove the rope from Naname's neck, I was told. "If you kill Yatu and she dies," they all admonished her, "You alone, only *you* Naname, must have the pigs and money to pay her brothers for her head (i.e., the "head" payments owed as death compensation)! You better have the means [to buy her head] *all by yourself!*"

When Naname's new baby became deathly ill at about ten months some of those who had ridiculed her wantonness accused her of lethal neglect. Women in her compound reacted with the same scorn, even contempt, they showed during her pregnancy, pointing out how Naname carried her sick baby to her garden through heavy rains. Mothers of sick infants were supposed to remain inside their houses all day long for days on end, hugging their babies close to the fire. When I looked surprised by the severity of the criticism, the women became impatient with me, repeated my name derisively as if to say, 'Come on. Don't *play around* with us. You know very well what happened!' They recalled the day Naname delivered her baby near a boulder on the narrow bank of the river. The women waited there for hours, napped, netted string bags, brought Naname tobacco and cooked sweet potato and, to my occasional inept questions about where babies come from, answered, "I don't know." Suddenly Naname met my eyes and told me to leave. I complied at once thinking I oughtn't to have been there. Now the women told me that Naname ordered me to leave because she intended to kill her child, which her mid-wives, especially her sister-in-law, prevented her from even attempting.

Her baby daughter's final illness was drawn out; and once it became clear that she would die, Kilo and Yatu, the baby's father and paternal grandmother, inserted themselves as chief mourners to supplant Naname's shows of grief. Kilo sat on one side of the house holding the dying baby in his arms, blowing continuously over her, his mother crouched at his back, Naname frantic by his side. "She is not yours," Kilo said when Naname tried to take the baby in her arms. Women who were scornful during Naname's pregnancy and after her failed suicide attempt now arrived to sob and wail, reciting the names of infants they had lost. Naname got up and walked out of the house. She picked up a bushknife, laid her left hand on an upended stump and hacked off the end of her left index finger. Inside, Kilo commanded the baby to "Wake up! wake up!" Handing the limp body to his mother, Kilo went outside to prepare an earth oven: he planned to hold his dying daughter over the rising steam, he told me, so she could imbibe the food's tantalizing odor and regain her appetite for life.

To find a remedy to save the baby, Kilo and his comrades rehashed the sins of his youth: as a young bachelor, Kilo smoked a marsupial out of its nest deep inside a cave, sent in his dog to drag it out and killed it. The marsupial's *kore* (lit: 'spirit' or 'ghost') had lain in wait ever since. The moment his child fell sick, the murdered marsupial's *kore* found its chance for revenge. Kilo and two other men went to the cave where he killed the marsupial many years ago, in low-lying marshy ground called *neki maha* (lit: *neki*, 'insane' or 'mad' + *maha* 'ground'), a place where life both teems and stagnates, where things arise and decompose quickly, disappearing into "wild" (*kore*) surroundings. A *neki maha* is rife with plants easily trampled and with small creatures—bats, snakes, frogs, toads and marsupials—easily destroyed. If a baby died with its teeth clenched, the vengeful *kore* of a bat that clenches its teeth when cooked was taking revenge; if a child writhed in agony, a snake's *kore* was avenging itself (Gillison 1993: 224–28).

All sorcery, even that perpetrated by measly swamp plants and creatures, operated on the principle that the perpetrator *stole* some part of the victim: if—even momentarily, remotely or indirectly—the avenging sorcerer were forced to come into contact with his victim, the spirit of the missing piece would be restored and the sorcery neutralized. The attack on Kilo's unweaned baby, still an integral part of Kilo, might be retaliation for what Kilo stole when he murdered the marsupial in his youth. Kilo chipped a fragment of rock off the entrance to the cave where the marsupial nested and brought it to Naname. "You tricked me, my child! You lied!" she keened, repeating her admonition in rhythmic intonations.

When the rigid unresponsive baby suddenly opened her mouth, Naname inserted her finger to make a place for her nipple to drip milk between the baby's teeth. "My one and only, you did not listen ..." Even when Naname's voice quavered, faltered and broke, her cries were cadenced and repetitious like riffs on women's "secret" songs to plants and pigs that plead with "my one and only," "my sweetest thing ... to come inside and grow big." Other women present counted the deaths of their own infants. From my genealogies I knew that children's deaths were common. Yet never did anyone say or suggest that 'this is the way life is' nor, in light of Naname's much-condemned mothering, that her baby daughter's death was in any way expectable, acceptable or routine. The baby would be Naname's last, Kilo announced. He had "sealed her shut."

* * *

Perhaps, I thought at the time, Naname's guilt heightened her grief. Perhaps the torment of losing a child she did not want, or that caused her shame, expressed itself in exquisite, inventive and excessive mourning. It also struck me how dissimilar were men's and women's styles of mourning. The father had recourse to remedies that required him to review his unmarried adventures with his comrades, go with them into the forest and perform a cure that interrupted the interminable death watch. The mother, on the other hand, had no ready escape nor easy comradery. She was perpetually present, adept at performing unmediated connection to her child.

Part II

Gimi women and men appeared to me to possess the same qualities: anyone might be intelligent, articulate, domineering, flamboyant, charismatic, courageous, eccentric, devious, obscene, cruel, craven, humourous, timid, tender, talented, kind-hearted, vicious or violent. Even the thing that supposedly set women apart and accounted for men's and other women's sometimes implacable hostility, what I call the *'I-thou' mode,* a symbiotic style that originates in the attachment of mother and child but extends through magic to plants, pigs, utensils and other adults, was certainly not restricted to women. Men who used magic or sorcery also relied upon the 'female' mode of intimate connection by stealing the body-leaving of an unsuspecting victim. But unlike men, women were not *entitled* to resort to violence, certainly not as a group, which meant that cultivating exclusive attachments as the way to exert control over others was considered women's specialty.

Violence was perhaps the ultimate source of prestige in the estimation of both sexes. In pre-contact Highland New Guinea, warfare was endemic. Men's preparations for battle, communal residence in barracks-like "men's houses" from which women and children were strictly excluded and kept at a distance, stockaded ridge-top settlements, rites of male initiation that created warrior cohorts and age grades, on-going strategizing for surprise attacks and for defense, shifting regional alliances and hostilities among settlements, indeed, the entire male-dominated political system was directed against the violent male 'enemy without.' But men's organizations and preparations for war in the past were also explicitly designed to combat the everpresent 'enemy within' best described as a noxious femininity that originated in menstrual blood and permeated women's 'way of being,' a specifically *dyadic mode of relating* to others inherent in the mothering role that was contagious, even 'promiscuous,' and could be co-opted by sorcerers. In times of war women's very presence was a menace: women could ruin men's weapons, implements and other artifacts like smoking paraphernalia and net bags merely by stepping over them or "passing them between her thighs," a danger Gimi women still embodied.

The 'female style' inspired women's grievances against each other and hampered their efforts to coalesce into consistent factions essential for success in wider conflicts. The following incident of violence and obscene taunts among two groups of women—skillfully deflated by two Big Women and a Big Man—illustrates the way women's tendency to rely on what I call dyadic connection impedes their attempts to come together as a group.

The Case of Keparano

A girl about twelve years old stumbled upon an adulterous tryst between Marot, the father of six children under fourteen and a newborn daughter; and Keparano, the wife of Marot's clan brother, Tamur. The pair were caught in a taro garden near the *bik rot*, the construction site of what the Subdistrict Headquarters at Lufa promised would be the first car-carrying road into the village. Work on the large project was a source of cash for both sexes who were paid at the same rate and came into contact with one another on a novel basis. It was the only setting women and men of different clans and compounds met without ritually-prescribed constraint. The girl who happened upon the adulterous pair informed Marot's wife, Arnantu, and she struck her husband in a rage. In retaliation, Marot cut off the top of Arnantu's left thumb and slashed both her breasts so that she could not nurse their infant daughter.

Towards the end of the day, in what I thought was a separate matter emanating from Situpe's compound in a different part of the village, Naname screamed for her husband Kilo to intervere in a fight raging between one of his paternal uncles, Kepu, and the widow of another named Tobali. Kepu was asserting his right to inherit his dead brother's wife, having contributed to her brideprice many years ago. Now Kepu was accusing Tobali of having secretly promised herself to Paronte, a charismatic Big Man like Situpe (and namesake of his sister's son 'Paronte' married to Situpe's daughter Kamale. See Fig. 2.2 above.) It was just before dark, the early evening hour of village-wide broadcasts shouted back and forth in a special call language, when complaints and grievances accummulated over the course of day were publicly aired. Kilo yelled to his uncle in another compound, "Tobali is still wearing widow's weeds! It is *unseemly* of you to demand to marry her now!" Paronte accused Kilo's uncle of shaming him but added provocatively that Tobali "likes" him. She "wants me," Paronte shouted from his own compound for all to hear, and she ought to "have" him.

After a brief lull, Marot the adulterer called out. He bought Keparano and gave her to his clan brother Tamur. But Tamur was a poor manager, Marot yelled, did not plant gardens nor raise pigs. In lieu of the pigs Tamur owed him in return for Keparano's brideprice, Marot now claimed Keparano as a second wife for himself. Then Marot's younger brother chimed in to berate him for slashing his wife Arnantu: "You just made a child and gave it [to her]. You were wrong to strike her! ... to wreck my 'mother' [i.e., elder brother's wife]!" To one and all Marot's younger brother announced that he intended to accede to Arnantu's demand to kill one of "her" pigs to compensate her father's widows and her father's brother for the injury Marot inflicted upon her. The back-and-forth ended at nightfall with the plan to hold a court the following day.

A cacophany of callings-out began first thing the next morning. As I stood beside Naname atop a boulder that separated our houses, she yelled, "Whoever beat up Keparano, speak up now! Come down here so I can shove my hand up your cunts and pull out your guts! You think we're all *dead* down here? ... we women of Keparano's lineage? Some of us are still alive so stop *playing around* with us!" Naname was Keparano's designated sister-in-law and helpmate. Standing behind Naname, another woman shouted, "Keparano is not the child of a dog! ... the child of a pig! ... the child of a tree! Keparano is the child of *men* [some of whom recently] died so you think you can *play around* with her!" Very early that morning, I now learned, a gang of women led by Arnantu beat up Keparano *with stones!* From our stance atop the boulder, we saw sticks flying above the neighbouring compound and rushed there to find Situpe and his fourth wife, Venet, brandishing sharp fence posts. Venet and her married daughter, Delaru, were part of Arnantu's gang. Situpe hit Venet in the eye and she retreated inside her house.

The rest of us, a group of ten or so women, climbed to Keparano's compound and found her sitting outside the door of her house, huddled under a blanket and bloodied, rings from pop-top beer cans arming her fingers (Fig. 2.4). The arriving women shouted abuse at her assailants and their allies who were already assembled, thirty or forty strong, some eight metres above us on higher ground: "Plentiful were the men who bore her but many have died so you dare to *play around* with her!" "*Rikipiooooooo!* " they yelled the name of Rikipi, one of Keparano's attackers. "Come down here *now!* .... That little passage you have for fucking! I can go up there, *toooooo!*"

After they beat up Keparano, three of her young married assailants, Rikipi and her co-wife Lantu and Venet's daughter Delaru, lifted up their string skirts and thrust their pudenda into her mouth. "You hit her with *stones* and then you put your *cunts* into her mouth?!" A concession came from above: "The women were wrong to beat her. They should have left it to the *komiti* and the *konsul*." With the exception of her sheepish husband Tamur, the contingent of women surrounding Keparano expelled all the men from the enclosure around her house and continued to scream abuse at the clanswomen of Keparano's attackers on higher ground: "She

Fig. 2.4 A woman subjected to a gang beating after a young girl reported having stumbled upon her during an adulterous tryst. Her fingers, like those of many young married women, are armed with metal rings pulled off pop-top beer cans. (© Gillian Gillison)

is not a woman of another place who came here to marry. She was *born* here! And you beat her! So now face us!" Addressing Keparano, Rano shouted rhetorically: "Arnantu beat you while we were far away. If we had been anywhere near you we would have fought for you. We are fighters!" Trying feebly to disperse the cluster of women surrounding his wife, Tamur told them she was not worth fighting for. She was herself to blame! "Her leg is badly wounded. Let her suffer," he said. "No," Rano replied. "She is *not* nobody. Even if her fathers have died, we, her mothers, are *heeeeere!*"

Fig. 2.5 After a woman accused of adultery was beaten by a gang of women, her own kinswomen joined forces to confront her attackers, the adulterer's wife and her allies seen in the distance. During the day-long confrontation between the two groups of women, a Big Woman of the victim's clan yelled abuse at their adversaries gathered on elevated ground some 50 metres away. (© Gillian Gillison)

From the higher ground, one of Arnantu's clanswomen blamed the men, the only time during the whole affair anyone did so: "Let Marot and Tamur fight [over Keparano]! You women should not fight [us]! What are [we] women doing?" Down the hill, Tamur continued to blame his wife Keparano, saying, "I told her to follow me when we left the garden but she dallied. Arnantu saw her chance ..." Rano told Tamur their fury was justified, recounting the beating Situpe gave Venet earlier that morning: "'This isn't *your* affair!' Situpe yelled at Venet. 'Why did you take up *someone else's* fight?!' He hit her and drew blood. If Delaru [Venet's daughter] sees the blood on her mother and comes down [into our compound], we will hit her, too." "It is not up to *men* to help us women!" another woman interjected. "We women want to fight [by] ourselves. Let's call on women everywhere to come down here and help us now!"

"Beating [Keparano] is one thing. Shoving your cunts into her mouth is another. You are not the only ones with cunts! ..." "I'm going to kill you Lantu! *Lantuoooooooo!* Get down here right now!" Rano screamed. "You and Arnantu are so pleased with yourselves for what you did to Keparano. Keparano is a married woman and Marot seduced her and ... you ganged up on her so we have come here [to fight you]!" Among a group of men also assembled on higher ground in the distance was the *komiti* Benaro (torturer of a mother rat and son of the over-eager would-be widow-inheritor Kepu) who ordered the women to be quiet, to stop their "nothing talk" (*natinikaina*, lit: *natini*, m.p. 'nothing' + *kaina*, 'speech'). "*natinikaina*!!" Rano yelled back furiously. "Keparano is covered in blood! Her head is broken and battered! She is beaten to a pulp." Benaro told her to bring Keparano up the hill so the men could inspect her wounds and assess damages. The women replied that Keparano could not walk! Benaro descended from higher ground and stepped into the women's midst. He lifted Keparano's blanket and examined her hastily. "25 pounds and two pigs," he announced (calculating in Australian currency), "and she has born two children. Her brideprice is gone [i.e., her two children cancel her patriline's debt]. We will just take her back."

"Lantu has a cunt!" Rano screamed. "We *too* have cunts to shove into your mouths!" Tamur began an incoherent defense of his wife: "We have courts where women speak, where a woman can say, 'I want a new husband,' and everyone can hear her." But there was no court so Arnantu has no cause to beat Keparano. "Keparano was just fucking around," Tamur continued, "so Arnantu has no reason to be furious and to beat her up." Rano repeated Benaro's pronouncement: "We will take Keparano back [home] with us!"

After more shouting and obscenities, Keparano's allies proceeded to the upper compound where the two *komiti* and other men were assembled and sat down. Behind them, supported by her puny husband, Keparano ascended limping, her face hideously swollen, her bark-string skirts splattered and matted with dark blood. She sat down at the end of the line of seated women and hugged her blanket. In what felt to me like a startling *non sequitur*, the men began to speak of upcoming *sep-gavmen,* elections to be held for representation in the Eastern Highlands District, which would soon be a Province in the independent country of Papua New Guinea, and the *bik rot* that the *gavmen* was paying them to build. After a while, Benaro instructed the *komiti* to go to Lufa, the Subdistrict Headquarters, and to leave it to him and other men to settle the fight over Keparano: "Arnantu just bore a child and Marot killed one pig and gave it to her lineage," Benaro said. "They will buy rice and celebrate the feast for the newborn. This is what we decided."

The men strutted, gesticulated, preened and rattled while the women sat together in silence, their backs turned away from the men. The men discussed pigs and rice while women mulled over wounds received and to be inflicted. Paronte the elder arrived and addressed the group of Keparano's allies, women of his own clan: "The other women [of Arnantu's clan] have not beaten you. You are their equals! Do you hear me?" Led by Rano, all the women stood up and walked out of the enclosure in silence and disgust, leaving Keparano behind them. "You will be taxed ten *kina*!" Kilo shouted at his wife Naname as she passed him by. "Why don't you call for a tax on the women who beat Keparano?" she shouted back at him. "If Keparano is *paid*, we can settle this," Benaro's wife Pame added. "Otherwise we fight!" The women proceeded to a spot on lower ground, sat down in a circle and began to go over once again the details of Keparano's beating.

Naname: "Why didn't you fight? I wasn't there [at the road construction site where Keparano was beaten]. If I had been there, there would have been a fight!" Pame, Benaro's wife: "Benaro forbid me." The women rambled and went back over the circumstances of the attack. While Keparano was taking a breather, sitting down on the section of road she was digging, Delaru and Lantu came at her, "pushed her head to the ground so her ass and her legs were on top of her." Attempting to defend herself, Keparano picked up a stone and threw it but, because of the impossible position she was in, it went astray and cut a man's foot. Furious, the man reached for a bushknife tucked into the belt of a man working beside him, sliced the belt and left the other man standing naked, forcing him to dive into the ditch for cover. Meanwhile, three other women—Arnantu, Marot's wife, and her allies Rikipi and

Venet—*and* the man with the cut foot; *and* Marot, the adulterer; *and* Benaro, the elected *kemiti* who decided the compensation for Keparano's wounds would be "25 pounds and two pigs;" *and* Arnantu's paternal uncle who just received one of Arnantu's pigs to compensate *him* for the beating Marot gave Arnantu had joined in pummeling Keparano.

Rano: "We do not fight with sticks and break open heads. We fight with our hands. ... Arnantu had a big gang and our numbers were small so we did not fight for Keparano. ... We could have shoved a stick up Lantu's cunt but we did not do that!" Naname: "If they *pay* Keparano we can settle but if they do not *pay* her then we fight!" There was agreement all around. Then one woman added, "When the women who beat Keparano compensate her, she should put some aside for [the man whose foot she inadvertantly cut open]." "And for [the man who lost his fore-skirt], too," another woman said. "Keparano should pay for his shame!"

Paronte the Big Man arrived to address his clanswomen once again: "If you take up another woman's fight you can go to jail! A man who does that [joins the fight of someone who is unrelated to him] can go to jail too! If you try to fight me, I will not fight back. I will just stare straight ahead. So you cannot fight me." The assembled women wanted to defend Keparano but were at odds. Paronte elder hit upon an important issue. What business *was* it of the four women who joined Arnantu in ganging up on Keparano—Venet, Situpe's fourth wife, Venet's married daughter Delaru, and the co-wives Lantu and Rikipi, none of them linked to Arnantu by clanship or birthplace or any other recognized basis—to fight on her behalf? In each case, it occurred to me, the motive might be vicarious: each woman was about to be, or had just been, displaced inside her own household by the addition of a newer wife. Perhaps each of the four identified with Arnantu's rage against the adulterous Keparano and dared to vent her fury in the novel setting of a construction site where people of many compounds congregated willy nilly.

Standing before his clanswomen, Paronte raised the topic of last evening's broadcast about his affair with Tobali, accusing certain of them of taunting his rival Kepu. He addressed himself mainly to Naname, 'outing' her for goading Kepu with mean gossip. Naname admitted to me that Paronte's accusation was true. Weeks before, when she told me how pleased she was by Tobali's liaison with Paronte, I sensed her own longing and attraction to him. Now she seemed to concede, confidentially, her clandestine role in trying to spoil the match she openly favoured.

The group of women supporting Keparano started to leave, issuing parting threats to "fight Rikipi." Keparano retreated into her house with Tamur. Her clanswomen's threat, first issued by the *komiti*, to "take her back" was apparently idle.

But the day was still new. No one had yet eaten breakfast! A short time later, by about 9:30 a.m., a court assembled to hear the dispute over Tobali. Kepu led off: "We men die and leave widows behind. If we do not inherit them, they are left alone, unable to marry." But the men of his age, including Situpe, spoke only of the upcoming vote and Papua New Guinea's Day of Independence: "We cannot elect a nobody. We should put a Big Man on the Council," everyone agreed. Younger men, like Benaro, avidly chewed betel, the insides of their lips and flowing nasal mucous stained a garish red. At the edge of the inner circle of men, the women groomed one another. Apini, a daughter of Situpe and his first wife Viru, groomed Nadule, her "true" same-named sister-in-law. A young wife recently purchased by Situpe for the son of one of his allies killed lice in Viru's head hair.

Kamale, her husband 'Paronte' the younger, and Kilo's mother Yatu, who had been picking coffee beans from trees planted at the edge of the compound, wandered into our midst. Coffee beans were spread out to dry in the sun on large sheets of heavy yellow plastic laid in the centre of the compound. Men spoke in irrelevancies or chewed betel; women groomed one another, swatted flies off pigs. Someone commented that Situpe was a man for coffee and ought to be elected. In the vote, women raised pointed index fingers and cried *"yeeeeee."* As Situpe and Paronte elder were elected, I wondered if I had missed the court over Keparano. But other men were now assembling in Keparano's compound. A group of us including Aramo, Rano, and Pame, Benaro's wife, made our way there, as the women remarked, to prepare to fight the women who attacked Keparano.

In the wide open space of Keparano's compound, as was typical, men sat on one side, their backs to the women and heads in the sun, speaking in subdued voices about self-government. In the shade near the compound's periphery, twisting string on their thighs, suckling infants and chatting, sat the contingent of women who supported Arnantu, including Delaru, the married daughter of Venet, Situpe's fourth wife; Sege, Aramo's second daughter married like Delaru into the clan of Arnantu's husband, Marot; and other clan wives, comprising a group in which were the daughters and sisters of the women allied with Keparano by affiliation to *their* husbands' clan. In the anticipated battle with sticks between the women of the two clans, each side was thus internally riven, its unity more a matter of show than meaningful solidarity. Suddenly, one of the women allied with Arnantu shouted, "You women [supporting Keparano] want to fight us!" Her husband told her to shut up, "We are meeting first," he said. Keparano's delegation of women gathered to go over yet again what happened at the road construction site, each iteration of the incident bringing to light new details. It was Pame, Benaro's wife, who told Situpe about Venet's part in beating Keparano, provoking his fury and Venet's bloody eye.

All of a sudden, the women around Arnantu came into view on higher ground above us: Aramo approached as Arnantu kept her distance up the hill (see Fig. 2.5 above). Arnantu yelled: "Marot said to me, 'I am not interested in you anymore! All you know how to do is fuck. You do not care for pigs. You do not make gardens!' *That* is how Marot spoke to me! He can marry Keparano. I have many children and can live without him. I can find another man." Aramo answered: "Arnantu! We have no problem with your beating Keparano. But you and other women *ganged up* on her. Women who are *nothing to you* backed you up! That is why we are enraged and demand compensation." Pame: "[Benaro's clansman] says he will break your legs!" Arnantu: "So let's fight!" [Kepu's wife]: "Venet was your leader. She sleeps here with you now but if she tries to come back home to us, watch out!"

A married daughter of Paronte elder stood like a sentry beside Arnantu, holding a large shovel. On Arnantu's other side stood her mother. Taking over as spokeswoman again, Aramo acidly remarked: "Venet's husband broke her face and now she's hiding up there [with you]!" whereupon Venet, her face bruised and bloodied, moved defiantly next to Arnantu. Aramo vented her anger at her co-wife: "When Delaru wanted to marry and you had nothing, I killed a pig and gave you food and she was able to marry. Now [Venet's younger daughter] wants to marry and

I – I! – killed a pig and got a lot of money together for her. Delaru is a big shot now, heh? She better not come anywhere near me. I want to take part in the elections but *you* want to fight. Fine! Let's fight!"

Arnantu (defensively): "My hand, my back, my whole body are broken [from Marot's beating]. For *that*, I took revenge and beat Keparano." Aramo (in retreat): "I did not eat Keparano's [brideprice] pigs. I ate [Paronte's daughter's brideprice] pigs. If *she* gets into a fight, then I will fight for *her*." Venet, responding in fury to Aramo: "*You do not eat?!!* When Marot dies, you will not come to eat his 'head'!?" Aramo: "When Sebol died you[r clan] did not pay me so I will *not* come to ask for Marot's 'head'!" Arnantu: "We just gave Keparano to Tamur and now *you come up here and want to give her to Marot*?"... Pame, another one of Keparano's "true" sisters-in-law, screeched abuse at Arnantu.

* * *

In this exclusively female forum, the women of two heavily intermarried coresident enemy clans, one clustered on a hillock and another standing in a compound beneath it, attempted to formulate their battle with each other in terms not only of blows inflicted upon Keparano but also of men's exchanges in brides and "head" payments. The implication of Aramo's taunts and Venet's responses was that their allegiances and alliances, and especially their willingness to resort to violence, were determined and made legitimate by the history and expectation of their roles as consumers of brideprice and "head" payments made on behalf of individual women and men. Big Women like Aramo were sometimes able to influence—but not to determine—the distribution of their own pig herds and to act as players in negotiating other women's marriages. But when an old man like Sebol died there was little room for negotiation: his paternal kinsmen were obligated to "buy his head" from his mother's paternal kinsmen lest his corpse and therefore his spirit (lit: *kore*) be lost to his own clan's ancestral reservoir. Women participated in exchanges as recipients of "head" payments alongside their husbands and of brideprice as mothers of brides; that is, as those who "eat" but do not donate.

Despite loud appeals as leaders of other women to the system of man-made rules and their places within it in particular instances, women like Aramo also recognized that the system was built upon abuse of their sex. By treating women as objects of exchange like pigs, the rules made married women into *isolates* who lacked any legitimate basis for recruiting allies and, therefore, for engaging in violence. This was the gist of Paronte's lecture to his clanswomen and of Aramo taunts to her co-wife Venet. What tied Venet to Arnantu, Aramo wanted to know. What was the source of Venet's borrowed rage against Keparano? What valid reason could there be for Venet to join in the attack? Consulting my kin charts, I noted that Venet's son-in-law—Delaru's husband—was Arnantu's father's brother's son, an obscure link that certainly could not explain Venet's violent anger on Arnantu's behalf. In allying herself with Arnantu and ganging up on Keparano, Venet seemed to be another jealous co-wife or prospective co-wife venting her fury against a target of opportunity, and getting fierce support from her daughter Delaru. Inside Venet's—and Aramo's—polygynous household, as Situpe's fourth wife, Venet was about to be displaced by a fifth wife.

While loudly proclaiming the ethic of ritual exchange and situating herself and her cohorts within it, Aramo well understood a woman's fundamental isolation and used it as a way to manoeuvre. As she repeatedly said, if Arnantu *alone* had attacked Keparano the attack would have been her affair. But when "*meri nating*" (m.p. 'nothing women,' i.e., women with no legitimate affiliation or tie to the aggrieved) take it upon themselves to join forces, then money has to be paid! Aramo did not let up her tirade against her co-wife: "Venet, you go around stirring up [the women around] Arnantu so do not come back home! Don't come back down to us! You beat up Keparano and everyone, even the *komiti, saw* you do it ... and [the *komiti*] told Situpe and he hit you! *Why* did you beat Keparano? Have you spoken [i.e., do you have some outstanding gripe] with her? Are you *angry* at her for something?" Pame, Benaro's wife, chimed in: "You ate Keparano's [brideprice] pigs! How can you beat her up?" "You want to fight?" Arnantu's mother answered. "Come on up here!" ... "We wanted to fight you this morning but there were elections ..." Rano answered. "That's enough!" Aramo declared.

But the fight and exchange of obscenities were not nearly over. From above, one of Arnantu's allies shouted: "One of you – Gaputi – ridiculed us. We want to beat you until you shit yourself!" Standing beside Aramo on the ground below, the wife of Paronte elder (the one romancing the newly-widowed Tobali) retorted: "You did not give us Sebol's 'head'!" Arnantu's ally responded: "You women want to give Keparano to Marot – *that's* what we are talking about – *that's* what we are fighting over!" and then she unleashed a torrent of abuse against the three leaders of Kaparano's faction, Aramo, Rano and Paronte's wife, accusing them of *sakma* or *saguma*, a Chimbu term for noctural cannibalism practiced by she-devils whose Gimi equivalent are forest-dwelling *kore badaha* or "wild women" (lit: *kore,* 'wild,' 'ghost,' 'forest spirit,' + *badaha*, 'woman'). Aramo tried once more to return to the topic of exchanges of "head" payments between their two clans: "You got [our clan's] money! We paid you. So why are you angry at us? You beat Keparano and want to give her to Marot but we want to get rid of Tamur and take Keparano back home with us!"

A little after noon, the hill was crowded with Arnantu's contingent, some thirty to forty women and children among whom was Delaru, the married daughter of Venet, Aramo's co-wife. "*Delaruoooooooo*!" Aramo yelled. "You are wrong to go against your own mothers!" "We are your mothers who 'cut' [i.e., sent] you to be married," Paronte's wife added. "We killed *big* pigs for you. You cannot fight with Aramo!" In a climatic move, Marot's mother made her way down the hill, sat down next to Aramo and began to rub her shin. There was a lull on each side as the two Big Women of opposing clans consulted intimately, Aramo counting on her fingers the names of those who beat Keparano. Afterwards, I learned that their conversation also touched upon a recent incident parallel to the present one in which women of Kaparano's clan, led by Naname, ganged up on the side of a third wife of Arnantu's clan to batter a newly arrived fourth wife.

Marot, Arnantu's husband, was almost never mentioned, although it was his mother who led the effort to come to terms with Keparano's clanswomen. Wasn't Marot to blame for Keparano's beating? Hadn't Arnantu herself declared that she attacked Keparano in revenge for wounds her husband inflicted after she struck him on account of his infidelity and then he cut her down, lopped off the top of her left thumb and slashed both her breasts? One on one, a Gimi woman was no match for a husband who, in the past, was a trained warrior and sometimes had the right to kill his wife if she transgressed. Since there was virtually no legitimate basis to recruit a female ally, some women vented their fury on each other in 'disorganized' ways that Big Women like Aramo declared were contrary to the principles of men's rules of exchange. But women like Aramo also knew that men's rules were the cause of women's misdirected fury. Ganging up on a defenseless target like Keparano, not to mention the way some women 'over-loved' infants with constant handling and frequent masturbation, fostered an image of women, even in their own eyes, as devouring "she-devils" (*saguma badaha*) or "wild women" (*kore bahada*) who dared to act in stealth or against the defenceless, forfeiting their place in civilized society.

* * *

By late afternoon, after the summit between Aramo and Marot's mother, the two groups of women dispersed. A group of men of the two clans, including Situpe, Paronte elder, and Benaro, sat in the center of Keparano's empty compound. There was a mood of subdued *bonhomie* as men talked and listened to Marot's younger brother describe Marot's habitual philandering. Tamur escorted his wife Keparano into their midst. She sat alone, still shrouded in a blanket, with her back to the group of men; and she remained there for hours, a motionless and faceless exhibit, while the men discussed her fate. At one point, the men removed her blanket to reveal the free-for-all her beating had been. *Everyone* had a go at her: Benaro, the *komiti*; Marot, her seducer and partner in adultery; the man whose foot Keparano accidently wounded in self-defense; Arnantu's paternal uncle (a former *komiti*) who received a pig to compensate *him* for Arnantu's injuries; Arnantu; Arnantu's mother; Venet, Situpe's fourth wife; Delaru, Venet's daughter; Lantu .... Quietly, the men recited the list of assailants. "I paid a lot for her," Marot testified, "and she rears no pigs to pay me back so I will marry her."

After the explosive war of words between the two groups of women earlier in the day, the women supporting Arnantu were mostly absent. In the shade at the compound's edge was a silent, sparse audience of women who supported Keparano, including Aramo and Paronte's wife and their daughters who were married into Arnantu's clan and had stood beside her earlier in the day. While Keparano was still center stage, the women shelled coffee beans, twisted shredded bark fibres into string across their thighs, groomed one another and waited. Aramo went to sleep under a banana plant and quietly left upon awakening.

Marot told the group of men that Keparano seduced him and that he was reluctant; that intercourse did not take place because the girl interrupted them and they fled. Men's deliberations centered almost entirely upon the question of *who seduced whom*. They badgered Keparano and coaxed her repeatedly to speak but she did not utter a word. And so, by her own 'default,' Marot won the case. The men determined that *no* compensation would be paid for Keparano's beating. Her wounds were the just desserts of a seductive, faithless woman.

Later the same evening, during the regular early evening news broadcast, I heard yelling at Situpe's compound. Benaro was raging at Tobali for humiliating his father Kepu and Tobali was wailing. Naname laughed and sent her husband Kilo to confront Benaro and take Paronte's side. From his compound, Paronte elder called out to Kilo: "Let's wait til tomorrow. Tomorrow we will sit down again at court. Go to sleep, Kilo! Forget the fight for now."

* * *

Notes

1. Pseudonyms are used throughout.
2. For details about the fieldwork upon which this book is based see Gillison (1977, 1983, 1993: xiii–xviii). The National Science Foundation and the Canada Council provided initial support. In later years, my former husband David Gillison and I received funds from National Geographic Magazine and the New York Zoological Society. In 1985, I was awarded a *Poste Rouge* by the Centre Nationale de la Recherche Scientifique to work at the Laboratoire d'Anthropologie Sociale in the Collège de France in Paris founded by Claude Lévi-Strauss and headed, during subsequent appointments by Professors Françoise Héritier and Phillipe Descola.

3. Mary Douglas describes a similar notion of fatal harm caused by the *return* or reingestion of something the body has already ejected or discarded. Among the Coorgs of India, "[a]nything issuing from the body is never to be re-admitted, but strictly avoided. The most dangerous pollution is for anything which has once emerged gaining reentry. A little myth, trivial by other standards, justifies so much of their behaviour and system of thought. … A Goddess in every trial of strength or cunning defeated her two brothers. … [so] they decided to defeat her by a ruse. She was tricked into taking out of her mouth the betel that she was chewing to see if it was redder than theirs and into popping it back again (sic). Once she realized she had eaten something which had once been in her own mouth and was therefore defiled by saliva, though she wept and bewailed she accepted the full justice of her downfall" (Douglas 1970 [1966]: 147).

   Obscenities like "Motherfucker!" and "Eat shit and die!" also convey the sense that going back, or taking back inside onself, what was originally part of oneself is fatal.
4. A Gimi individual normally receives many names over the course of a lifetime—at birth, initiation, betrothal and marriage. Most proper names are not marked for gender. I use single quotes around the name of a person named after a close relative in the parental or grandparental generation, as Kamale named her two daughters after her own father and elder half-brother; and as her husband 'Paronte' acquired the name of his mother's brother Paronte at his first stage initiation. The practice of "same-naming" applies to an initiate and his or her chaperon and to designated sisters-in-law as the indication of their special relationship and mutual obligations. See *ahamoina* in Gillison 1993: 385.
5. Mythic figures and artifacts are capitalized to distinguish them from their ritual counterparts. But pronouns that refer to mythic figures appear in lower case. Big Man and Big Woman, individuals recognized as important persons and leaders in the community, are also capitalized.

References

Anonymous. 2017. *The Incest Diary*. London and New York: Bloomsbury Circus.

Douglas, Mary. 1970 [1966]. *Purity and Danger: An Analysis of Concepts of Pollution and Taboo*. London: Pelican Books.

Gillison, Gillian. 1977. Fertility rites and sorcery in a New Guinea Village. *National Geographic* 152 (1): 124–146.

———. 1983. Living Theater in New Guinea's Highlands. *National Geographic* 164 (2): 147–169.
———. 1993. *Between Culture and Fantasy. A New Guinea Highlands Mythology*. Chicago: University of Chicago Press.
———. 2001. Reflections on *Pigs for the Ancestors*. In *Ecology and the Sacred: Engaging the Anthropology of Roy A. Rappaport*, ed. Ellen Messer and Michael Lambek, 291–299. Ann Arbor: University of Michigan Press.
———. 2016. Whatever Happened to the Mother? A New Look at the Old Problem of the Mother's Brother in Three New Guinea Societies: Gimi, Daribi and Iatmul. *Oceania* 86 (I): 2–24.
Mimica, Jadran. In press. *Of Humans, Pigs, and Souls: An Essay on the Yagwoia Womba (Cannibal) Complex*. Hau Malinowski Monograph Series. University of Chicago Press (forthcoming July 2020).
Wagner, Roy. 1967. *The Curse of Souw: Principles of Daribi Clan Definition and Alliances in New Guinea*. Chicago: University of Chicago Press.
———. 1977. Analogic Kinship: A Daribi Example. *American Ethnologist* 4 (4): 623–642.

3

Portrait of Karapmene

One very early morning in August 1985, as I staggered back from the out-house, I found Karapmene sitting outside my door. Although she was not one of the women whom I knew well or saw every day, she had visited me about a week or so before in the company of an older half-sister, the wife of one of her husband's "fathers" visiting from another village. The two of them wanted to record the women's stories they'd heard I was putting on tape and playing back to the story-tellers. I remembered Karapmene vividly from the first time I saw her years earlier when she arrived near the end of a feast with several other women, moving in single file along the shaded edge of a compound, to pick up large packages of cooked pork and rice, wrapped in banana leaves, which the hosts had allotted to their husbands. With the large bundle balanced on her head, Karapmene seemed to glide along the shaded path, her bark-string skirts swinging elegantly from a cord slung below the navel. Her taut sleek torso and thick, short-cropped hair glistened with pig fat. The women's husbands were not in attendance because sorcery—whose main targets and only practitioners were men—was rampant.

After the *Pax Australiana* and suppression of open warfare in the early 1960's, Gimi sorcery flourished, perhaps as never before. For a man

G. Gillison, *She Speaks Her Anger: Myths and Conversations of Gimi Women*, Culture, Mind, and Society, https://doi.org/10.1007/978-3-030-49352-3_3

neither old nor decrepit to eat, smoke, and casually converse with men of other clans inside the other clans' compounds—to put himself in a situation where he was liable to *forget himself* away from home—was to take needless risk. One simply never knew who harbored a grudge or might be the accomplice of someone who did and for whom one's presence provided the opportunity to steal a bit of his person—a shred of threadbare, sweat-soaked clothing, a discarded sweet potato skin or sugarcane husk, a morsel of tobacco, a pandanus seed or other ort or a drop of fluid leaked from one's nose or a sore—and then to spirit it away, turn it over to a collaborator or middleman who would arrange for it to be deposited in a woman's corpse (through a slit in the abdomen) or destroyed by equivalent means, instigating the same vile decomposition and absorption of female 'elements' in the rest of him. The thief's identity was almost impossible to guess because his or his sponsor's motives were usually based upon misunderstandings or lies about oneself or other members of one's lineage or clan. The epidemic of sorcery created ubiquitous peril that made Gimi men prefer to send their wives onto other clans' turf to receive the prestations of food and other valuables that were their due. The first time I saw Karapmene she was part of such a delegation.

It was years later that Karapmene and her visiting sister came to record their stories. But when the play-back was over, the women did not get up to leave. Karapmene held up the swollen second finger of her right hand. It was covered with tiny black slits, incisions made by the miniature bow and obsidian-tipped arrow Gimi use to "shoot" a wound or ache to release the pain. Smiling broadly, Karapmene told me that her husband broke her finger in a fury. She and her sister decided to visit me that morning because she could not work in her garden nor cut firewood. I glanced down at her hands to see the condition of her other fingers. Gimi women amputate fingers above the middle joint—as many as two or three by late life—to mourn the death a child or husband or husband's father or brother. I noticed that the top of the baby finger on Karapmene's left hand was missing. Karapmene showed me her deformed left ring-finger, an old break inflicted when she raised her hand to shield her head from the blow of her co-wife's heavy stick. The pain in her right finger now, she said, was as bad as the pain in her left finger was then. It tormented her day and night without letup so she could not sleep, not even fitfully nor in the exhaustion before dawn. As the women rose to leave, Karapmene bent over to whisper that she had something more to tell me.

A week or so later, I found Karapmene outside my door. We entered the house and remained in the back room as Karapmene requested. The house was raised on stilts, about three feet off the soggy ground, with a floor made of loosely-woven bamboo panels that squeaked when walked upon and through whose ample interstices children playing beneath the house could see and hear what was going on overhead. As we sat cross-legged facing each other, Karapmene started to speak in a rush I could hardly follow. I reached for the tape-recorder and, as I did when she and her sister recorded their myths, set it down between us. With great animation, Karapmene spoke about the hell of marriage to Vapa, using her injured hands to demonstrate on herself and on me exactly where she suffered blows or landed them on her co-wife. She began her story at the time she still lived with her parents in another village and Vapa often visited to sleep with her.

> When Vapa first knew me, I was strong. I did not want to marry him! I said to myself, "He's got one wife already." I did not want to live my life in anger and fighting all the time. I told him so and he said to me, "My wife is not a good wife. She does not look after me. She does not wash my clothes. She has no shame. She does not plant sweet potato and I go around hungry. I am fed up with my wife! I do not sleep with her anymore. I just give her children. You think she is my wife – not really! I sleep wherever I happen to be. I eat with my mother and father. I do not spend time with my wife. She does not know how to work and I do not like her. I want to marry you! I want to marry you only!" The man was stubborn.
>
> He was strong. He did not live at his place. No, no he did not. He stayed with me all the time ... and I said to him, "Stop it. Go back home. I do not want to get pregnant." I told him to go and he said, "No!" So I said to him, "If you make me pregnant, I will tell everyone it was you." "Oh no you will not," he said to me. "I will say it was someone else. I will say, 'Another man made her pregnant.' But if you hurry up and come to live with me then I will say, 'Yes, the child is mine!' ... You are too hard," he said to me. "You live here with your mother and father and I come here to sleep with you. We have been sleeping together a long time now."

That is what he said to me. That is the way he spoke to me and I thought, "This man will abuse me. 'Another man made you pregnant,'" – he would say that?! Yes, he would! ... Vapa slept with me for a long time. Twenty times he slept with me. I counted. And I said to him, "Soon I will be pregnant." ... "Come quickly to live with me in my place," he said, "and then when you are pregnant, I will say, 'She is my wife and I made her pregnant.'" But I refused! "I do not want to marry you!" I told him.

Vapa did not give up. He kept on and on so I decided to trick him! "Let's go to live in your place," I started to say whenever he came to see me. "Let's go to your place!" But he was still furious at me [because I did not keep my word]. He made love magic and brought it with him in the night. He banged on my door and I opened it. "I want to sleep with you," he said. "It's the middle of the night," I told him. "Why have you come?" "Because you are my wife," he answered. I opened the door and the man came inside.

He started to look for [a bamboo container of] water. "Don't you have any water in the house?" "Water is there," I said. ... (*Whispering to me*) he went outside and *emptied* the bamboo! "There is no water!" he cried. He came to trick me! He wanted to give me that stuff [the magic] ... and he put it in the cigarette he was making. He bought *Root* [a tobacco brand] and rolled a very long cigarette. "Smoke this and you will be thirsty," he thought to himself. That is why Vapa had to empty the bamboo *before* he gave me the cigarette [because a drink of water ruins the magic]!

He took the bamboo outside and poured out the water. "What's this? There is no water here! I am pouring out dirt." He was tricking me. Then the two of us sat down on the bed. We slept in one bed. "Light the cigarette," he told me and handed me matches. "Smoke it and then give it to me." I struck a match and lay down on the bed and smoked the cigarette. "Are you smoking?" the man asked and I said, "I am smoking," and passed him the butt. "Never mind," he said. "We can smoke later." He tricked me. I gave him the butt and he stubbed it out and put it aside.

Vapa put *that* cigarette aside but he had made another one! He lit that *other* one and smoked it. Now I did not know this! No way. It was dark and we were lying down. (*Giggling*) I did not know about the cigarette he gave me! And I went to sleep. In the night I awoke and said, "I want to smoke." And he gave me back that [first] cigarette and I lit a match and smoked it. "You are not smoking," I said to him, "I am the only one smoking here." "No," he said. "I am smoking." He tricked me.

He tricked me with that cigarette! ... *Yeeeeeee!* I felt ... I thought about Vapa ... I did not want to stay with my mother anymore! No way! "I want to be with *you only*." The man gave me [the stuff] and then he took [the rest of] it away and the matches, too. And he thought, "I have given the woman *something*. Now she will come to me!" ... That is what he did and ... in the morning I could not think. I cried and cried and cried because Vapa had gone away (lit: 'I did not see his body'). I cried and cried and climbed a mountain ridge to see the place where Vapa lived. How I cried. ... "Come and get me," I said to him. In the afternoon he came and I said, "Vapa, you gave me something ..."

After an interruption Karapmene continued:

Vapa arrived in the afternoon and said to me, "I am your man and I want to marry you." And I said to him, "Come back tonight and get me. I will prepare my things." ... In the dead of night the man came. ... He brought money and put it in the house where I slept. ... I cried so hard. I was leaving my mother and father ... for what, I was thinking. I cried a lot and he heard me and wanted to run away. "You cannot run away! I am crying for my mother and father. You can take me ..." He was proud and he took me.

We arrived at his compound. We went inside one of the houses where no fire was burning. The house was empty. There was no firewood so we could not make a fire. We were sitting there and Vapa's first wife arrived [after Vapa had called out to her through the closed door,] "Heh, bring us some firewood and a lighted faggot so we can make a fire." But she had it all figured out already! "Oh," she was thinking, "so you want to marry this woman and you bring her into your house and you are in there with her and you call for me?" "Open the door!" she yelled.

"Why should I open the door?" Vapa answered. But the woman insisted, "Open the door! I want to look inside first. The woman has come and I want to look at the two of you!" His wife spoke these words and I said, "Vapa, what are you afraid of? Open the door so she can come inside and look at me." Vapa was angry but he opened the door. "The woman is here," he said. "If the two of you want to fight and make trouble, it is up to you." The woman entered the house and hit Vapa with her hand. "Why hit *me*?" he said. "*Here* is your enemy. Fight with this woman. The two of you can fight each other. Do not fight *me*! If you are angry, then fight with Karapmene," Vapa said. "Try hitting Karapmene!"

The woman hit Vapa again and said to me, "Find another man! There are plenty of men. You have not looked." "No," I said, "I want to marry Vapa and I have come to stay. You are here for nothing." I spoke boldly. "Is this man your husband?" she asked me. "You come here so sure of yourself, how come?" and I answered, "Too bad. I want to marry him. You have nothing to say (lit: 'your neck is dry'). He is already mine." And the woman got up and struck me. And I hit her back and we fought. I am a woman who knows how to fight!

I hit her hard and nearly killed [i.e., seriously wounded] her. "Aye! They are fighting!" Everyone came running in the night and watched us fight. "Hey, she is not very big," they said to me. "She is nearly wrecked. Leave her alone." "I came here peacefully," I told them. "Why did she start with me? She did not greet me. She said, 'Why do you come to my place?' She would not take my hand. I was just sitting there and she hit me. And I hit her back. You cannot stop me from fighting her," I said. And I kept hitting her. And I pushed her into a corner. Then I pushed her out of the house and broke the door.

Now we fight all the time. At night Vapa takes me to the house of his mother and father. He goes there with me and does not stay in the house [of his other wife]. ... His mother and father get up and make a fire. They like me. "We do not like his other wife. 'Get a new wife,' we told him. And now you have come!" They are happy with me and we live together and they miss (lit: 'cry for') me whenever I am gone. But no! That woman is determined and wants to fight. So they said to me, "Do something (lit: 'find a remedy' [a magic potion]) and she will leave." And I listened.

They [Vapa's parents] spoke to my mother and father. They [my parents] arrived one morning and said to me, "The woman is already married to him. Now you have come and you are second. They will get rid of you. What are you going to do?" and they showed me something. "Give this to your husband and he will think only of you and stay with you only." I took it and put it into his cigarette. It was payback! I thought, "You put something in a cigarette and gave it to me to make me think *only* of you. Now you will think *only* of me!" I prepared the cigarette and lit it and gave it to Vapa. He smoked it and now ... no way! He thinks only of me now!

I interrupted Karapmene to ask about the 'stuff' she received from her parents. It was another variety of love magic made from the bark of a tree that grew at lower elevations in a place called Unabi. For "two, three or five *kina*" a woman could purchase one 'shot' from other women known to possess it.

> Men do not know about it and we hide it. We hide it very, very well. If a man were to see it he would say, "What is this?" He would ask us and we would have nothing to say. We hide it. And when the man is not around we make two cigarettes. One is just ordinary. The other is for the man. It has *the something* in it. We put the two cigarettes aside. And when the man asks for a smoke, we light the two of them.
>
> We light them when he is not looking. We smoke one to fool him. The other we give to him. And he smokes it. When he is finished, he gives us the butt and we put it out and put it aside. Our own cigarette, we smoke. Later, he calls for his cigarette and we light it again and give it back to him and he smokes it all. "Good, you smoked it all!" we see and we are happy. We are happy because now the man says, "I do not think about my other wife anymore. I just think of you." ... "Why do you think of me so much?" we [coyly] ask and he says, "No, I do not like the other woman. She is there. And I should go to her. But I do not want to. I want to stay with you." He says that and we think, "We have won! We have him now," and we are happy.

After Karapmene slipped Vapa several more cigarettes loaded with "the something," he "forgot" his first wife completely:

> When Vapa is away on a trip, he thinks of me and comes running back. He stays with me all the time. "Karapmene, did you give me something?" And I say, "I did not give you anything." [But I think to myself] "What you gave me made me give something to you. I gave it *back* to you." I thought that way and gave him the cigarette [loaded with magic] and he smoked it. The first time I made one and gave it to him, he smoked it. The second time I made one and gave it to him. ... The third time I made it and gave it to him ... and now, no way! He thinks *only* of me. He forgot his first wife. He left that woman altogether. He left her and now she keeps to herself.
>
> I am strong! I am like the first wife now. I *am* the first. And that woman comes second. I get [whatever he holds in] his hand. His money, his *kago* (p.e. 'cargo,' factory-made goods) whatever he has, he keeps in my house.

He does not give her *anything*. And men, too, give me food and visit me only. ... And because of what I gave him [the love magic], everyone is angry at me. "What did you give him?" they say to me. "You old women do not know how to do what I did," I tell them. "He was married to her and I came and I was strong!" I have been very strong and gave him something and now Vapa says, "You gave me something and I left my other wife." He gets angry at me and I tell him, "This is the kind of woman I am. When one wife is already there and another one arrives, this is what we do. What do you *expect*!?"

How to Get Rid of a Co-Wife: Lessons of Girls' Initiation

Karapmene was reminding Vapa of the remedies men know women have for the bane of polygyny. Karapmene's visiting half-sister, with whom she recorded several stories, came here to help initiate two girls and instruct them, among other things, on how to get rid of a co-wife. During the initial seclusion, which may last five or six sleepless days and nights, the duration of a typical menstrual period, women crowded into a hot, airless woman's house or, in the past, a menstrual hut. A cage-like "sugar bed," a raised platform made of sugarcane stalks lashed together with liana vines and surrounded by thin bamboo poles decorated with poinsettias and other red foliage, was erected inside the small space to hide the pair of initiates from view. Inside the "sugar bed," chaperons sat between the girls and slapped them if they nodded off or slipped from the crouched position, with buttocks raised off the platform, a posture they were forced to maintain day and night lest even momentary contact with the sugarcane lead to early pregnancy.

To end the initiation's first phase, the chaperons took the girls by the hand and pulled them off the platform and out the door of the woman's house where other women were assembled. The group ran out of the compound hand-in-hand, the chaperons yanking up the cramped and bleary-eyed initiates when they stumbled. Reaching the forest above the settlement, the women began a two-day "wandering" to continue the girls' education in married life. To demonstrate how to get rid of a co-wife, the women used the aerial rootlets of fern-trees, masses of fine, densely-tangled black fibres, as giant substitutes for the back of a co-wife's head. "'When another woman arrives and wants to marry your husband, break her head with a stick,'" one woman instructed as she hit the fern-tree's massive black roots with a long sharp stick. "That is what we tell her. And this is what we sing:

> *idu idu adu Aduao 3da edau*
> *siru siru saruba*
> *simiri ubo ubo ubo baine ubo ubo ubo*
> *idu idu adu Aduao 3da edau*

> That woman will not answer you back! She will put her hands over her head [*Karapmene's sister crouched and crossed her arms over her forehead*] '*Eeeek!* Help!' ... Your [would-be] co-wife will cower and be unable to return your blows. *siru siru saruba* will make your stick as mighty as *simiri* ['bow and arrow' in Chimbu] and you, as irresistable as *baine* [a cuscus used as metaphor for a beautiful girl]!

Another chaperon added, "'And then she will go to another man!' We send the second woman to another place! This is what we tell the girl while we smash the fern-tree to pieces." Afterwards, the chaperon passed the stick to one of the initiates, then to the other, to do likewise. "[The girls] break the heads of the tree-ferns [with great vigor]! We give them good, strong words and they break everything all around and we are pleased with them. And then we come back [home] ..."

The Nature of Magic

To *persuade*—to make the one you want to go away, go away, or to make the one you desire most desire you most of all—requires magical assistance, the use of specially-concocted instruments like a stick or cigarette infused with "secret" words or spells. The cigarette Karapmene said Vapa made for her and the several cigarettes that she, in revenge and in cahoots with her step-mother, made for Vapa; and the long sharp stick with which women teach initiates to beat aspiring co-wives, become magically effective—imbued with the efficacy of a bow and arrow wielded by a wife as irresistably beautiful as a cuscus—because the added "something" or secret song transforms the stick or cigarette into a near-perfect extension of the preparer or spell-sayer. The magically-induced connection between Vapa and his cigarette, Karapmene and her cigarettes, a co-wife beater and her baton, transforms the manipulated object into a 'mindless' vessel and vehicle of the spell-sayer's wish and command. What is more, the magical condition is *contagious*: once Karapmene smoked the cigarette Vapa manufactured as the 'unknowing' repository of his desire to marry her, she took on the attribute of his doctored cigarette and herself became the 'mindless' extension of Vapa's desire.

The principles governing Gimi magic are necessarily hard to discern because, like most sorcery, most magic operates *ex post facto*: the *effects* of love magic—the senseless or even harmful attachments it inspires or, in the case of sorcery, the illness and death it precipitates—determine its presence as cause. When magic is at work, the person who is the target is not responsible for his or her heedless devotion just as the victim of sorcery is helpless to separate himself from an attacker he cannot recognize or identify. Magic achieves a state of dual unity that *excludes all others*; a state that originates, and has its purest expression, in the symbiotic attachment of mother and child. Efforts to conjure the magical condition mimic maternal behaviour by employing gentle carresses and intimate ministrations of the kind a mother performs; and by uttering nonsensical 'sweet nothings,' mellifluous, rhythmic, repetitious, rhyming, sing-songy vocalizations like the private language a mother invents to soothe her baby into blissful unknowingness and sleep.

In songs, spells and incantations—like *abracadabra* or *doobidoobidoo* or *hachachimoo*—and actions—like soft blowing and careful stroking and meticulous wrapping and enfolding—the techniques of Gimi magic imitate, encapsulate and elaborate upon idiosyncratic and 'incomprehensible' maternal communications as the means to create a sealed dyadic connection: magical spells and verbalizations project into another being or object *a part of oneself*, a piece of one's soul or animating, volatile inner being which Gimi call *auna*. Secret magical formulas accompany each stage and phase of gardening, pig herding, thread-making or any other activity in women's long list of tasks, including co-wife thrashing. Virtually every incantation opens and closes with a refrain that is "the *aund*'s own song," an emanation of pure self that, by inviting the object to merge with the spell-sayer's inner being, attempts to refashion it as the perfect instrument and repository of her volition. Women also adorn, alliterate and play with the two or three meaningful words of the "main song" to make them resonate with the surrounding "song of the soul."

The "main song" of the chaperons' spell to endow a sharp wooden stick with the lethal impact of a bow and arrow has only two meaningful words: *simiri* which means "bow and arrow" in Chimbu, a language most Gimi, especially adolescent girls, do not understand but whose use enhances the incomprehensibility essential to magic. The other word in the spell is *baine,* Gimi for a marsupial cuscus, one of the forest creatures who incarnate the "wild woman" or *korebadaha* (lit: *kore,* 'ghost,' 'forest-dwelling spirit,' 'wild' + *badaha,* 'woman') in women's myths and insults, a creature who may be wicked or violent but who is also impossibly beautiful, rebellious, irresistable and unattainable. "Wild women" escape every social constraint because they never menstruate nor marry. Just uttering and embellishing the sounds in the word "cuscus" help to endow the spell-sayer with wild-woman powers and allure.

Karapmene's Tale of the 'Wild Woman'

On the same occasion when Karapmene's half sister, visiting from another village to chaperon a pair of female initiates, recounted the women's "wandering" in the high forest and lessons on co-wife beating, Karapmene recounted a myth about the "wild woman" who flaunts the rules of being a wife. A Gimi myth is like a dream in the sense that everything in it, all the characters, situations and events, express the *singular perspective* of its heroine or hero. In rare but highly revealing instances a woman may 'cut and paste' excerpts of several myths to compose a virtual autobiography. Most of the time the storyteller chooses a single myth whose heroine's adventures portray in an iconic way aspects of her own attitudes and feelings. The heroine of Karapmene's tale is a "wild woman" who, in order to keep her child with her forever, willingly exchanges the 'benefits' of life in society for the freedom of the forest.

hoEEEE bada

A Trickster (*koreda,* "wild man, lit: *kore,* 'wild,' 'ghost' or 'forest spirit' + *da* = *ba[na],* 'man' as suffix) came upon (lit: 'saw') fruit skins lying on the forest floor and realized there was a marsupial eating in the tree above him.[1] He returned to the spot at nightfall with bow and arrows [to shoot the marsupial but instead came upon] a Wild Woman carrying her Child on her back inside a net bag. The Man approached her and stood before her [silent and utterly still] and the Woman thought he was the trunk of a tree.

She poked her finger up his nose and felt that it was not hot. She poked her finger into his mouth and felt that it was not hot. She poked her finger up his anus and felt that it was not hot. And although there was a Man standing *right there* [in front of her] she thought she was standing in front of a tree! She hung her Child on his shoulder [as if it were a low branch] and climbed the tree. She broke off the fruit at the top and ate it and, while she was eating and eating and eating [to her heart's content], the one on the ground took off and ran back to the settlement (lit: 'house') with her Child.

The Wild Woman continued to eat the fruit in the tree top. When she finished, she climbed down the tree and saw that her Child was gone .... She followed [the man to the settlement]. On and on the Wild Woman went and, as she got closer, she realized (lit: 'saw') that her Child had been put inside one of the houses.

[In the meantime] the Man summoned all the men and women of the settlement. "All you women, everybody, come to the men's house," he cried. And everyone gathered inside. "I stole the Wild Woman's' Child and brought him here." And to all the women (sic), to everyone inside the men's house, he said, "Be quiet. Do not speak. Do not utter a sound." Then he closed the door with everyone inside. The Wild Woman arrived in the settlement and listened. She put her ear to [the wall of] each house, going from one to the next to the next, but she heard nothing. She heard nothing. She heard nothing. Then she arrived at the men's house and heard everyone!

"Hey!" she cried. "You people inside the men's house!" "What is it?" they answered. "Someone stole my Child and I have come [to find it]! Give me back my Child and I will give you every kind of food! But if you do not give my Child back to me, I will not give you anything to eat!" They gave back her Child. "You gave me back my Child so I will bring you bananas, wild bananas. And I will bring you greens, delicious wild greens. And I will bring you wild yams. I will give you all these wonderful foods," she said, "and I will eat only the bad-tasting (lit: 'ugly') foods of the forest [i.e., berries, fallen fruits and leaves unfit for human consumption]."

Saying this, she carried her Child back to her house [inside the forest]. Where she lives today we have no idea. This is true.

hote 'aba aba he'i3pa 'aba aba
hoEEEE bada

hoEEEE dada or *hoEEEE bada* means literally "call of the wild woman," (*ho*, 'do' or 'say'; *badaha*, lit: *bada*, 'woman' + *ha* 'one') the magic-word bracket Gimi women used to open and close their stories. Two Gimi words in the incanted penultimate phrase connect Karapmene's tale to first-stage male initiation ritual. *hote* are tongs used to remove cooked sweet potatoes from hot ashes; and *he'i3pa* is a long stick used to make a depression in the ashes to bury raw tubers. Men used both implements to beat adolescent boys after forcibly removing them from their mothers' houses and secluding them inside the communal men's house to be 'unborn' from their mothers and "reborn" from the men. The "wild woman's talk" at the end of the myth reiterates its theme, leaving no doubt in the listeners, who likely included pre-adolescent sons, that their mothers knew all about the "secret" ordeals they would one day have to undergo inside the men's house.

The Child cradled inside the Wild Woman's net bag, whom the Wild Man-Trickster stole and hid inside a communal house far away, refers to the boy-initiates men "steal" from their mothers and seclude in the men's house at the start of male initiation rites. But the Child the heroine carried "on her back inside a net bag" and carelessly hung on a man disguised as a tree also refers to the pair of sacred bamboo flutes, disguised as containers of salt, a Gimi bride transports to the groom on the day of her marriage supposedly without knowing her bag's real contents. Traditionally, Gimi men wrapped the flutes in the same bark cloth women used to swaddle infants; and they described the flutes' haunting music as "cries of the newborn." At the climax of men's rites, they reveal the flutes to the initiates by placing the uncovered bamboo instruments in the boys' laps. Although men once forbade women to *see* flutes on pain of death, women have *heard* the flutes' "crying" all their lives and easily recognize the distinctive tunes associated with each clan.

Fig. 3.1 Shooting a possum up a tree. Two male performers, one dressed as a woman, portray a typical scene from myth in which an "ugly old man" shoots a possum up a tree in the forest while a "wild woman," wearing a net bag on her head, watches. (© David Gillison)

The Trickster-Wild Man who spies a marsupial up a tree is a stock character in Gimi women's myths: he is an ugly Old Man, an Ogre who haunts the forest and uses "tricks" instead of brideprice to obtain a lovely wife and child, just as Karapmene accuses Vapa of tricking her into marriage, and just as the Moon "tricks" every nubile girl into losing her virginity. The suggestion that the heroine is not entirely innocent—that she may indeed be complicit in the "theft" of her Child—is another theme of women's myths. The Marsupial-Woman hangs her Child on the Wild Man-Trickster's shoulder, believing it to be a low-lying branch, supposedly because he disguises himself as a tree and stands rigidly still before her—silent and 'cold on the inside'—without apparent menace. But the Wild Woman suspects that the tree is really a man because, before climbing to gorge herself on the "fruit" at the top (lit: "head"), she pokes her finger into his every orifice to make sure he is *not hot* like a man ready to 'burst forth.' Where there is doubt, there is never any doubt. Knowing, or rather, denying what she knows, the Wild Woman gives in to her selfish hunger for highborne delicacies and hands her Child over to the thief. Once sated, she changes her mind. She leaves the forest in search of her Child and hears him "crying" inside the men's house. To get back her Child and keep him for herself alone, the Wild Woman makes a deal to live in permanent exile. She chooses to return to the forest and subsist on foods unfit for human beings in order to keep her Child with her forever.

A short time after recounting her story of the Wild Woman, Karapmene began her tale of married woe. Like most heroines in women's myths, Karapmene said about her marriage to Vapa that she had every reason to *know at the outset* that she would regret what she was about to do. "That is the way Vapa spoke to me and I thought, 'This man will abuse me.'" Karapmene said she foresaw and dreaded "fighting all the time." Yet, like the Wild Woman in her myth, even after she acquiesced, Karapmene stubbornly refused to comply with men's demands. "Men taunt me," Karapmene said. "'Why don't you go away and live in a cave or tree hollow?' they say to me."

Karapmene and Her Co-Wife Came to Blows and Went to Court

> ... That woman says to Vapa, "You do not give me money. You do not help me with clothes or soap or other things. The two of you go about in fine, fine clothes. ... As for me, you ignore me completely. And I go about in what? My old bark-string skirts! That is not right. *What is it* with you two?" This is what she says and they [she and Vapa] argue! I do not do anything. The two of them argue and argue and then she turns to me, "You are not a good woman! You go around in fine clothes and enjoy yourself before my eyes." "Sorry," I tell her, "I buy my clothes and I wear them. I did not come here with nothing!" I speak this way and she gets furious. ...

> Once I got a huge stick and ran her down. She took off the net beg she was carrying and picked up a huge stick, too. ... I hit her. And she hit me. I cut open her head. And the blood ... it did not fly! It *shot* out of her! And she said, "I want to go to court." "Go on!" I said. "Get the *konsul* and the *komiti*. Let's have a court!" And she made a report and brought the two *komiti*. ... I was in my garden wrapping up bunches of bananas. I wrapped up one bunch and then another. ... The first bunch was loaded [onto my back] and I was about to load up another when they arrived. "Come here, woman. You make trouble and then go about your business!"

Locally elected officials like the *konsul* and the *komiti* were not in the habit of intervening in fights between two women, especially co-wives. When two or more women spontaneously came to blows some men, if they happened to be nearby, liked to watch from the sidelines. Women's 'illict' fights could be sexually arousing. The same day Karapmene began her story, nine women of 'Fandi's lineage confronted a woman whose husband had just made a down payment of pigs and money to mark 'Fandi,' Kamale's now grown-up elder daughter, as his next wife. (See Fig. 2.2.) "If 'Fandi' touches me I will knife her!" the woman was overheard to threaten. During the women's hours-long altercation, no blows were exchanged but one man crouched on the sidelines the entire time hoping there would be because, he told me, the sight of women fighting "makes me feel sweet." Gimi men had the leisure and prerogative to be voyeurs and seducers, indulging sexual urges spontaneously when an occasion arose. But to achieve a measure of personal freedom, sexual and otherwise, an intelligent and desirable woman like Karapmene relied on premeditated magic and her own capacity for violence and articulate outrage.

> "Are you taking me to court?" I asked the *komiti*. "For what? ... Too bad, I will not let you sue me," ... and I went to get my bushknife. "Go away or I will cut you," I said. "We *are* going to court!" [said the *komiti* and I replied,] "You want to take me to the Police or to a Patrol Officer ... and put me in jail ...? You cannot do that!" ... They shouted at me and then they went away and left me alone.
>
> But they came back! "Come with us! We want to hold a court. You have to *pay* this woman you beat up and then we will leave you alone. She has a lot of relatives and if we attack you, you will be *dead*. And *then* you can go

away and live *all by yourself* inside a cave or hollow of a tree!" That is what they said to me. "You are *strong*, alright," Akito said: "Find a cave to live in [i.e., go be a wild woman]! There is no place for you to live here [among us]." And I said, "This is my husband's place and I am not leaving it. I can stay here. If a woman or man lays a hand on me, I will use my axe on you." And they all left.

But in the morning they were back again! Three women and Akito and another man said to me, "We want to hold a court. Come to our house." And they all sat down outside. "I will *not* go to court," I said. "Try it and you will have to take me to the Police! ..." "You speak too violently, woman. You are stubborn and will not make friends with your co-wife. You just fight her. But she does not spend time with her husband and he does not take food from her hands. ... You are the only one with him! ... But you have no pity for her," they all said to me.

"She came looking for trouble and I hit her. I did not provoke her," I said. They held a court and one woman, Kata, got up and said, "She is not going to hit *me* and make *me* run away!" Kata took off her net bag and came running at me. She was going to strike me. I got a big stick and I was ready. (*Karapmene reached for a bamboo pole standing in a corner of the room where we sat and held it up. Smiling broadly, she continued*) I gave it to her! Kata held onto the fence, ready to hit me and jump over it. But no way! I was ready and I gave it to her! Here (*Karapmene touched her right temple and forehead).* "She hit me!" [Kata] yelled and looked for a stick. But I hit her again and she went down.

Once I cut [my co-wife's] nose, as I told you ... (*Returning briefly to the incident with Kata ...*) They [those who had convened the court] said, "This woman is too strong to take to court," and they left me alone. Then Vapa said, "I do not want this woman. She does not know how to stop! I tell her I am going to leave her but still she does not say to herself, 'I will behave.' No. She likes to go around with other men, to have affairs. That is what she does. And I am one total nobody!"

"I am a man," Vapa said [during the court]. "I am a man and I married her. She is my second wife. I liked the way she did things. Whatever I said, she listened to me. She stayed in the house. When I said, 'You cannot go there,' she listened. But the family of my first wife insists that she be *paid* [to compensate for the slashed nose]. Karapmene cut her. That is enough! I do not *want* her anymore. ... And she sleeps with another man. She tricks me. She does that. But I am *not one total nobody* ... and I do not want her *at all.* They [Karapmene's parents] cannot ask for her payment."

My co-wife's family feel sorry for her, "Ah, poor you," they say. "You do not have a decent life. You drool [i.e., salivate with unsatisfied desire] when you speak. You are not Vapa's wife. ... She hit you. That is enough." But they left her and went home. ...

Karapmene bemoaned the life of a co-wife:

... [W]hen there are two wives, we get angry fast and easily and we fight. That is the reason. When there is one wife, it is a good thing. When there are two, it is bad. Men abuse us. They trick us. ...

Once I cut her nose with a knife. ... Here is how it happened. I went to my garden because Vapa said to me, "Let's go into the forest [for a tryst]. Get some sweet potatoes for us to take along." I climbed to my garden to dig up sweet potatoes and bring them to the house to dry out. That's what I was planning. [Before I left] I gave Vapa [other] sweet potatoes, "Here are four tubers," I said to him. "You eat two and leave two for me in the ashes." When I came back from my garden with the sweet potatoes [for our trip], I took the sweet potatoes [I had given Vapa earlier] out of the ashes. I was so hungry! "These potatoes are not cooked!" I said to Vapa, "You just put them in at the last minute!"

Now that old wife of his had *seen* [me leave for my garden] ... and she went down to the river to fetch water and ... (*whispering loudly*) he followed her and the two of them did it beside the river! [Meanwhile inside my garden] I finished digging up the sweet potatoes and came back to the house. I was standing at the gate and I saw the two of them running. Vapa saw me and shook. "Hey, Vapa, where have you been?" I asked him. "What have you been doing?" He had nothing to say. And she ran into her house.

"Woman, what do you want?" he said to me. "Hey, you sent me to the garden and I told you, 'Cook this food.' ... Did you put the potatoes in the ashes as I asked you? What were you doing with her? What were the two of you *doing* [while I was gone]?" Vapa had no answer. "Sorry," he said. "You found me out." I was angry and I yelled at him, "You did not put the sweet potatoes in the hot ashes! ..." And the man said – he did not speak – I said,

"*What were you doing*? I am very hungry. ... [These potatoes] are *raw*!" And the man got angry at me. He became furious. "You want to eat?" he said to me. "Why not swallow 'something'? ... I shot my wife and came back here."

"Is that 'something' for me to eat?" I asked him. The two of them had sex and then he said to me, "Why don't you drink it?' (*Aside to the clueless ethnographer*) He was talking about his semen. "You want to eat ...?" he said to me. "Go eat what I left in her vagina." He said that and I went into a rage. "Too bad you speak to me like that," I said. "The Moon is going to kill that wife of yours." ... "Do *you* want to give me *your* filth?" he said to me!

I am a strong woman, you know. "Fine," I said to him. "You said you would put the sweet potatoes in the ashes but – thinking about sex with her! – you put them in wrong! You two did not want to do it in the house! Why not try it in the house? Why did you have to go to the river?" He was fuming. He was about to strike me and I said, "This wife of yours ... the one you tell me to *eat* from ... I am going to fight her. You gave me something [love magic]." "Go ahead," he said. "Try her out. You cannot beat her ... you do not have what it takes!" ...

So I got my knife, a long knife, and said, "Vapa, the thing [cigarette] you told me to eat [smoke] .... What all men eat, I ate ...." "They do not really eat it," he said to me, "they just play around and leave it!" ... "But *you gave it to me*," I said, "and I ate it. ... Take a look at me! See this knife? I am going to stab that woman!" ... I showed Vapa the knife and went outside. ... I went out of the house and [ran toward] his wife's house. "You cannot attack her," he shouted. "You cannot. You are crying." "Yes," I said. "I am crying."

"So you have come," she greeted me. "'So you have come,'" I said back [mockingly]. "Are you talking to me?" I said. "I did not come here for nothing. I came to fight!" And the woman stood up ... *(Karapmene related the details with relish.)* "I did not come here for nothing," I said. "I came here to fight you!" And the woman stood there shaking. So I stabbed her. Look! (*Karapmene traced a semi-circle above her right nostril.*) I cut her nose open! The mark is still there. I can show it to you! I stabbed her [in the nose]. Then I stabbed her in the back.

People tried to restrain me but they could not. I stabbed her in the nose and again in the back! The woman cried, "Vapa!" and ran outside. "What did you *say* to her to make her stab me?! She stabbed me with a knife and I am going to die." "'What we two did at the river,'" your husband said to me, *'Eat it!'* I came here to stab you in revenge. And if your husband comes I can fight him, too. And if your relatives come, I can face them," I said.

Vapa entered the house in a rage and struck me. I tried to get out but Vapa was standing there [blocking the door]. "Okay, hit *me*," he said. ... I said to Vapa, "*You gave me something* ... and I stabbed her. Get it?" I said to him [it is your fault on account of the doctored cigarette you made me smoke!] ... "Have you got the *savi* now?" I asked him. "Are you pushing me?" he answered. "I killed [badly wounded] your wife and she is going to die [be a total wreck]."

Vapa hit me ... and I hit him back. ... Vapa's mother came and hit me and the woman who was nearly dead held a stick and was about to hit me. I was holding a huge stick and I struck Vapa. Then his mother approached so I turned my back on Vapa and fought his mother. Then the wife came at me so I turned away from his mother and struck his wife! I stood up strong! ... The three of them ganged up on me. I was alone. I was alone but I had a stick and hit the three of them. And they fought me. ... We kept fighting and that woman was nearly dead. So they carried her into another house. They brought her to her own people. In the morning she came outside and *(laughing broadly)* they wanted to take me to court!

I said, "The three of you ganged up on me. You want to sue *me*? I can sue you, too." So we went to court. The dead [badly hurt] woman said, "When I urinate, there is blood and when I defecate, there is blood." And then she laid down on the ground. This is what I said. ... "The man gave something to me and it made me wild and I stabbed her. And they said, "Okay, now you *pay* her. A knife is taboo. Why did you *stab* her?" "I was enraged and I stabbed her," I answered.

The woman [Vapa's first wife] had no money. And the man [Vapa], too, had no money. I held the money and I was stubborn. "It is mine," I said. "Vapa, you can get your own money and your wife can get hers, too." Vapa's money was there. I had it all. I said, "Your wife, your mother and you, Vapa, you get some money and pay me! I have money. I can pay you." But they did not want to pay me. So the court did not end. It went on and on and on and we fought on and on and on.

I insisted they pay me and the three of them refused. "We have no money," they said. I had six *kina* [Papua New Guinea bank notes]. "I am giving this to the woman so you can pay me [back]. I can give her the six *kina*. But if you do not pay me back, sorry! I am not giving my money away." I was strong. The *konsil* was strong, too. I said to him, "No. I will not give you my money. If she takes my money and spends it around, that would make me angry. But if she gives me money, then I can give her money, too. But if she wants to take my money on *one side only* then I will not do it!"

I refused and they all cried out, "Give it to her! Give it to her!" I was holding the six *kina* and tore them up. "The money is gone now," I said. "I tore it up." (*Karapmene took a sheet of paper from my notebook to demonstrate how she tore up each of six one-kina PNG bank notes and let the pieces flutter to the ground on either side of her).* I said this and tore up the money and threw it away.

"Leave her alone," they all said. "This woman is too strong. We take her to court and she beats us. She beats us every time! Let's leave her alone." The six *kina* I tore up I burned in the fire. "You give me and I will give you," I said. "This six *kina* of mine was a lot of money!" I fooled them like that with *six kina*! I have other money! I fooled them ... tearing up the six *kina* ... I said, "I have no more money," and went inside. I was strong and they left me alone. ... I said I did not have anything [left]. I fooled them. "I have no pigs,' I told them (*laughing*). I fooled everyone. I have pigs and I have money. But I am not *giving them away*! They want to hold a court. ... "I will not speak," I say. "I will just stare straight ahead." ...

Karapmene Ran Away

As Karapmene began to recount what happened after the court case, her air of triumph dissolved.

I decided to run back home. I was not going home, but to find another husband. I was angry and got my things together. And Vapa went away, too. I did not know where he went. I did not see him. That night, I gathered my belongings and went onto the big road. I walked all the way to Mane and arrived at dawn. When my Mane cousins saw me in the early morning, they cried. I cried for me, too. "You arrive here at dawn and we are sorry to see you [in such a state]. You can eat here and go [on your way]." They made tea for me and heated sweet potatoes and gave them to me. [But] his relatives followed me. While Vapa went to Goroka, his relatives followed me [to Mane].

Then Vapa arrived. He came in a car. ... and I hid. My cousins hid me in a house. "The woman is not here?" they [Vapa's relatives] asked. And [my relatives] said, "We do not know." While they were saying this I was asleep [i.e., lying down]. They put me in a house and I lay down to sleep but I could hear them, I could hear them talking. "She ran away," they said. "And we followed her here." I went to sleep. My cousins heated stones [for an oven] and they woke me and said, "Vapa's relatives are here putting pressure on us to make you go back to him. ... Vapa came back [to Ubagubi] from Goroka and heard that his wife had fouled him. ... He went to Agotu and heard from my parents' lips, "She did not come here!" And so he rushed to Mane.

He came to see me. I got up and went outside. I stood there. He was holding an axe and gave it to me in the back. Vapa is a stubborn man! He hit me and other men tried to restrain him but he did not listen. "I want to cut up this woman," he said. He hit me in the back but I did not fall. I stood up straight. And then we fought! We fought and fought and he beat me up. Then he said, "Let's go back to Ubagubi," and he pushed me. We came back together [in the car] ... on and on and on we drove until I got to an infirmary.

I took the medicine [i.e., was treated for my wounds] and we came back here. That is how we are living. I am very angry.

So I made another potion. I asked all the women, "Give me some." And they gave it to me and I did the same thing as before. I gave it to Vapa and after a while he came back to me. He left that other wife altogether. [She lives in another house and] he sleeps with me now. He takes food from my hands. He goes places with me. Money, everything, clothes, he buys them only for me. He does not like his [other] wife.

I asked Karapmene about current living arrangements.

She lives in her own house, a lousy house. She sleeps there. Her mother and brother came to live with us ... live with her. Me, I sleep in a place where she does not sleep. She lives with her mother at Korebi ... I live here, near the bridge, inside the fence ... She does not speak to her husband. Not at all. She does not speak to Vapa. He does not give her food, nor buy her soap, nor give her anything. When men butcher pigs and allot portions and put Vapa's name on them, I am the only one who receives them. *I am the one* who cuts the meat [he receives] and gives out the portions. And I am the *only one* who eats it .... Vapa – whatever there is, a plate, a spoon, a pot – he does not buy it for her. He puts it in *my* house. And he stays with *me*. He does not go places. He does not go places with her. He does not *look* at her! No way!

That woman is strong. She says, "I am going back home." But she lies and she stays. Vapa looks after her children. Both of them. He buys them soap and things. And I give them things, too. They ignore their mother. We look after the two children. We buy them soap and clothes and give them food and they sleep with us. Sometimes they sleep with their mother ... but we [Vapa and I] keep his children and leave their mother to herself. The two of us do this and she keeps looking for a new spell [to make Vapa come back to her]. She wants to get rid of me again. She wants to find [a new potion]. She wants to get hold of it and give it to him. But the man *does not take food from her hands!* So she leaves it [the love magic] in the house and it gets lost. She gets it again and prepares it again. If Vapa would take food from her hands, she would prepare it, give it to him, and he would not think of me anymore! He would go back to *her*. And *me*, I would be left alone and angry.

Marriage to one wife is fine. There is no anger. Men can go around as they please, and women too [i.e., wives can have affairs]. But men trick us and have sex with other women. They abuse us. "I came from this place ..." But I see what is going on! I know right away. "Vapa, you came from there." "Yes," he says, "I came from there." "You went there. ... I know where you went!" I speak the truth, I do not lie. ...

A woman who wanted to marry Vapa made friends with him. "You did this..." I said and we fought. I am not going to be easy on him. I am a strong woman. Other women are afraid of me. They say, "Vapa, get rid of Karapmene first and then I will marry you. If you do not get rid of her, I will not marry you." "How am I going to rid of her?" Vapa says. "Come and marry me and *you* can fight with Karapmene and then one day, eventually, she will let up...." That is what he says. Women are afraid of me. (*Karapmene gave me an example of how she ended one of Vapa's liaisons*). ...

All the women say, "What has this woman got [lit: 'what does she see,' meaning 'understand' or 'possess']?' Marop's two wives ask me. Other women ask me. "Whatever you know, give it to us so we can use it." They ask me but I tell them, "I do not know anything. I do not know about such things [as magic]. In the past, women knew such things but we who have grown up since the [Australian] *gavman* arrived, we do not know. "Show me what you have!" other women say to me. They try to give me twenty *kina* or ten *kina* but, "Never mind," I say to them, "I do not want to steal your money. The money is yours! This is *your place* [natal village] but you do not know how to look. ... it does not come from somewhere else. It comes from Unabi," I tell them.

And they say, "Show us! We will kiss your sweet ass." They give me money but I say, "I do *not* know!" I fool them. "I do not know such things," I say. "You are a good woman, now show us," they beg me. "We can give you a lot of money!" "I have seen a lot of money but I will not take it," I say. The women ask me. And they get angry at me. "How is it that you – your husband has two wives but the other wife keeps to herself and your husband lives with you only. That is *too* good!"

I lie to them. If I were to give it to them and they were to use it and give it to their husbands, and [their husbands] were to get rid of their other wives, one after another, [the men] would come to me and say, "Why did you give that stuff to make one wife live by herself and the other one live with her husband? That is *not* good! We bought the [now discarded] woman with pigs and money." [The husbands] would be angry at me so I hide it. I use it for my own husband. That is enough.

Rules of Allegiance in Wartime Still Determined Men's and Women's Relationships

Karapmene refused to share her know-how in winning her husband's exclusive attention because she feared that doing so would make the women's husbands angry at her. The rules of war still dictated that a woman's loyality was first and foremost to her husband and his comrades, in Karapmene's case, to Vapa and his age-mates and to Vapa's father and his age-mates, all of whom she addressed as *her* "age-mates." In times of war, a woman who secretly provided wives of "her" age-mates with the magical means to manipulate the men's affections and sabotage their co-wives marriages would be guilty of treason. Before pacification, any threat to the cohesion of a cadre of fighters was strictly taboo. Flirting with her husband's brothers or his age-mates bordered on a 'death wish' toward her husband, Karapmene was at pains to explain, because, if her husband were distracted in battle and killed, those men were first in line to inherit her as his widow. Making common cause with the co-wife of a husband's age-mate—a man whom she addressed as "age-mate" and might one day be her husband—in order to estrange another of his wives was as distracting and subversive as seducing the man herself:

> "No, [wives of my husband's] brothers and age-mates *you* cannot ask me," I tell them. Marop is my [husband's] age-mate. Imper is my [husband's] age-mate. … We call each other "age-mates." If I speak to Imper, Vapa would be angry and hit me. And if I speak to Marop, and flatter him, he and Vapa would fight. ... We share our food with them ... but we do not sleep in their houses because they are age-mates. [A man] would think his age-mate and his wife touched. He would think that and they would fight.
>
> "He is an age-mate so you cannot sleep in his house or talk with him." We can give them food. But if we speak to other men, our husbands get angry. And their wives would ball us out, "He is an age-mate. He is your [potential] *husband* so lay off!" If Vapa dies, I can marry Marop. If Marop dies, Vapa can marry his wife. A man can marry the wife of his age-mate. If Vapa dies, I will marry one of his age-mates. If I leave the age-mate and go off somewhere else, they (his age-mates) will poison me. I can only [re-] marry an age-mate.

In the ethnographic present of 35 years ago, more than two decades after open wars were ended, the dangers of sorcery and attendant risks of infidelity intensified. The sorcerer's *modus operandi* was to "steal"—not just any of his victim's leavings—but particularly his semen, which made the target's wife or paramour, wittingly or not, the sorcerer's ideal accomplice. To recruit her, he had first to seduce her—to become the "adulterer" (*udabana*; lit: *uda,* 'theft' + *bana,* 'man') with whom she "steals" sex. Gimi men's obsessions made the sorcerer a virtual third party in every act of heterosexual intercourse.

The exclusive twosome Karapmene described as the marital ideal seemed to be attainable, according to her, only when conjured by magic that mimicked the mother-child dyad as a relationship of which one party was unaware and therefore incapable of treachery. Just as love magic operated by recreating the sealed perfection of a mother-child bond so was sorcery the *perversion of motherhood* by men who—despite having been initiated and regularly purging their bodies of the vile traces of female influence—remained attached to their mothers and became ghastly parodies of them. Rather than turn into a man capable of killing other men in open battle, the imperfectly-severed son surreptitiously procured other men's leavings in a travesty of a mother's 'unnoticed' care. Like the babe-in-arms he once was, the sorcerer's victim is relaxed and unsuspecting in the sorcerer's presence. "Since the government arrived and banned warfare," Gimi men lament, "we have all become little boys working sorcery!" (Gillison 1993: 297).

A woman's reliance on love magic to dampen her husband's ardor for other women and keep his attentions riveted on her, women pointed out, stemmed not merely from selfish desire but mainly from her primary duty to protect his seminal fluid by detering him from the adulterous liaisons that sorcerers were bound to instigate. It also meant, of course, that a wife herself could not engage in adultery nor seduce her husband in places where sorcerers might lurk. Before her first marriage to a man before Vapa, Karapmene received advice from her father's third wife:

> "Be strong!" she said to me. "If you are not strong, sorry, you will be left by the wayside. Your husband will not speak to you. He will not break firewood for you. No. You will be one woman alone. Your eyes ... your throat will hurt from crying. You will go around like that, sleeping in your house all alone. ... (*Excitedly,*) When your husband is with you, make this love magic and give it to him! He will eat it and think only of you. He will stay with you. And you will take good food from his hands." That is what she told me.
>
> "But, no [if you do not heed what I am telling you] ... You will not receive good food. He will only give you *something* [his semen] and that is all you will be left with. He will think that way and you will eat by yourself. 'The first wife who stays beside me eats the good food. You, you can eat what is left.'" That is what my stepmother told me to make me strong.

"We looked, we all looked ... one angry woman went looking for it, for the magic. She asked all the other women, 'Have you got the stuff? Give it to me. Give it to me. I want to buy it. I want to make it for my husband and give it to him.'" We who are angry keep looking [for better and better remedies.] Do you search, too? "They want to beat us," my stepmother told me, "so we look – no – what I have [now] is strong so I stay put. But *that* woman [who may be any woman] she keeps looking. ... She is furious!"

This is what they tell us: "When you are married, you cannot steal [commit adultery] with another man. If you go with another man, your husband will cut you with an axe or shoot you with an arrow. Behave yourself and think only of your husband and do not flirt with other men. If you are flirtatious, other men will get hold of you .... They will tremble [with desire] and take you fast! And if you do that, the man [your husband] will give you whatever is no good, and he will give his [other] wife the good food. He will stay with his first wife and give her *gooooooood* food and buy her *gooooooood* clothes. And you, he will have sex with you for nothing [i.e., like an adulterer who *steals* sex and gives no food or 'cargo' or brideprice in exchange]." That is how our mothers speak to us.

"Your own husband will feed you well and care for you and buy you soap and find good things for you to wear. He will make you a fine house and you will sleep on a good bed. But if you steal too much, your husband will not give you good food. 'My wife is conceited and sleeps around with other men. ... I see what she does and will not give her good food. Go ahead, everybody, eat! My wife does not deserve anything to eat.' But if he sees the way you are, if you wait for him, if you sleep only with him and then you want to do something, he will do it for you. That is good. He can look after you and buy you nice clothes and ornaments. And make you a good bed ... but you fool around, sorry, he will not give you good things." That is what they tell us.

"When you serve your husband ... when he takes you to the garden or into the forest and wants sex right away, sing this song. When he holds you tight and has an erection, sing this song and he will lose it! Then you can come back to the house and have sex there [where a sorcerer cannot get his hands on the semen that spills on the ground]. ... When a man wants sex with you right away, sing this song. Sing this song [under your breath] and his penis will go limp:

asaro asaro asaro asaro
da ine damosu nareo nareo
asaro asaro asaro asaro
'go limp, go limp, go limp
[you tree] branch ...'

"'I want to hold her, but my thing is limp,' he will realize. Then go back to the house and when *you* want it – when *you*, the woman, want it – then say:

da ine more uke uke uke uke / repeat

"... call him the branch of a tree! Say to him, '*uke uke* ... Stand up!' and his thing will stand up straight! ... In your garden say, '*asaro asaro* ... Go limp, go limp.' He will tremble and try to take you but – sing this song – and he will not [be able to]! When his penis goes limp, the two of you *run* to the house. When you are there and you, the woman, want it, sing this and the man's thing will swell fast. And he will take you in a hurry."

Like Karapmene's myth of the Wild Woman, her step-mother's ditty refers to the penis as the branch of a tree. In Karapmene's myth, both the low-lying branch where the Wild Woman hangs her Child cradled inside a net bag, and the tree itself that puts forth delicious fruit at the top or "head," represent a giant erect penis. The branch in the ditty belongs to a real-life husband whereas the tree in Karapmene's myth stands for the First Husband, the Trickster Moon or primal Father upon whose "head" the Wild Woman—knowingly but unknowingly—dines contentedly all by herself. Allusion to the phallic imagery of myth in the wife's song, sung inside her garden and under her breath, increases the song's efficacy by identifying the wife with her pleasure-seeking and heroic counterpart.

"But when you are in your garden and he wants you, sing this song: '*asaro asaro...*'" ... The women are thinking of sorcery! A man who fools around in a garden or inside the forest lets his medicine [semen] fall to the ground where a sorcerer can get hold of it .... The man [who has sex out of doors] will have a short life! [Sorcery] is a powerful thing. ... He will not live one day more. He will go to sleep and in the morning he will be dead. That is why they tell us, "When a man has sex with you and you get up quickly or carelessly and spill his semen onto the ground [where a sorcerer will surely find it] and then run off, that kind of woman is a bad (lit: 'ugly') woman!"

"The man's parents tell him [to say to his wife], 'Wife, be careful with my semen. Check to see where it is. Then stand up straight and go about. Then you will be my true wife. And you will stay with me a long time until you are old.' Tell her that. Women do not think of these things. You play with them, and they get up and wipe away your semen and go off. That kind of woman is no good. She does not look after her husband. You can say to yourself, 'I married a bad woman.' So turn your back on that woman and find a new one!'" That is what a man's parents tell him.

"... and outside the house, too, when a man does it [copulates with us], we check to see if any of his fluid has fallen on the ground and we get rid of it before we come back home. 'You are a good woman. You look after your husband and he is well and will live a long life. He will not be poisoned in a hurry!' ... Now, look at this other woman. She has sex and says, 'It [semen] is bad, dirty stuff.' And she gets up and runs away. She is not careful. 'Sorry, I married a no-good woman,' the man says to himself and *he gets rid of his own emissions*. That is one angry man! He takes a new wife. ... He does not give good food to the [old] wife. When men present him with a huge pig, he does not show it to you. He gives it to other men and to his new wife..." That is what they tell a man and tell us women, too.

"... if another man comes, run away from him. Run away and wait for your husband. 'I can do it and he will not find out,' you say to yourself. But he *will* find out. He *will* see you. 'That is what my wife does with another man .... I will find them and beat them up.' The two men fight with arrows and axes." That is why we do not go with other men, no way! We wait for our husbands. But some women do not. Ubagubi women play around a lot! ... But not me. I do not steal because I am afraid. If another man holds me, I look the other way to show him my shame. I sleep with my husband. So he has nothing to say. I am happy to sleep with him. Another man makes me afraid and I tremble. If I am alone and a man finds me, I make a face. I do not speak to him. I keep to myself.

Suspicion of Adultery Comes with Being a Wife

According to Karapmene, the men of Ubagubi had reason to fixate on adultery because their wives were promiscuous.

> Vapa asks me, "How was your outing?" And I say, "I thought only of you. No one but you," that is how I answer him. "I am your wife. I am not thinking of stealing [with] another man." "Karapmene, did you think of me or did you do something else before I came?" he asks me. "No. I am your wife," I tell him, "and I think only of you." I tell him that and take him in my arms.
>
> "If you think of me, then it is alright to hold me. But if you do not think of me, then you cannot embrace me.' (*Karapmene went on to complain about how much reassurance Vapa demanded.*) "Sorry! I think about you. You are my man." I say this and hold him. We speak to each other in a funny way. Other women! No way! They have sex all over the place. Ubagubi women are arrogant and big-headed. ... They sleep around – in the forest, in their gardens, in their houses – and cause fights! They take off and sleep with other men. I do not like that kind of thing. I say: "My husband and I made our house and we sleep in it. No other man can sleep in my house." If we find out about that other man ... they [other women] do not accuse him! But not me.

Karapmene disapproved of women who were complicit in other women's infidelitites. She did not keep secrets, she insisted, neither her own nor other women's. After complaining that Vapa demanded constant reassurance from her, Karapmene remarked that such solicitude coming from a man could only be the "trick" of an adulterer.

> I came to Ubagubi [from another place]. If a man touches me, I will tell my husband. ... To the man I say, "You want to steal? I do not do that. If you try to do that with me, if you touch me, I will tell all!" "No, you are a woman. Women are not like that," he [the would-be adulterer] persists. "We trick you and you have sex with other men." Men fight us and trick us. They say, "You, I saw you do this in my dream." They say that to trick

us. "No," we say. "We were *here – not there in your dream!* We did not do what you saw us doing in your dream ..." We resist the trick. In the past, our mothers tell us, "They speared us when we were unfaithful. They saw us and speared us here (*Karapmene touched her upper thigh*) ..."

Now, the women of today, big shots, you think it is nothing. But not before. In the past it was different [adultery was serious business. Still today] they shoot us with arrows! Our husbands – when we go to work in our gardens – hide and watch us and make noises [in the bushes]. We turn around to look (*Karapmene twisted her head to look behind her)* and they shoot us! So when we hear a noise, we think [it is either an adulterer or a husband trying to catch his wife wavering...] and we *do not turn around to look!* No, we just keep working. We hear it and forget it. We keep working and our husbands say, "You are my woman. You are my wife."

Our ancestors spied on their wives and men today still do. Vapa has done it to me. At night, too, he comes to trick me. At night, he says (*whispering*), "Karapmene! Karapmene! Vapa has gone off somewhere. Let's you and me do something." "I have nothing to say," I answer. "Vapa, you have come to trick me," I think. "I am staying here." I am not a crazy woman who would get up, open the door and go out, no way! If I were to get up, "Oh, a man has come, I will take him ... I will open the door for him," ... were I to think that and go outside, Vapa would hit me hard! ... "You do that!" he would say. "I came to fool you and you ran to the door and opened it and came outside!"

I would eat a huge stick. He does this when I am lying down. I hear him. He has done it many times, tried to trick me. But I know. I think of what my mother told me. "If he comes to trick you and you say, 'Who is that?' and go outside, if you open the door and go outside, you will find your husband." He will give it to me! Hit me and hit me ... And I think, "Ah, you want to hit me so you come to make trouble [as the pretext]. I know what you are like!" and I do *not* go outside. ... Once he came, "Karapmene! Karapmene!" he called me, "Are you there? Vapa has gone away to another place. Karapmene, let's do it. Let's do it, Karapmene," he said. "I am not talking," I said. "Who are you? Say your name." And he tricked me and spoke another man's name. "It is I. I have come." "Fine," I said. But I could see that it was Vapa.

> "Karapmene, open the door and come outside. Come outside! We cannot let Vapa find us. Let's do it fast and you can go back inside!" ... But I was strong. Vapa kept tricking me, on and on, and I was fed up. I sat there and he went on and on and on. "Karapmene, come open the door." [Finally] I opened the door and I said, "It is *you*, Vapa." And he said, "You knew it [was me] so you would not come out."
>
> Men trick us all the time. That is what their ancestors taught them and that is what they do. ... An adulteress would go outside right away. And her husband would give it to her! He would hit her hard, in the nose, in the mouth, make her blood run! She would sleep badly. "We trick you so we can see you, see what you are *really* like." ... these kinds of things, kinds of stories, do you hear them from men? ... When we were young, we kissed. We do not tell our husbands. We do not say, "We kissed this one or that one." No. They would hit us. They would be angry and hit us ...
>
> But men say to us, "I kissed so and so. Did you kiss ...? I am your husband ..." Sometimes we answer, "If you kissed so and so then I kissed so and so." So when men ask their wives and then confess their own dalliances, then, only then, do women reply, "Yes, we did as you did ..."

Karapmene ventured onto the topic of marriage before the Australian-mandated peace, when wars were ongoing and men's vigilance over their wives extended beyond gardens to the neighbouring hamlets where their wives were born and where their wives' fathers and brothers, often the husbands' enemies, resided. In the days of war, a woman might "leak" not only her husband's semen onto the ground where a sorcerer might find it but also his lineage's plans for ambush or attack. Despite my expressing interest in the way things were in the recent past, Karapmene rarely digressed from the subject of her tumultuous marriage.

Karapmene Fought Her Co-Wife from the Start

> I have not been lazy about fighting that woman. I fought her while we were still in Hagotu [Vapa's natal village] ... I tore up her house ... [and] ... I set it on fire. She and her mother tried to fight me but I burned the house down! Her family came in mourning. They gathered up her belongings and took them to their place. (*Smiling broadly*) ... then I burned down the house!

Karapmene's account of setting her co-wife's house on fire began at the time Vapa's father was killed by sorcerers in a misguided act of revenge. Killing a man in his prime, especially a Big Man like Vapa's father, usually meant wiping out his entire lineage to ensure that no one was left alive to avenge him. After Vapa's father's murder, Vapa and his two wives and the rest of his lineage had to get out of town in a hurry. Their destination, as was usual in these circumstances, was the clan's ancestral home, in this case, Ubagubi, the place where Vapa's father's patrilineal forebears were born. In advance of their move to Ubagubi, Vapa and his kinsmen sent their pig herds and acquired land to cultivate sweet potatoes.

> They [Vapa and his lineage] brought the pigs and left them here. ... Vapa was sitting with his wife at Hagotu. She said, "There is nothing to eat. There is no sweet potato." I was hungry and gave Vapa two *kina* and told him, "Buy me some rice." I got the water ready. But that man did not buy the rice in a hurry! That woman got the rice – and [tinned] fish! "Vapa, you did not bring me [the rice]." "Sorry," he said, "she took it." And Vapa pushed me. "Go and fight her," he said.
>
> He pushed me and I went outside and spoke the woman's name. "Garganu!" I yelled. Vapa was carrying something of mine and she stole it. She was angry and watched the road and [when she saw Vapa coming] she took the rice. "That is my rice, Garganu! Give it to me!" "Why should I give it to you," she said. "I have it now." "I did not use your husband's money to buy it. I sent him to buy rice with *my* money. I am hungry. I have just come here [to Hagotu] and you have not shown me your garden. You take food from that garden and eat it. You do not say, 'I will look after you who are a newcomer.'"
>
> She was stubborn! "I will not give it to you!" Her mother, too, was stubborn. "Is this something of *yours*?" I asked them. "Are you two so strong? Give it to me, I am hungry." Vapa said, "Hit them and wreck their house!" He said that to me and he left. "Give me my rice!" I shouted. And the woman, in her fury [came outside and] spilled the rice on the ground and the two of them went [back] inside the house. I could hear them closing up the door. "Open the door," I yelled. But they did not listen. I kicked the door and broke it. And she and her mother came at me with a huge stick and stabbed me. It went up inside me. Then I entered the house, grabbed the stick, and smashed the house, smashed the wall and pulled it apart ... and they just sat there. "There," I said, "There was nearly a fight!"

Vapa arrived and smashed the wall again. In the morning the woman went crying to her relatives ... to her mother's relatives. And they came to beat me up. "Why did you wreck her house?" they demanded. But in the morning I was even angrier so I burned the house down! The house was destroyed. The woman went to live with her relatives. After that, we [Vapa and I] brought our belongings and came here.

But she came [here] later on. (*Vapa's first wife Garganu – whose name Karapmene finally spoke – took time to recuperate from her wounds and to look for a new husband. Then she followed Vapa and Karapmene to Ubagubi.*) We left her there [in Hagotu] and we came here. "Why don't you find a new husband?" we said to her. "The two of us are truly married and have come to live in Ubagubi." But that woman came later. Vapa did not build a house [to live in] with her. No. Vapa built a house and lived in it with *me*. He did not go into her [room] in the house. *He really did not!* He stayed with me. And he went around with me. When he was hungry, he took food from my hands. He did not take food from her hands. No way! ... and he gave me all kinds of things. To her he gave nothing.

When we first arrived in Ubagubi, Himepepo gave us his old house to live in ... and we gave her a place inside it to sleep. Vapa and I slept together in one bed and she slept in another room. She slept alone. Vapa and I slept in one room. We held each other and slept. That woman was angry, angry. ... "Aye," she thought, "that woman and that man sleep in each other's arms and I sleep alone." And one night, in the middle of the night, she was not sleeping. Vapa and I were asleep. She made a fire and sat there until dawn. "Heh!" she thought to herself, "You two [sleeping in each other's arms] do not make the fire."

Finally she said, "Why don't you ever make the fire?" So I said to her, "I can make the fire if you do not want to get up and make it yourself!" And she got mad. It was dark. She was angry at me and I got up slowly and took a piece of firewood and hit her in the head. It was the middle of the night. I hit her and she grabbed hold of me and I hit her again and again. I broke this part of her (*gesturing to her chest*) ... I hit her here and here (*pointing to her eye*). I hit her in the eye and it swelled terribly. I beat her badly and in the morning that woman gathered up her belongings and went to her own lineage, to the lower part of the village.

She went down there and I stayed inside the house. "That woman went into the infirmary with her wounds and lives with her lineage," they all said to me. "She stayed [in the infirmary] and came out and now says, 'I want to go back to that house.'" "You will not come back into my house!" I cried. I insisted! I threw her out of this house! I got rid of her and she went to sleep with her old mother ...

Then we built an enormous house in the compound. While I was working on the house I did not say, "Help me and we can work together." No, I never said that. I worked alone and finished the new house and moved in. That woman stayed with us in the old house and slept in her part of it. She slept there and we lived that way. Then I made a new house! "When you make the house we can all live in it," she [had the nerve to say to me]. "No you cannot! You cannot," I said. "I want to build a house for *me* to live in. You can build your own house!" I said that, and got rid of her, but she came back. "I am going, I am going ..." she kept saying, but she never left or went [back] to her place. "I am going to marry another man, ... another man," she said again and again but that woman is *still there!* She is in her part of the [new] house!

So I gave her something ... to defeat her. It [the love magic Karapmene put in Vapa's cigarettes] defeated Vapa! Our mothers tell us about it. Our ancestors used it and passed it on to us. "When you marry a man already married to another woman and she tries to get rid of you, and she stays with her husband, and you are left by yourself and he does not give you food and you go around finding food on your own while they go around together ... try this, try making this ... and the man will leave that woman and come to you." That is what they tell us.

"When another woman comes to marry your husband," our mothers and fathers tell us what to do. "Do this .... You go to live with your husband and you are the first wife. You stay with him and eat all the food he has. When men give him pork or other things, he thinks of you and gives you some. If you live like that and stay in your place, another woman will take it! And then where will you go?! There is no place for you to live. 'Get out,' she will tell you and try to get rid of you. You have to be strong and fight her! (*Karapmene laughed softly.*) Hit her!" That is what our parents tell us. "And make this [potion]." And they show us what to do. "Make this and give it to the woman. And give it to the man and he will eat it. And then he will think *only* of you. He will think of *yoooou* and sleep with *yoooou* and stay with *yoooou!* When he goes places he will go *only with you!*" That's what they tell us.

> "If you do not watch what we show you now, you will not know how to make it [the love magic] and give it to them. The first wife will be too strong for you. You will lose face and be by yoursaelf. And together the two of them will cook pork and other delicious things and eat them together. And whatever is no good they will pass on to you! He will have sex with you *for nothing*, and give you his *marasin* (p.e., 'medicine,' a euphemism for semen). 'Eat this,' he will tell you." That is what our parents tell us. ...

Karapmene's Early Life

I asked Karapmene about her young life.

> My father had three wives. Two of them died. The first one died. My mother left me when I was very small. I had not yet lost my umbilical cord. She died and left me. I did not know her. I do not know the kind of woman my mother was. No. My mother died and left me. She cut the cord and she died.
>
> My father looked after me ... not another woman. My father was strong and he looked after me. He was not supposed to look after me but he did! He fed me sugarcane juice. He fed me and fed me until I was big. I did not see my mother. I do not know what kind of woman she was. I wonder about her. Some women have mothers who look after their children and help them work in their gardens. It makes me cry. If my mother were alive, she could help me work and spend time with me, weed my garden and make net bags and give them to me. That would be so good! I am alone and that is not right. When I see parents visit their children, I cry. I say to myself, "I did not know you, mother, and you died." My father is alive.
>
> Another wife, the wife [after my mother], told me the story [of] ... how my mother was murdered by sorcerers [who inserted poison into her vagina after forcing my birth]. *(Karapmene's mother was her father's second wife whom he married after his first wife was killed by sorcerers.)* He married again. And she died [too]. They poisoned her and she died. One sorcerer held her belly ... the others pulled me out of her. First they gave her poison, then they took me out of her, then they inserted [more] poison into her vagina. She gave birth to me ... they took me out of her ... and they poisoned her. ... They cut the cord and put in more poison. *They put me back inside her.*

... They did not give birth to me. They had already taken me out and [put me back inside her again]. It was a faked birth. They took me out and she died.

My father was furious because they killed another one of his wives! "I will kill five or ten men [to avenge her]!" he swore. "They took out [the child] and put in more poison. They cut the cord and put the child back in again! We will kill them all! We are sorcerers, too!" my father vowed. ... Another woman told me these things. My father's third wife told me these things.

Karapmene departed and returned several days later, taking up her story by repeating many of the things she already told me, especially her step-mother's instructions about how to protect a husband from sorcerers. The topic of sorcery led back to her mother's death.

I never saw my mother's face. The sorcerers hid in her pig house [the hut where her mother slept with her pigs in a separate enclosure]. My father was away, they told me. He had gone to Mane ... where they were feasting. My mother was pregnant. I was still inside her ... and they poisoned her. Men held her and dragged her down to the river. They laid her out [on the bank] and poisoned her. They put a stone inside her and inserted pieces of wood. *(Karapmene pointed to her neck, shoulders, underarms and upper torso to show me the places on her mother's body where the sorcerers inserted sharpened slivers of wood.)* Then they took out the child. They put their hands inside her and pulled [me] down. Me, it was *me*. They pulled me down and put me into a net bag.

They pulled everything out of her, out, out, out, out, and cut the umbilical cord. Then they put everything back inside her, back into her belly. They got a stone, a huge stone, and placed it at the bottom [to keep everything from falling out]. They put the stone into her vagina. They took me out with their hands and [put me back inside her]. They sealed me inside her with a stone so I would not fall out. Then my mother came up from the river. "I am going to bear the child," she announced, falsely. "Yes, she is about to give birth," the women said and kept watch over her. "She is about to bear the child. We will hold her and look after her." "No," my mother said, "I am *not* going to bear the child." And they looked and saw – no! – it was the stone they used to close her. ... They looked inside her and saw the stone. They removed it and me and the afterbirth. The two of us came out of her completely.

Speaking of "the two of us," Karapmene referred to her newborn self and the afterbirth. A woman's death in childbirth was generally considered an attack on her husband: to make sure no trace of his seminal fluid, embodied in both newborn and placenta, remained inside the dead mother an autopsy was usually performed. The husband's 'remains' left to rot and *indissolubly combine* with his wife's decomposing corpse placed him exactly in the position of a victim of sorcery. Once a sorcerer obtained a piece of his victim, ideally, his seminal fluid, he wrapped it in a tiny leaf packet and inserted the packet into the abdomen (via a slit below the navel) or vagina of a woman's corpse, preferably one "killed" during childbirth as Karapmene's mother had been or, if no female corpse were available, by an equivalent ritual means (Gillison 1993: 312). The sorcerer's *modus operandi* was to send his victim—a grown man reduced to the stolen morsel of his person—"back up the road he first came down," forcing him to return to the place where the Moon issued his "firstborn" as dead blood. Both sexes identified the sorcerer with the Moon.

Corpses of women, especially those who died in childbirth, were routinely examined before burial for signs of sorcerers' tampering. In 1985, a Gimi man described the autopsy of his much-loved lineage sister.

> She had a *kore arak* (lit: *kore*, 'wild,' 'ghost' or 'spirit' + *arak*, 'child') and she died. The *kore arak* was there. The *dusa arak* (lit: *dusa*, 'domestic,' 'living,' 'real' + *arak*) was there. The two lay together inside the mother's belly. She bore the *dusa arak* but the *kore arak* stayed inside her and she died.

During the autopsy, the men found the *kore arak*, an enormous blood clot that they said was "black" and "hard as stone." It lay beside the *dusa arak* and grew at the same rate but—because it stayed inside the mother and was not delivered immediately after the *dusa arak*—it hardened and blackened. "It was a stone," the man said.

Karapmene continued the story of her mother:

> Everything came out of my mother and she was close to death. They said to my father, "You did not kill a pig and give it to her." "Kill a pig and give it to me," my mother asked him. "I looked after a lot of pigs," she said. "Kill one for me and then I will die." But my father did not kill a pig. He killed a dog, they say. The dog was bad-tempered and my father was fed up with it. "I killed a dog and gave it to your mother," he told me. "I am not going to eat it!" my mother said. "The dog will find (lit: look at) me and bite me! I am a woman who reared many pigs but you will not kill a pig and give it to me! ...
>
> "I am about to die. Kill a pig for me," my mother begged my father. But my father would not do it. He refused. He killed a big dog [because it was snarly and unruly] and gave it to my mother. "Once, when I went to see [who was coming along the road] that dog bit me," my mother said. "I am not going to turn around now and *eat the dog* [that ate me]!" She said this and then she died. And no one ate the dog ...

A dog is an animal that tracks and kills other animals inside the forest. If Karapmene's mother had eaten the dog that bit her, the dog's vengeful *auna* would have hunted down her *auna* after she died and devoured it. A pig, on the other hand, is an animal reared to be eaten.

> My father ... I am angry at my father. "You did not want to give my mother a pig to eat before she died! No. You killed *a dog* and gave it to her." He gave her the dog and she died. My sorrow is double. "Father, I do not want to look at you," I say to myself. "One day, I will go to see you. You killed a dog and treated my mother with no respect. That makes me twice as sad." I do not go to see my father. And my mothers [my father's other wives] did not make net bags for me nor help me with my work. They just wanted my brideprice. They demanded my brideprice but I said, "You are not going to get it." I missed my mother. And I did not see my father.
>
> But my father worked hard to look after me. He gave me water and sugar-cane juice until I was grown. He looked after me well. In some ways he looked after me like a mother. But in other ways he was arrogant and made me sad. "You would not kill a pig and give it to my mother. You killed a dog!" ... I think about the dog and when my father comes here, I am not

kind to him. "If my mother were alive she would be good to me. But you [my father] went away and they poisoned her [while you were gone] and you would not kill a pig for her [when you came back]." I think about this and I am angry at my father.

Only, my father. ... Nobody made net bags for me. I made them myself and they tore because I made them wrong. I did not have a mother to come to see me. I am married but not like other women whose mothers come to help them with gardening, make net bags for them, bring them food. I have no one. I am alone.

I am a strong woman. I can cut the forest and make a garden. I think of my mother being there and helping me while I work and I make a *huge* garden! I plant a lot of food! Everyone takes food from my garden and is pleased with me. "This is a *goooood* woman!" they all say. ... Everyone puts food inside my house. Pork and other good things people eat they give some first to me ... and my house fills up with food.

My father was angry when my mother died because [the sorcerers] pulled out the child and [put in the poison]. In return, he said, he would kill five men. "We will get poison and kill five of our enemy." [His wives told me,] "Your mother died and your father worked hard to look after you so, in return, when you are grown, you will find a man and marry him ..." and they took my pay. They said, "You are such a fine girl!" and all the men from the coast, from Goroka, from everywhere – I could not count them! – they all came to buy me. I said, "I am fed up." [Those men who] brought payment for me ... two, three, four men. They were all the same to me. ...

Karapmene Bore a Son by Her "Crazy" First Husband

Karapmene was married to a man before Vapa.

I married a man and went to live with him but Vapa pulled me away and married me. ... In Chimbu, I had a child, one child, and I came with him to look after Vapa. My first husband was crazy ... when I lived with him I was sick ... that man was always angry at me. "Are you drunk or are you crazy?" I asked him. "I think you are crazy." The man ... shot me with an arrow and tried to cut me. He went around shooting pigs. ... Me, I am strong. He tried to shoot an arrow and I grabbed it. And he tried to cut me with an axe but I got hold of it. (*Karapmene raised her hands to demonstrate her agility in grabbing hold of the arrow and the axe her husband wielded against her.*) I could have cut him. ... I ran away.

I slept in another house but he came there to shoot me. He came to that house and people said, "You are a good woman. Too bad you have to be afraid and run away." "I am not running away. I am not scared of a spear or an axe," I said. ... "I can keep an eye on him. I can handle him. That is how I am."

"If he tries to strike me with a stick ... or an arrow ... or an axe ... I can grab hold of it *fast*. I can see him coming and restrain him." That is how my husband was. They sent him to the hospital in Chuave. He went to Chuave and then to Kundiawa. From Kundiawa he went to Goroka. I thought he was dead. I lived alone, made a garden alone, looked after pigs alone. And after a long time he came back. The hospital car brought him back *crazy as ever!* "He is not crazy anymore so you have brought him back to me?" I asked. The doctor said, "No. It is not finished. Keep your distance. And he, too, should be put at a distance." He said this to me and I went *far* away.

I ran away with my child. The man was crazy. He did not say to himself, "You stayed here while I was crazy. You made a garden and reared pigs and lived here and did not think of going back to your place. I cut you and shot you several times with arrows but, still, you did not think of that and run away. No, you stayed here!" He did not think like that. He came back and started hitting me again! ... I was holding the key about to open the door [for him] and he hit me in the back. I screamed. "Too bad," I thought. "I stayed here and waited (lit: 'thought of you') and you hit me. I am leaving. When your craziness is over, I will come back." I took my child and went back to my [father's] place. …

I was living there and Vapa said to me, "You are my good friend. I want to marry you." And I married him. I brought my child and was living with him ... I want to tell you, that man ... I was in Hagotu for a year or so and then I married Vapa and came with him here to Ubagubi. I had been here one or two nights ... and that man arrived *here!* He took the child and went away. The child left me. The man was strong. "He is not yours, he is mine and I am taking him." And he took the child. The boy's name is Nako. I bore him on a Thursday and I named him Thursday and Nako. He was a beautiful boy. That man [my crazy first husband] was handsome. ...

> I miss that child and I cry. I cannot forget him. No, I cry all the time. Vapa said, "Have [another] child." "No, I miss that child. I want to wait a while." These thoughts possess me. It has been five years and I want a child with Vapa but I do not have one. … I have not eaten any contraceptive. I have not closed myself up. I think to myself, "I think about that child too much." He [my first husband] said I could have another child (lit: 'cut new skin') and took that one away from me but the child still remembers me. This is what I think about. And maybe that is why I do not have another child. I think that child possesses me.
>
> Do you have a remedy, something you can give me to make me pregnant …?

I told Karapmene that fertility treatments might be available in Goroka and suggested we go there together on our next supply trip. Karapmene said we would have to find a pretext, some way to conceal the real reason for her going with me. She continued to speak about her first husband:

> I think he is [nearly] dead. That is what I have heard. A lot of women from Mane are married here in Ubagubi and have told me. His mother is alive but his father is dead. … his elder brother is dead, they tell me. Only his [brother's] wife is alive. That man said, "I knew I was a crazy man but I thought I would go back to her. … but Vapa married her and he would cut me. … that is why I live here. She is married to Vapa now." And they say, "He has not lost his madness. He talks to spirits. … he talks to the ground and we have almost stopped speaking to him. He is very thin. He seems close to death."
>
> That is what they tell me. … maybe I am wrong. Maybe he is married to a "wild woman" (*kore badaha*). He thinks she is an ordinary woman (*dusa badaha*) but he has befriended a spirit. … The man has been that way for a very long time. … He stays inside his house and the wild woman comes there to charm him. The man is going to die, that is what I think. I worry about my child. Who will feed him?

Karapmene's "Crazy" First Husband Married a Wild Woman

Karapmene's portrayal of her former husband married to a "wild woman," whom he believed was real, and her fear that he would soon die and become "wild" like his wild-woman wife, envisaged the same kind of 'fatal regression' that sorcerers inflicted on their victims. Several months after Karapmene's account of her "crazy" first husband, a young man from a Chimbu village offered a tale about a besotted lover 'holed up' with a "wild woman," one of a category of hybrid stories, told by men, that seemed to adapt tales the men heard as children living in their mothers' houses. In this story, which combines allusions to both female and male initiation rites and to men's Flute myth in which the First Woman seduces an innocent Boy, the irresistably beautiful "wild woman" seals the hero's doom.

> *One* In [the Chimbu village of] Kiyati there were a Girl and a Boy who made love and wanted to marry. And so they were betrothed but the Girl died. Her Mother and Father went to their pig-house and killed and cooked a pig. They decorated the Girl ... completely [as a bride] and made a fire. The Mother and Father placed the pig on the [overhead] rack for drying firewood and returned [to the compound].
>
> *Two* They told her fiancé [where she was] ... and he went there. He knocked on the door and her spirit (lit *kore*) said, "Open the door and come in!" The Boy opened the door and went inside. He blew on the fire and saw her decorated body lit up by firelight. Lying there, she was as beautiful as she had been the first time they lay together.
>
> *Three* He climbed onto the [platform] bed and made love to her. When it was nearly dawn, a cold wind blew. He held her and realized (lit: saw) that the woman's body was very cold. "I'll make a fire," he said to himself. He got down off the bed and blew onto the embers until they were alight. He saw the pig fat above him. He looked up and saw the pig that had been ... butchered, cooked, and stuffed into bamboo tubes and the innards placed on top of them (i.e., the wedding pork). Nothing had been eaten: it was all there. And the man thought to himself, "The pig was killed and put there when the woman I slept with died."

Four He thought and thought and thought. ... Seeing the meat, the man realized he had just slept with a Wild Woman! He ... searched for the door. "I must pull out the door-planks but I cannot find the door (lit: the door is hidden)!" Back and forth, back and forth, back and forth he paced but the door was shut tight. The dead woman's spirit was holding the door shut. And where there had been a door there was none! He shouted and shouted and shouted. Not far away was a men's house (lit: initiate + house, i.e., place where first-stage male initiation rites were in progress). His shouts did not have far to go but they were hidden [shut up] inside the house.

Five On and on and on [he paced and he shouted but soon] his voice was gone (lit: closed). In the morning he thought, "I have my voice." He tried to shout but only a tiny thin sound—a high-pitched squeal—came out. ... In the morning, the hidden door reappeared and he rushed outside and went over to the men's house. He stood at the door and was about to enter the house but he collapsed and died on the spot.

Six Why did he die like that? He had come from sleeping with the Wild Woman. He died on account of that. He took a mistress (lit: 'he fell in love') and entered her house. ... That Boy slept with the Wild Woman and so he died. They dug one hole and put the Boy and Girl inside it together.

The story-teller's companion, another young unmarried man from the same village, interpreted his tale. (Some of his exegesis, presented inside double quotes, and my commentary refer to material presented in summary form in the Introduction Chap. 1 and again at length in later Chapters, for which I ask the reader's forbearance. For a quick look ahead, see Appendices I and II.) Paragraphs *One* and *Two*, my interlocutor pointed out, describe the Girl's "funeral arrangements," preparations for *haro* (lit: 'roof'), the rite of first menstruation which, like every Gimi rite of passage, celebrates the subject's symbolic death and rebirth (van Gennep 1960 [1908]). The Girl's initiation takes place inside her mother's "pig house," also used in the past as a menstrual hut. She is "betrothed," "decorated completely as a bride" and "dies" because she is married to her "first husband," the Moon. When the hero "'climbs onto the bed and sleeps with her' (Paragraph *Three*), he climbs onto the roof of the house

Fig. 3.2 At the climax of a girl's initiation to celebrate her first menstruation (*haro*, lit: 'roof'), her future affines, men who have paid her brideprice, climb onto the roof of the woman's house where she is secluded, tear open a hole in the thatch and insert a long sugarcane pole, enacting the mythic onset of menstruation when the Moon sends his Giant Penis out of the night sky to copulate with every nubile girl. (© David Gillison)

where the initiate is secluded" and where her future affines, acting as surrogates for the Moon's Giant Penis, open a hole in the thatch and insert a long sugar pole (Fig. 3.2).

When the Hero "blew the fire alight, he saw what was above him!" Entering the woman's house, making a fire, blowing it alight and looking up reiterate what the Hero did: he [*re-*]entered the First Woman—his illicit first love—whose Vagina was on fire because, as he now could see from *inside* her house, she was already married to the Moon. Stashed in the rafters above him, the Hero saw the wedding pork, slabs of fat and cut-up chunks of meat stuffed into bamboo tubes; that is, he saw *the flutes* disguised as containers of salt that a bride carries from her father to the groom inside her net bag, supposedly without knowing what she transports (see Chap. 1). The Hero sees the wedding pork for the her marriage to the Moon and knows "the woman I slept with died" (Paragraph *Three*).

"He thought and thought and thought," and realized he had slept with a Wild Woman (Paragraph *Four*). To sleep with a dead—menstruating—woman is to be "killed by the Moon" *oneself*, to become the Moon's "firstborn child," the one dancing beneath him—pacing "back and forth, back and forth"—at / as the "head" of the Moon's Giant Penis. Looking up, he saw the Giant entering through the roof of the house where he slept: he witnessed the 'primal scene' from a vantage point *inside the womb* and knows he is doomed. His pacing "back and forth" shows him moving 'in step' with the Moon because he is as yet *unsevered* from Him. The love-struck Boy is still (attached to) the Giant's "head" because, as long as the Giant 'dances' inside the Wild Woman, he remains in tact: "Nothing had been eaten: it was all there" (Paragraph *Three*).

The First Woman / Wild Woman seals herself shut—like the Sister in men's Flute myth who closes the instrument's blowing hole with a plug of her pubic hair—to protect the baby-boy Hero from the Moon's murderous wrath. But the moment the love-struck Boy *stands up at the door* and tries to enter the "men's house," where other boys are being initiated, the Moon strikes him dead (Paragraphs *Four* and *Five*). Although his cries for help 'did not have far to go' they were unheard because he was shut up inside the womb while his parents—lying above and right beside him—were not listening.

Once "the hidden door reappeared and he rushed out ... he collapsed and died on the spot" because the only way to exit the First Woman is *as* her menstrual blood, *as* the Moon's murdered "firstborn child," the severed "head" of his Giant Penis. The Hero and his "cold" beloved end up in "one hole" because the Moon / Giant Penis copulates with the Wild Woman inside her forest niche, the cave or tree hollow where she and her murdered "firstborn" reside all alone.

* * *

Only a short time before Karapmene described her first marriage to a "crazy man" and her unending grief over his "theft" of her only child, she told the story of the Wild Woman embarked on a desperate search for her Child after thoughtlessly hanging him, cradled inside a net bag, on a low branch of the Tree-Man Trickster who stole him and imprisoned him inside the men's house (see above).

> I worry all the time. Vapa is impossible, too. I should not have married him. I should go away. I think, "One day I am going to hold that child." (*Karapmene told me that Vapa supported her first husband's right to take her son away from her.*) "You are stubborn," Vapa said to me. "Let the man go with the child. You know Chimbu men do not give up their children. They will not let the mother take the child to a new husband. No way! ..." That is how Vapa spoke to me and now I say to him, "You pushed me and he took the child! 'Give him to him. Give him to his father. If you do not give him to his father, I will throw you out.'" Vapa mistreated me and I sent the boy away. ... Vapa abused me. "Send the boy away, send your child away. You can be with me. If you are attached to that child, you cannot be with me," he said.
>
> Vapa said that and summoned the child. ... "Karapmene, Karapmene ..." [my child] was calling me while [my first husband] carried him away. I cried and cried. (*Tears came now to Karapmene's eyes.*) ... I worry and am crying still. I put scraps of his pants around my neck [in an amulet as mothers do with relics of a dead child]. I worry so much about this child.
>
> I would not stay here if Vapa had not paid my brideprice. I would leave ... I would cross the river and climb to the other side. I would hide [somewhere where I could] see my child. I would watch him and steal him and carry him away. But I am married to Vapa and I am waiting. He has thrown me out many times. Ten times, at least. ... And he is close to doing it again. "Good," I say. "I am a strong woman. I make gardens and look after pigs and bring you prestige. Men will not like it if you throw me out. If you get rid of me, I am going to get that child and bring him to my family. They can look after him." I am thinking these things.
>
> "... send the child away and you will want him back but then you will have *another* child. And you will look after it and forget about the other one." That is what Vapa told me. I want another child and I have tried hard! But I do not have one and Vapa says to me, "If you have a child, I will give it

food and help the two of you. ... And if I get rid of you, it is for no other reason. It is because of the child [you do not bear me]! Give me a son and I will be happy." Vapa talks this way. He is going to get rid of me.

... I talk about having a child and go all over the place asking, "Do you have something to make me pregnant?" I ask all the men [the sole experts in rites that cause pregnancy]. "Did you close something inside yourself?" they ask me. "No," I say. "I did not *close* anything. I have done nothing. I want to have a child but I cannot ...." They say, "We do not know. Only you can think of it. ... Did you close something inside yourself?" ...

Vapa says to me, "You took a contraceptive. *I* have children. But *you*, you are stubborn. I have children and can give them to you. But you do not *want* to have a child. Alright! I do not *want* to sleep with you and flirt with you. No, you can stay by yourself." Sometimes, when Vapa wants to sleep with me, I say, "Fine, if you are so sick of me, then never mind! ... You would be wasting your semen," I tell him. And Vapa is thinking of marrying a new woman to have a child. He has no child, just two daughters. He has no son. He says, "Try and ask [someone for a remedy] ...

(*Whispering*) I want a child and I do all kinds of things but ... no way! Vapa says, "I am going to cut you open and look inside." He is angry, "I am going to cut open your vagina (*laughing*) and see what is closing it! ... And me, I think about my child and cry all the time. "You are stubborn," Vapa tells me. "You are a good woman and you can remove [the thing that is closing you. Otherwise] I will marry a stupid woman and the stupid woman will give me a child!" But one after another I get rid of them [Vapa's prospects for a third wife]. ... I get rid of them and he cannot get a new wife.

"You *have* a wife," I tell him. "You *can* have a child." But he does not listen. He wants to be rid of me altogether. "I want a new wife," he says. "With her I will have a child. If there were a child, I would be satisfied. The child would speak and we would live contentedly. But the two of us sit in our house and talk only to each other. We have nothing to say and then we go to sleep. A child plays and speaks .... We are alone and that is not right."

... Other women say to me, "I will have a child and give it to you." ... But when a woman has a child she says, "No, I will *not* give it to you!" That is what they all say. "Fine, but I am not a man. I am a woman and I need a child. Something is closed [inside me]!" I say [to myself] and I cry. I cry all the time for a child. If I could hold a child it would be so good! I go around with empty arms while other women carry babies. ... I look at the women who are pregnant and say [to myself], "What did you do? I am the same as you and you are pregnant. Take out what is inside you and put it in my belly," I say. "Then I would be pregnant and have a child." I talk this way because I want a child so badly.

Note

1. Because of their intimate connection, Gimi myths and rites are often discussed together. Mythic figures and artifacts are capitalized to distinguish them from their ritual counterparts. But pronouns that refer to mythic figures appear in lower case. Big Man and Big Woman, individuals recognized as important persons and leaders in the community, are also capitalized.

References

van Gennep, Arnold. 1960 [1908]. *The Rites of Passage.* Translated by Monika B. Vizedom and Gabrielle L. Caffee. Chicago: University of Chicago Press.

Gillison, Gillian. 1993. *Between Culture and Fantasy. A New Guinea Highlands Mythology.* Chicago: Universityof Chicago Press.

4

Totem and Taboo in the New Guinea Highlands: The Collusion of Sisters and Brothers

> One day the brothers who had been driven out came together, killed and devoured their father and so made an end to the patriarchal horde. United, they had the courage to do and succeeded in doing what would have been impossible for them individually.
> Sigmund Freud, *Totem and Taboo*, 1972 [1913]: 141

Before "pacification" of the Eastern Highlands of Papua New Guinea in the early 1960's, warfare among neighbouring settlements was endemic and Gimi women practised cannibalism as part of funeral rites for men of their husband's lineages, many of whom were killed in battle (Gajdusek 1973; Berndt 1962; Gillison 1983a, 1993: 65–152). In elaborate rituals of conspiracy and rebellion that, in actuality, were parts of a charade and joint exercise, women "stole" the corpse of a man his comrades had installed on a platform outside the settlement supposedly to rot in peace. Once the bones were washed clean by the rains, men declared, they intended to decorate them with coloured vines and disperse them inside caves, in the cleft branches of trees and other sacred "female" niches deep

G. Gillison, *She Speaks Her Anger: Myths and Conversations of Gimi Women*, Culture, Mind, and Society, https://doi.org/10.1007/978-3-030-49352-3_4

inside the clan forest. According to men's accounts of what happened in the past, women conspired to spoil men's best laid plans. After the men had installed their fallen comrade on the platform and left him there, women gathered below the platform in secret, pulled the corpse to the ground, cut it into sections and loaded them into their net bags. Stealthily, one or two at a time, the women returned to their separate houses and, together with their young children, consumed most of the man before their husbands discovered women's "terrible deed."

Gimi death rites were staged as a contest between warriors and cannibals. To compare it with the last chapter of *Totem and Taboo*, one would have to say there were not one but *two* "tumultuous mobs:" a band of brothers who "murdered the father" and a conspiracy of sisters who devoured him. Like every Gimi rite of passage, cannibalism *depicted* the primordial past, the era of "wild men" and "wild women" before marriage or society existed, within the constraints of present day rule-governed norms. By "stealing" the corpse, as ritual dictated, women behaved *as if* social rules had yet to be invented and there were no taboos. The historical cannibal victim was usually a man killed in battle by men of an enemy village so that he was not related as a father to his killers: murdering a member of one's own clan or settlement was strictly forbidden. Nor was the dead man related as a father or brother to the women who ate him; rather, he was likely to have been a real or classificatory father-in-law, brother-in-law or a husband. But in the primordial era which the Gimi mortuary rites enacted, every dead man and every murder counted as the very first. From a mythic perspective, in other words, any man for whom cannibal rites were celebrated stood categorically for the First Man or primal Father.

Gimi cannibal ritual revived a mythic era as contructed mainly by men: the rites *dictated* that women behave like an "unruly mob" of cannibals so fierce and devious men could not anticipate nor prevent their vile deed. Women's savagery left men no choice but to punish and attempt to reform them 'after the fact.' As ritual prescribed, any woman who participated in the cannibal meal became *faba badaha,* literally, "nobody" (*faba*, 'nothing,' + *badaha,* 'woman'). She lost her name and kinship status and membership in society on account of her own "wild" behaviour. Men used various ritual means to force cannibal women to 'disappear' from the human social world: the women had to remain in seclusion inside their separate houses and to 'black out' their faces by covering them with a mixture of soot and pig fat. Whenever the cannibal women appeared out of doors, especially in harsh sunlight, the shiny black mixture smeared over their faces flattened their features so that they became virtually unrecognizable. Paradoxically, in order to impose such conspicuous anonymity and shame as part of the ritual, the men made a spectacle of finding out the names of every woman who participated in the cannibal meal. As soon as men "discovered" women's crime, they say, they searched for the *one* woman or older child of either sex who had "kept her head" amidst the supposed carnage and frenzy. Once men had identified the lone alert eyewitness, they demanded that she give them an account of precisely who ate each and every part of the man. According to men's and women's descriptions of what transpired during cannibal rites in the past, and in keeping with what I witnessed when cannibalism was no longer practiced but women still secluded themselves, blackened their faces and wore elaborate mourning garb made from the dead man's attire, men selected, slaughtered, butchered and cooked pigs reared by the women on their list of 'perpetrators.'

The men set out rows of banana-leaf 'plates' and onto each one placed cooked vegetables, rice and a section, subsection, innard or organ of pork that corresponded anatomically to the part of the man each woman was reported by the 'expert witness' to have devoured – a thigh for part of a thigh, a rib for a rib, a liver for part of a liver, etc. Then they summoned each woman *by name*, calling one after another into the open compound to receive men's matching gifts of pork in outstretched hands. The public spectacle both exposed women's "secret" crime *and* 'undid' it as part of the exchange. By compelling each woman, one by one, name by name, to accept men's gift of perfectly-matched pork 'in the public square,' the men forced her to release the part of the man she *stole* and devoured out of men's sight and kept trapped inside her body and her house. Once the men had liberated *every aspect* of their dead comrade from the cannibal women by forcing each one to accept perfectly-matched "other meat" in exchange, they restored the recipients' names and identities so they were no longer "nothing women" nor banished from civilization. The men retrieved their comrade's bones from women's houses, decorated them

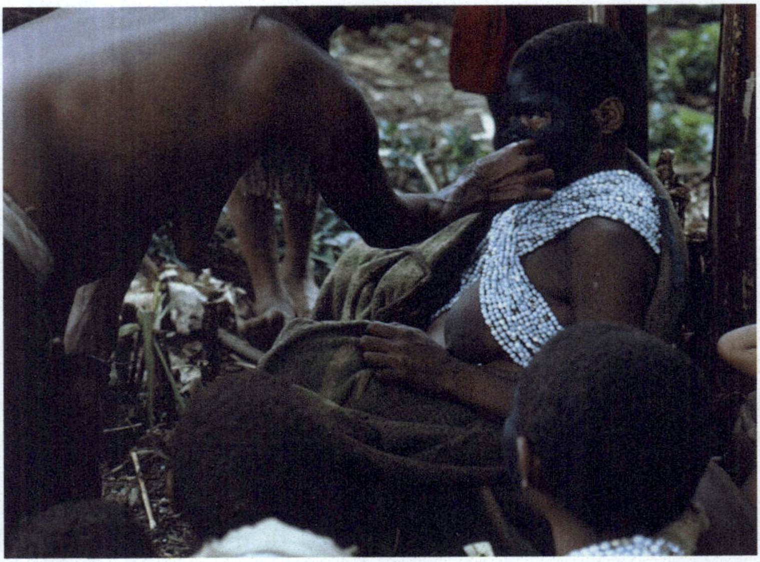

Fig. 4.1 When a man dies, women mourners blacken their faces with a mixture of soot and pig fat and wear neacklaces of Job's tears as part of their elaborate mourning garb. After a period of weeks or months, a rite is held to remove the blackening: a woman of the dead man's lineage uses a tiny bamoo loop to peel off a token ribbon of blackening from each woman's face as another woman, right behind her, places a chunk of salted pork directly into her mouth – an immediate exchange of food for 'return' of the deceased's spirit absorbed in the black mixture worn by each mourner. (© Gillian Gillison)

with coloured vines and carried them into the clan-owned forest to install in sacred "female" niches inside caves and the clefts of tree branches (Gillison 1983a, 1993).

Men's meticulously-matched gifts of pork (or, in the past, cooked marsupials) – presented and received *in public* – compelled each woman cannibal to liberate the part of the man she "stole" in a criminal conspiracy that supposedly annulled her individuality and very humanity. According to the logic of men's ritual, any cannibal who refused their gift of pork would remain a sub-human creature of the primordial past, condemned to live as a "wild woman" alone in the forest.

Like all Gimi rites of passage, cannibalism was highly conceptualized and theatrical: it dramatized events and relationships that disguised a contrary and deeper reality revealed in women's myths and performances of ritual theatre. The ritual men orchestrated made a great show of civilising a mob of cannibal women, undoing their savagery by forcing each one to 'return' the man she surreptitiously devoured and kept hidden. In ritual terms, the men first mythologized the cannibals – treated each one as if she were the counterpart of the Flute-owning First Woman who *appeared* to be alone or with only her Sister but actually – as *women's* myths show – hid the "head" of the Father who lurked unseen inside her. The men 're-socialized' the cannibal women by forcing each one to release the Father she held captive and made disappear, bringing to an end the primordial era of chaos the First Woman created inside her body. But according to *women's* myths – and part of the reality underlying the historical cannibal ritual – the sexes were in cahoots all along.

The Myth of the Dream Man[1]

In women's myth of the Dream Man, a heroic "wild" or "spirit" couple are counterparts of the Gimi women and men who in the past staged the cannibal rites together. As creatures of myth, they are 'the first ones' which means the couple are also sister and brother. Unlike their ritual counterparts, the Man and Wife/Brother and Sister in women's myth murder and dismember the Dream Man as a team and distribute the pieces of his body to *everyone* to eat, thus ending the primal era dominated not by the lone First Woman, as Gimi men's Flute myth and cannibal ritual declare, but rather by the elusive Dream Man who hides in his tree-top house and leaves a bloody trail behind him. The three women's myths to follow show that the primal Father – who, like the Moon, operates at night – is no helpless victim like a male corpse or like a small Boy seduced by the siren sounds of his Sister's Flute, but rather a cannibal ogre personified by the Dream Man, the Giant Penis and the vicious Python. The primal Father in women's myths raids the place where babies come from and takes up residence there, inside the Dream Mother's body, trapping everyone inside *his* "house." His blood lust, devouring every life before it begins, is the reason women menstruate. *He* is the relentless cannibal whom no one saw until a pair of his unhappy progeny decided to lie in wait, follow his bloody trail, kill him and every one of his like-minded brood and thereby usher in the world we know today, the one we see everyday with our own eyes.

hoEEEbada

A spirit Couple set marsupial traps all the way up the mountainside. … The first trap held only a head and tail. Thinking the trap was full, the Woman cried "Hurrah! Hurrah!" Seeing there was only blood, her Husband said: "There is only blood here!"

The two discovered [the same thing] in trap after trap after trap until they reached the top of the mountain. There they saw a heavy vine hanging down from a tall tree and dripping with blood. Then they caught sight of the Dream Man as he disappeared through the door of his tree-top house. The bloody meat he clutched under his arm left a trail of blood behind him.

The Marsupial Hunter left his Wife on the ground [beside the tall tree] and built a platform to lie in wait. As the Dream Man shinnied down the vine, his body lit by flames from below, the Hunter shot him dead. The Dream Man fell out of the tree and landed on the ground with a loud thud. The Wife dragged his body next to her, close to the fire.

One of the Dream Man's Sons appeared in the doorway of the tree house and the Hunter poked him with the butt of his arrow. "*de de de de de de* …" the Dream Boy cried. "Who has come to *play around* with you?" the Dream Mother called out. "The one we have been eating has come back to eat me!" the Dream Boy answered his Mother. [One after another after another, the Dream Man's many progeny appeared in the door of the tree-top house. Each time, the Marsupial Hunter poked the Dream Child with butt of his arrow and each one cried out "*de de de de de de*…" The Dream Mother called out after each of her children, "Who has come to *play around* with you?" she asked and each of her Children replied in turn, "The one we have been eating has come back to eat me!" ….

The Hunter shot each of the Children and one after the other they fell dead to the ground with a loud thud. Finally …] the Dream Mother appeared in the doorway and the Hunter shot her dead and pushed her out of the tree. She too landed at the base of the platform with a loud thud.... [One after another after another, his Wild Woman/Wife dragged all the Dream Man's family next to her, close to the fire...]

The heroine's "hurrahs!" uttered each time she approaches another trap, believing that it holds a whole marsupial, express her joy at being pregnant. The beady-eyed marsupial covered in soft brown fur, its white 'hands' tightly curled into tiny fists, symbolizes the foetus nestled inside the mother's pubic hair in the myths and rites of both sexes. When the Marsupial Hunter/Spirit-Husband says, "There is only blood here," he is telling his Spirit-Wife that she is menstruating. The Dream Man has already come and gone. He steals the marsupial in every trap/the baby in every belly and leaves nothing but a bloody trail. The couple follow the trail of blood all the way up the mountainside and catch sight of the Dream Man just as he disappears through the door of his tree-top house where he stashes his bloody plunder and feeds his enormous brood. As the Dream Man and each of his tree-dwelling family members appear in the doorway, the Marsupial Hunter picks them off one by one. But first he pokes each one with the butt end of his arrow, eliciting mournful bird-like cries of "*de de de de de de.*"

At this point in the narrative, one story-teller remarked, "The child is waking up now. He is moving inside the mother." Unlike me, Gimi listeners needed no prompting to understand that the primordial drama occurs *in utero*. To induce birth at the end of a pregnancy, the husband has to go back inside the mother after a period of abstinence to "wake" the foetus. After the many copulations required to install a child inside the mother, the couple abstain from sex. But in order for the child to be born, "a man has to have sex with his wife one more time. If he does not go *back* inside her to wake the child it will sleep forever inside the mother!" The Marsupial Hunter's poking the Dream Child with the butt end of his arrow, the myth teller commented, represents a man's "waking" the foetus to induce the birth. The bird-like "cries" of "*de de de de de de* ...," as someone else pointed out on another occasion, mimic the stifled sounds of partially-hatched chicks. Like birds that rot in the nest, the Dream Children will never be full-fledged human beings. Everyone in the Dream Man myth is

Fig. 4.2 Marsupials symbolize the human foetus in both myth and ritual.(© David Gillison)

"wild" or unborn – trapped inside the womb – until the end when the first Couple, having laid eyes on the elusive Dream Man, kill him and each of his identically-made component family members, forcing all the Dream people to exit and converting them into a meal for everybody.

In unabridged versions of the Dream Man myth the Marsupial Hunter's provocations and the Dream Children's responsive refrains are repeated many more times. *"The one we have been eating has come back to eat me!"* reiterates over and over what it means to be unborn: to be both nourished on the Dream Man's ejaculate – fed on his "endless" food supply – *and* devoured by him inside his "house" where everyone is held captive and reduced to bloody meat. He is their only food and they are his! Everyone is doomed, including the Marsupial Hunter-Husband who keeps going up the tree and coming back down again to lie on the platform in the position of a corpse waiting to be eaten. The Hunter is the Dream Man's "firstborn," the one at the "head" of his Giant Penis who goes back and forth to kill each Dream Child as soon as it appears in the doorway of the treetop house – repeated episodes that magnify the ones on the ground at the start of the myth when the Hunter finds "nothing but blood" in trap after trap, representing the heroine's monthly periods. Women's myth portrays the Hunter-Husband lying in wait and then climbing the tree, and the hunted-Dream Man going in and out of his tree top house, as *both* separate *and* the same; as both in conflict and united in their goals, just as the Dream Children both constitute the Dream Man's hoard and feed upon it. The Marsupial Hunter is another of the Dream Man's offspring trapped inside his slaughterhouse who behaves just like him.

In the primordial era women's Dream Man myth describes – the time before a child exits the womb alive and opens its eyes – eaters are eaten; everyday distinctions are lost; opposites dissolve. Instead of rescuing the Dream Children, the Hunter kills them one after another, behaving just like the Dream Man he came to depose! He turns the Dream Man's doorway into a site of carnage just like the marsupial traps where, over and over, the wild Couple discover "there is only blood here!" The Hunter executes the Dream Man and his ilk but, because he is his firstborn Son, also repeats what he does.

The Dream Man family's appearing one by one in the doorway, letting out bird-like cries of "*de de de de de de*..." and falling murdered to the ground "with a loud thud," lit by flames from below, creates a *moving picture* – complete with mournful sound effects – of menstruation on a world-size scale. The repeated "thuds" and stifled utterances of unhatched birds evoke *what is not heard*: the hypnotic rhythms of men's sacred flutes, called "birds," echoing the "cries" of babies born alive. Each "loud thud" – a lifeless body dropping heavily onto the ground beside a blazing fire – pictures for Gimi listeners the monthly demise of a severed *piece* of the primal Father glowing red. The myth of the Dream Man continues:

After he killed the Dream Man and all his kind, the Hunter leapt onto the vine and climbed up and up and up.... He entered the Dream Man's house and looked around. He saw the bones of men and the bones of pigs and the bones of marsupials the Dream Man had killed.... He saw bones from long ago and bones from recent meals! Bones of *every kind* filled the house! some were not yet eaten [still had meat on them]! All these bones the Hunter dragged outside ...

"Hey! Woman!" he shouted down. "Look up here!" And he threw down the whole pile and she gathered it up. "Hey! Man! Come on down here!" she cried ecstatically. "You keep finding marvellous food and giving it to me! Come on down here!"

Her Husband climbed down the tree.... "Cut some firewood," his Wife said. The Man cut firewood and heated stones and dug an earth oven and cut up the Dream Man [and all his ilk].... When the two of them had cooked all the pieces, they loaded them into net bags and carried them back to the settlement.

The Husband divided the meat into portions and gave some to everyone.... "Marsupials and pigs and children and men would not exist as we do now," he said, "if we two had not *seen* the Dream Man with our very own eyes! and killed him! and made an end of his kind [lit: made him disappear in every facet of his being]! No one would look upon the things we now do [marsupials, pigs, people – the entire visible/edible world – because the Dream Man would steal from every trap and devour every morsel]! But the two of us *saw* the Dream Man and we killed him. So it is told.

hoEEEdada

To compare Gimi women's myths and cannibal rites of the past with the final chapter of *Totem and Taboo* is to place Freud's hypothetical prehistory, culminating with the murder of the Father, *inside* the Mother's body; and to see the Father's transgression as *ceaseless copulation/cannibalization*, his simultaneously ejaculating-and-devouring every offspring so none escapes the Mother's body alive. She is *always* "dipping blood." The *primal crime* becomes a *primal scene* in which the *act of looking* – from an intrauterine perspective – is tantamount to murder or the essential preliminary to it. And the *singular* transgressor, the Dream Man in Gimi women's myth – like the First Woman in Gimi men's Flute myth – is revealed to be *both parents*, one 'residing' inside the other and impossible to tell apart. After seeing the Dream Man disappear into his treetop house – watching Father enter Mother – "with our very own eyes," the heroic spirit-Couple kill him and cut him to pieces, a 'renting asunder' precapitulated by separate eliminations of his every offspring, all his proto-sons and proto-daughters who poke their heads out the door.

The conflation of primal crime and primal scene in Gimi women's narratives introduces the female players missing from Freud's scenario. The Mother, or her womb, appears as passive site of the drama, the Dream Man's "house" at the summit of his mountain top tree-size penis where he hoards all the food and all the family. To each of her brood, the Mother calls out forlornly and then gives herself up to their same fate. But the Wife/Sister/Daughter standing at the base of the tree is the Mother's counterpart and polar opposite: although her "trap" is always empty, filled likewise with "nothing but blood," she is a demanding co-conspirator as vigilant and blood-thirsty as her Husband/Brother.

The heroine of women's myth, left on the ground beside the burial platform, always looking up, inspires the Hunter/Brother/Husband to climb the tall tree and murder the Dream Man and his entire clan. Her avid desire to fill her trap with more than just blood moves him to enter the Dream Man's house filled with all the "bones" – food/penes/unborn babes – in existence. Unlike his ritual counterparts, who purchased the dead man's bones from supposedly outlaw cannibal women, the Marsupial Hunter of women's myth triumphantly throws all the "marvellous food" down to his jubilant mate standing on the ground in the place where, in the ritual version of men's Flute myth, the outlaw cannibal women cut up the corpse "in secret" out of men's sight. And then – again in contrast to the charade enacted during the historic death rite – Man and Wife/Brother and Sister work together to cook, cut up, carry back to the settlement and distribute the Dream Man's remains to *everyone*, providing a meal that establishes kinship – the "one kind of bond which was absolute and inviolable" – on a totemic basis (Freud 1972 [1913]: 134).

Women's Dream Man myth describes the murder and partitioning of the primal Father as the hidden cause of menstruation, the "death of the firstborn," which happens repeatedly, every time the Marsupial Hunter shoots another one of the Dream Man's progeny until, finally, he enters the Dream Man's house and empties it out. The Hunter sends *everything* he finds inside the Dream Man's house down to his Wife/Sister and together they convert him into a communal meal. In the following myth of the Giant Penis, the heroine has no male partner with whom to collaborate in the primal Father's murder and partition. She acts alone and suffers the consequences.

Adventures of the Giant Penis

Before the *Pax Australiana* of the early 1960's and the arrival of the fundamentalist American missionary Ben Wurtz, a menstruating Gimi woman went into seclusion for the four or five days of her period inside a tiny menstrual hut built on the edge of the settlement. There she "cohabited with the Moon," her "first husband," who stood for her father in a mythical and metaphorical sense. But menstrual seclusion might also have brought a woman physically closer to her actual father and men of her natal patrilineage who resided in a neighbouring settlement and were her husband's enemies, men for whom her husband and his patrilineage believed she harboured lasting affinity. One reason men forbade women even to approach the periphery of men's houses, they said, was to prevent wives' overhearing their husbands' war plans and running home to warn their fathers and brothers.

But according to women's myths, women have little sympathy for their 'prehistoric' fathers and make every effort to evict them from their houses and their bodies. To add Gimi women's perspective to the story-line of *Totem and Taboo*, one may say that if the "band of brothers" were enraged by a father who denied them access to their sisters and who hoarded all the "food" – delicious unborn babes – then the sisters whom the father continually raped and whose bodies he occupied in perpetuity (making them sing like sirens or plugging them up like flutes unable to utter a sound) were just as angry or even angrier. The heroine of women's Giant Penis myth has no husband or brother to spur into action nor serve as co-conspirator. She takes matters entirely into her own "hand."

In the same way that women's Dream Man myth provides a running commentary and counter-narrative to the historic rites surrounding Gimi cannibalism, women's myth of the Giant Penis parallels female initiation ritual (*haro*, lit: 'roof'; see Fig. 3.2 above). During a four-or five-day period, one or two initiates who are actually or supposedly menstruating for the first time, are secluded inside a cage-like "sugar bed" specially constructed inside their (real or close classificatory) mother's house or, in the past, menstrual hut. The initiate's seclusion represents at once the duration of her first menstrual period *and* her own early gestation. The "sugar bed" is a 'womb-within-a-womb' designed to replicate the situation of every female embryo or foetus installed inside her mother and nourished on the semen her father delivers on his regular visits, the many ejaculations necessary to bring a child to life and ensure its viability. When the child is female she is, of course, a miniature version of her mother – a womb within a womb or house inside a house – which means that her father's installing/feeding her is also a repetition-in-miniature of his regular 'visits' to her mother whom he necessarily enters first in order to gain access to her. Impregnating the mother is *simultaneously* feeding/impregnating the unborn daughter. Women portray this 'unholy threesome' in both myth and initiation ritual as the Giant Penis' invading the virgin Girl as she "sleeps" – lies gestating – inside her Mother's house.

Because of the way she comes into being as the Giant's 'offshoot,' every Gimi girl is *congenitally pregnant*, so to speak, and remains so until adolescence when she starts to menstruate: when she has her first period, she delivers her "firstborn" who is "the child of the Moon," the vernacular term for the Giant Penis women portray in myth. The Giant is father *both* to her *and* to her "firstborn child." In terms of the initiation ritual's reduplicated and encapsulated imagery, the initiate *both is and has inside her* the Giant's "head," or glans penis, the part he uses to 'make entry' into Mother's house.

The heroine of the Giant Penis myth, whom the female initiate incarnates, lies asleep inside her Mother's house when the Giant invades her body. At the start of the myth, in daylight, the Penis enters the forest to stalk and kill marsupials while they sleep in trees. The Penis is blind and hunts by smell through the only orifice he possesses, the "first mouth" on top of his head at the site of the urethra. After the Penis slithers up the tree and "shoots" the sleeping marsupial, he slides back down with his head still lodged inside his prey at the bloody site of penetration. The First Man coils his huge length round and round like a rope of liana vine with the Penis' head still stuck inside the bloodied fur-covered marsupial concealed at the center of the pile. The events that transpire in the forest by day foretell – or '*fore-image*' – what the Penis does at night.

> *hoEEEdada*
>
> A Penis was once an enormously long thing. It was not short. It was so long that while the [first] Man slept in his house his Penis went out exploring. It did not know about women.... Women slept in women's houses and men slept in the men's house.
>
> When the Man went into the forest to hunt marsupials, he took along his dog and that Penis of his, coiled round and round like a rope [of liana vine]. He put the coiled bundle into his net bag and hung the bag around his neck [so it protruded over his belly] ... and went out to hunt. Inside the forest, he opened the net bag and let out his Penis. The Penis stalked and killed marsupials just like his dog [by smell alone]. When the Man was ready to come home, he wound up his Penis [into a pile of coils leaving the bloodied marsupial, with his head still buried deep inside it, hidden at the centre]. He put the bundle of coils back into his net bag and hung the bag around his neck.
>
> The Man came home and [after hanging up his net bag on the wall] went to sleep. During the night, his Penis entered the Woman's house. While the Man was asleep inside his house, that thing of his roused itself and went out the door – the Penis alone! – and [making its way by smell] reached the house where the Woman slept.... She was sound asleep. The Penis searched ... it touched her here and there. It moved over her body for a long time but could not find [the Vagina]. It lifted her string skirts and slid between her thighs.... The Man slept. The Woman slept. Only the Penis moved.
>
> The Penis searched [for quite a while] but could not find the opening.... That Vagina of hers was shut tight! The opening was tiny and the Penis thought, "She has none!" The Penis smelled the Vagina but could not get

> inside. So he ate open the hole and slipped inside her. Semen flowed into the Woman. The Vagina was opened … and the *whole* Penis went inside. An enormous thing entered the Woman and she awoke with a start. She took the Penis in her hand and went out the door of her house. A stalk of sugarcane was growing in the doorway. She cut a section and a half of the cane and, holding the Penis in her hand, followed it all the way into the Man's house…. She looked at him as he slept. She took the piece of sugarcane and measured it [against his Penis] and cut it [to the length of the cane]…. Then she threw the [huge severed portion] into the river.
>
> The Man awoke with a start. And the Woman said to him, "That was a heavy thing you carried about with you! When you wanted to have sex with me, you did not come into my house! You did not *get up and move yourself!* You lay here in your house and sent your Penis. It went inside me and that is not right! So I did you a favour! I cut off your Penis!" …
>
> … That First Woman had a good idea! … She measured a section and half of sugarcane and cut the Giant Penis … that is why men have two marks on their penes – one on top and one below.
>
> *hoEEEdada*

The house in the myth of the Giant Penis, as in the corresponding rite of female initiation, is a symbol of the Mother occupied by a Child made in her image. Like a Child of the Dream Man, the heroine of the Giant Penis myth is "poked" by an invasive Marsupial Hunter. But instead of lamenting mournfully to her Mother, "the one we have been eating has come back to eat me!" she gets up, grabs hold of the Giant, goes out the door of her Mother's house and follows him all the way to *his* house. Still holding the Giant in her hand, and while he lies asleep, she cuts him 'down to size.' She tries to force "the first man" in her life to wake up and approach her with his whole self: instead of a rapist who comes stealthily in the night while she sleeps *and while he sleeps* far away in another house (suggesting that she is masturbating) the heroine tries to transform the Giant into a man who can satisfy her waking desires. But, acting alone, she makes a fatal mistake. Unlike the Couple in the Dream Man myth who apportion and distribute the primal Father and all his ilk, she angrily discards the Giant's huge severed length in a river.

Her selfishness backfires. The myth foretells the heroine's mistake by the way she pursues the Giant in the first place: taking him "in her hand," exiting her Mother's house – emerging from the womb – *through the same door the Penis entered*, the place where a stalk of sugarcane is growing. Like a Child of the Dream Man, she leaves her Mother through the *only* door which is the site of "nothing but blood." To stop the Giant's nighttime invasions and cut him down to size in a lasting way, the heroine/initiate cannot act alone nor spare any part of him. She has to enlist the help of a Brother/Husband to reduce the rest of his enormous length to portion-size pieces fit for consumption by others. To accomplish that, the primordial Brother/Sister Pair have to create a new kind of "house" equipped with a *second door*, a separate way out that will end the deadly two-way traffic in the first one.

The Rape of the Python: The Menstruating Girl Acquires a 'Second Vagina' on Her Face

The Python myth, longest of the Dream Man trilogy, is a prequel that describes the era before the "wild" Couple caught sight of the Dream Man, slayed him and converted him into a communal meal. In the Python myth, the huge severed piece of the Giant the heroine angrily threw into a river comes back to take revenge in the guise of a vicious nocturnal snake. The Python enters the heroine's vagina, passes through her whole body and comes out her mouth, opening a "second vagina" in the her head and losing his own head in the process. According to women's Python myth, the "pubic hair" men tattoo on a woman's face memorializes a brutal rape, contradicting men's elaborate rationale, derived from their Flute myth, about why they tattoo a "beard" on the bride before her departure in marriage (Gillison 1993: 263–64, 266–67, 269–70; see Chap. 1, Fig. 1.1).

In the Python myth, the severed portion of the Giant Penis that the heroine discarded returns as a spiteful snake. He comes back to invade her house and the one "sleeping" inside it again. But on this *second visit,* he rips open a new door. The Python myth begins, as does the myth of the Dream Man, with a Hunter playing the part of the primal Father's like-minded firstborn Son. Like the Dream Man and the Giant Penis, the Cassowary Hunter in the Python myth has a habit of 'going in the out door,' a practice visualized in this myth by his climbing into the anuses of the Cassowaries caught in his traps. The giant bird's droppings contain morsels of undigested fruits that look uneaten, as Gimi remark, making its anus a convenient symbol of a body orifice with 'two-way traffic.' The Python myth also reveals that the Giant Penis' blindness is utterly willful: before he enters the Cassowary's anus to devour her insides, the Cassowary Hunter removes his eyes from their sockets and places each one on a leaf of wild taro. Taro leaves are covered in a soft fuzz whose touch, Gimi men say, produces an itch which is the source of *women's* insatiable desire for sex.

Like the Dream Man's tree-top house stocked with an endless supply of "marvellous food," the huge, flightless Cassowary is another of Gimi women's portraits of the primal Mother as a *one-holed* inert creature, filled with food, whom no one escapes alive.

hoEEEdada

A Man went into the forest to set a trap for a Cassowary. Back and forth, back and forth he went to check on (lit: 'look at') it. But again and again he found nothing there. He took his Daughter, a little girl, and went to check his trap again. He left her on one ridge [of the mountain] and went to the other ridge [where his trap was set]. When he saw that the trap held a Cassowary he called out to the wild taro:

O Leaf of hiba Taro, O Leaf of kabo Taro
Here are my eyes!

He took out his eyes and laid each one on a leaf of wild taro. Then he disappeared into the anus of the Cassowary and ate and ate and ate. He ate up the liver and the intestines and finished all the meat so there was nothing left but the empty skin. He came back down [the Cassowary's fecal tract] and cried:

O Leaf of hiba Taro, O Leaf of kabo Taro
Bring me my eyes!

And he put back his eyes. He hung the Cassowary's empty skin on the branch of a tree and went to inspect the other trap he had set. [The scene is repeated after which the Hunter] fetches his Daughter and brings her home. He gives the two empty skins to his Wife telling her, "I didn't check the traps right away and … a couple of marsupial cats [*Dasyuridae*] finished up everything!"

The Husband lied to his Wife and went back to his traps, taking his Daughter with him again. He left her on one ridge and went by himself to the other ridge and ate and ate and ate …. Later, he fetched his Daughter and brought her home.

He kept *lying* to his Wife! "You brought me empty skins before," she said to her Husband…. "What am I supposed to eat?" His Wife decided to follow him, thinking, "I'll see for myself what you are up to!" And so the Man went and his Wife followed … to see for herself. She hid behind the trunk of a tree and heard,

O leaf of hiba taro, O leaf of kabo taro
Here are my eyes!

She saw him take out one eye and put it on a leaf of *hiba* taro. She saw him take out his other eye and put it on a leaf of *kabo* taro. Then she watched him disappear up the Cassowary's anus.

… While her Husband was inside the Cassowary eating [to his heart's content], the Wife thought, "Now I see you!" She broke off a section of bamboo and put his two eyes inside it [to keep them moist …]. Then she ran home. [Meanwhile …] her Husband climbed out of the Cassowary and called,

O leaf of hiba taro, O leaf of kabo taro
Bring me my eyes!

Nothing happened. Again he called,

O leaf of hiba taro, O leaf of kabo taro
Bring me my eyes!

And again, nothing…. And again, nothing…. (The storyteller repeats the refrain five or six times.) Finally, the Husband left the empty skin behind and set out for home, stumbling and falling as he went. The Man crawled along the ground and his eye sockets filled with mud and worms and debris.

When he appeared in the doorway, his Wife was inside the house rolling bark string across her thigh. "Ah!" she cried. "What happened to *you*? Tell me the meaning of this!" "The branch of a tree stabbed me in the eyes. Come here and clean out the mud and worms and debris!" Seeing his ghastly eye sockets, his Daughter said [to herself], "I pity you." She took his eyes out of the bamboo container her Mother [left lying at the head of her bed] and hid them in the palms of her hands. She cleaned out her Father's eye sockets and [discretely] put back his eyes. He opened them and asked, "What kind of *trick* are you playing on me?!" ... He was *furious!* ...

In the morning the Cassowary Hunter said to his Daughter, "Let us go into the forest again. Come with me. We will sleep the night so bring some [cooked] sweet potatoes with you." Off they went.... He left his Daughter in the usual place and went to look in his Cassowary trap. He wandered around until he found a Python. "Do this thing. I will bring her [here for] you to look at."

... During the night, while the Man and his Daughter slept inside their bush house, the Snake drew near, calling "*ki ki ki ki ki ki*" as he approached the side of the house [where the Daughter was asleep]. Father and Daughter slept in different places [on the sloping forest floor], the Man below the fire and his Daughter above it. The Python entered the house and went inside the Daughter while she slept. He entered her vagina and came out her mouth, shaking his head. The Snake shook his head inside the Girl's mouth and shook his tail inside her vagina.... Her Father awoke, stoked the fire alight and looked at [the two of] them. He watched his Daughter die.

The Man left his Daughter in the forest and came home.... "I went alone and I came back alone," he lied again to his Wife.... At dawn of the third day, the Wife and her Brother set out to find the Girl. They followed the Husband's tracks into the forest and came upon (lit: 'saw') the Python still shaking his neck (sic). The Wife's Brother said to the Snake, "Hey, Brother-in-law! Your neck must be sore by now! Why don't you rest your head on this piece of wood." They [the Girl's Mother and Mother's Brother] cut a branch and slid it under the Snake's vibrating head.

Then they cut off the Snake's head with an axe and pulled his enormous length out of the Girl's mouth and out of her vagina. They carried the

> Snake and the Girl back to the settlement and made a huge fire. Then they cut the Snake into pieces and cooked them. And they held the Girl over the fire.... They were bringing her back to life [i.e., celebrating her first menses].
>
> The Mother's Brother laid in wait. The moment the Husband appeared in the doorway of his house, the [Mother's] Brother shot him dead.... If he had not shot her [First] Husband ... every day of our lives would be like this story! Our husbands would lie to us time and time again and bring home nothing but empty skins [flaccid penes].... But we got rid of our First Husband ...
>
> *hoEEEdada*

A grandmother whom I knew well, and who was widely revered as an expert in ritual and myth, told me another version of the Python myth in which the Daughter enticed into the forest for a tryst is still an infant at the breast. Her Mother *alone* – without the aide of her Brother – rescues her Daughter and gets rid of her First Husband. While he had their Daughter "inside the forest" ...

> The Snake stuck its head out the Girl's mouth and cried, "Daddy!" The Snake called out "Daddy! Daddy!" and [the Father] left her where she lay and ran to the house. "Where is the Girl?" her Mother asked.... The Mother tied some firewood into a bundle and set out at dawn the next day to find her Daughter. She walked and walked and walked to the place where the Snake had entered [her Daughter's] stomach (sic) and come out her mouth. The Snake was still shaking his head from side to side. Holding the Girl to her breast, she cut off the Snake's head and pulled its body out [of her Daughter]. She cut the Snake to pieces and loaded the [dead] Girl into her net bag. And that [is how the] little Girl came [back to the settlement. The Mother] dug a hole and buried her. Then she married another man.
>
> And so would things be to this day but for the fact that the little Girl was "killed" [initiated]. Otherwise men's eyes would still be inside the Cassowary!

At the Dawn of Time and Human Existence …

At the dawn of time and human existence, which Gimi myths and rites of passage and exchange revive, the heroine-initiate was both the Giant's child and his consort. In the primordial/prenatal era, the Girl "asleep inside her mother['s house]" was both fed by and sexually united with her Father. Oral and genital functions were wholly fused: the repeated ejaculations which conceived and nurtured the Gimi girl *in utero* also "impregnated" her. By the time she is born – the *first time* she leaves her mother's house – a baby girl has already "eaten" many "heads" of her Father's/the Moon's/the Giant's Penis. Women's myths and initiation rites represent the primordial copulation-within-a-copulation as the Giant Penis' entering Mother-and-Daughter simultaneously: he enters the mother's house where the heroine – herself a second house-in-miniature – "sleeps alone," *using the same door* to gain access to both females. And the part of the Penis that goes through the only door and enters Mother first, the top of the Giant's head equipped with the urethra or "first mouth," itself repeats this highly condensed visual image: the opening through which the Giant "shoots" *at one and the same time* kills and devours the nourishment he supplies. The Giant eats back up every morsel of himself that he deposits as new life inside Mother. In the highly condensed and superposed images Gimi women's myths create, the Giant's lust turns *both* his one-orifice "head" *and* the Mother's single-doorway "house" into the same bloody site of carnage.

Something monumental has to happen for the child to escape its mother's house alive. The unborn are sexually undifferentiated. The [proto-]female who is a miniature mother and 'empty house' the Giant invades is also, like any foetus, a miniature version of the Giant himself. In women's myth, the Penis is blind and hunts by smell through the only orifice in his head – his "first mouth" – which is also the term for the fontanelle. Gimi of both sexes say that the First Man could not speak because the place on his face where his 'second' mouth should have been – where our mouths now are – was sealed over by a caul of skin behind which jostled the food he ingested through his open "first mouth" as it dropped from the top of his head through the hollow core of his body into his stomach. The First Man's closed 'second' mouth, in other words, ressembles a newborn's throbbing fontanelle, the "first mouth" on top of the baby's head overlaid by a thin layer of translucent skin. During the long "sleep" of gestation, the foetus' fontanelle is wide open – a mirror image of the Giant's "first mouth" that works in reverse and ingests the stuff the Giant "shoots" out the "head" of his Penis. To prepare the foetus for life *outside* the womb, near the end of a pregnancy after the period of abstinence, the 'second husband' has to "go back inside" the mother one last time to "waken" the child (see above page 129). This essential 'return to the mother' "finishes the child" by feeding it a 'last meal' of ejaculate that will *close* the "first mouth" on top of the foetal head.

Without a father to "finish the child" with new food, the mythic Giant's "first mouth" never closes which means he *never leaves the territory of the Mother's body*. The Giant's "first mouth" remains forever a deadly orifice of two-way traffic that works *both* as a urethra 'shooting out' food for the foetus *and* as a gaping maw that relentlessly devours the incipient life he engenders. (For this reason, a Gimi man avoids even remotest contact with his newborn [see Chap. 2]. While the father who is subject to strict post-partum taboos after the birth of his child is *not* the mythical Father or mother's "first husband," represented in ritual by her father and brother, the distinction between First and 'second' husbands has to be vigorously maintained. Like the primordial era brought to life in rites of passage, the past tends to intrude upon the present and to overwhelm it by doing away with critical distinctions in kinship.)

Like all the unborn, the female initiate is a child of the Giant, which means that she is also his consort and that her "gestation" inside her mother is also a "pregnancy" – the gestation of the Giant's Child inside the Giant's Child who is herself. And like any foetus, she has to be "finished" before she can emerge from seclusion "reborn" as a marriageable woman. In everyday life, the man who installed the child and 'fed it to life' inside the womb "comes back to finish the child" by feeding it one final ejaculation to close the fontanelle and induce the birth. But the Giant has no father so that his "first mouth" is *forever open*: he never provides food without also simultaneously devouring it. Someone else, therefore, a look-alike replacement, will have to "finish" the initiate and enable her to emerge from her mother's house.

Myth and Rite: A Meticulous Match-Up of Giants

Gimi women's myths are inextricably connected to female initiation and other rites of passage and vice versa: myth and rite *together* create multimedia images that shift back and forth between stories spoken aloud in intimate surroundings inside women's houses at night and scenarios acted out before a crowd, both mixed and sexually segregated, in specially-constructed settings. Myth and rite run closely parallel until almost the end when their scenarios diverge in ways that dramatize the life-saving alternatives ritual offers to the catastrophe myths present. The meticulous match-up of myth and rite shows that ritual is the best 'way out' of myth's dead-end redundancy and encapsulation, like the Giant Penis coiled up inside the First Man's net bag with his head stuck inside the murdered prey at the center of his body. The first phase of female initiation closely 'matches' the myth of the Giant Penis. Like the heroine asleep inside her mother's house, the one or two female initiates are hidden inside the cage-like "bed" of sugarcane erected inside the mother's house. But for the initiates to emerge reborn as marriageable women, they have to exit by a *new door* – one the Giant uses at his mortal peril. (See Fig. 3.2.)

Female initiation ritual brings about a 'new ending' to the myth of the Giant Penis because this ritual changes the personnel: the role of the Giant goes not to the initiate's paternal kinsmen (who include her own father and brother) but rather to her future affines (men who paid her brideprice on behalf of her 'second husband'). A day or so before the girl's expected emergence, her male affines arrive bringing with them a bulky package called the "sugar pig." The "sugar pig" is a cooked and dismembered shoat or marsupial encased in 50 cm. lengths of sugarcane and wrapped in layer upon layer of a continuous liana vine – the translation of the Giant Penis' amazing adventures inside the forest and the First Woman into a gift of food. The affines' "sugar pig" converts women's myth into the archetypical object of exchange called a "head" payment. Each initiate's prospective father-in-law or major contributor to her brideprice enters the stifling hut ahead of a small delegation of other male affines, holding the "sugar pig" in his outstretched arms. He dances up to the bamboo cage covered in red foliage where the one or two initiates are secluded, and then prances backwards toward the door, repeating his advance and retreat many times in a drawn-out tease and mimicry of copulation on a giant scale. The "sugar pig" is an 'exact copy' of the Giant's mythic exploits manufactured by a *new* husband, one who is *not* heir to the Giant who made her. The girls' future affines 'impersonate' the Giant's incursion into the Mother's house-size body to "wake" the initiates from their "sleep of gestation" and to induce delivery of the Giant's issue – the girls' first menes – by offering a substitute (Fig. 4.3).

To end her ordeal, each girl emerges from the "sugar bed," sits down before the fire blazing in the middle of the hut and prepares to undo the Giant-impersonators' special delivery. Dripping with persperation, she sets about the task of finding the end of the vine – the "head" of the Giant still lodged inside his prey – which her affines have carefully concealed amid many coiled layers of liana vine. If her ordeal lasts a long

Fig. 4.3 A female initiate (left foreground) faces her future father-in-law who offers a "sugar pig," the edible translation of women's myth of the Giant Penis into an object of exchange. The initiate's emergence from seclusion is contingent upon her acceptance of the "sugar pig." (© David Gillison)

time, which is a near certainty, her chaperons and, eventually, lineage brothers arrive to help in the search. And if they, too, are unsuccessful, another near certainty, one of her brothers hands the initiate a knife and she cuts through the layers of vine "in a fury" that is both ritually prescribed – to enact the mythic heroine's cutting the Giant 'down to size' – and often genuine. "I was angry and did not use my hands to look.... We searched and searched for the end. Then I cut the vine!" But the initiate herself does not eat the contents: "How could she *eat* the meat?" one of her brothers replied aghast at my question. "It is 'the head of the child' ... [the payment] for her flesh. Her affines are buying her vagina!"

Female initiation rites follow the mythic scenario very closely by staging large- and small-scale dramatizations of the First Penis' exploits, including his return as the vicious Python. Like the package she receives – the cut-up piglet or marsupial encased in lengths of sugarcane and bound with coils of liana vine – the menstruating girl hidden inside a "sugar bed" decorated with red foliage and vines is herself a replica of the angry Giant's bloodied "head" – the part of himself that got away – *and* that he comes back to eat in revenge. In this embedded and reduplicated image, the heroine/initiate is *inside herself* – both encompassing and encompassed, both as big as an adolescent girl and as small as a foetus. Like the 'before' and 'after' sizes of Alice in Wonderland after she drinks the potion labelled 'Drink Me,' the visual motifs in women's Giant Penis and Python myths and in their ritual recapitulations undergo radical shifts in scale: the menstruating girl is also a life-size version of her prenatal self. She is both a "sleeping foetus" and gestating a "firstborn child" of her own. Each aspect of the initiation ritual has parallels in the mythic adventures of the Giant Penis who shoots marsupials by day, vaginas by night, wraps them "at the bloodied head" of his enormous length and comes back to kill again.

The same play with size and proportion occurs at midday of the following day, at the climactic conclusion of the initiation, when the initiates' future affines return. On their *second intrusion*, the men do not enter the house through the only door. Instead, they climb onto the roof (lit: *haro*), the term for the initiation rite itself, rip open a hole in the thatch and insert a sugarcane pole, some four to five metres long, its leafy "head" intact and lashed to a casuarina sapling, and engage in a protracted tug of war with the women below (see Fig. 3.2 above). Inside the dark hut, the initiate and her chaperons gather in the shaft of light beneath the new hole in the roof and the chaperons – but not the initiate herself – reach up to grasp the sugar pole. As the women are about to take hold of it, the men on the roof withdraw the sugarcane. The women lower their arms to feign disinterest and again the men above them cautiously lower the pole. The women reach up again, and again the men on the roof retract the pole, repeating the back-and-forth tease they used to present the "sugar pig" to the initiate the day before.

But on this second occasion, the future affines conduct the coital tease through the new "doorway" they tore open in the thatch, an enactment of the climatic episodes in the Giant Penis myth when the Giant blindly noses his way beneath the heroine's bark-string skirts and "eats open" her tightly-closed vagina; and, in the Python myth, when the Python's head emerges from the heroine's mouth shaking in fierce coital abandon – creating a "second vagina" on her face, represented in the bride's tattooed "beard" (see Fig. 1.1). But the Giant who opens a new "door" in the roof of the mother's house merely *looks exactly like* the one in women's myth. The ritual dismemberment of this Giant will get rid of his blood and set the girl free.

As female initiation ritual dictates, the women win the tug-of-war with the men on the roof. Eventually, again with crucial help from the initiates' lineage brothers, the women succeed in breaking off section after section of the sugarcane pole until only a small piece remains. "We hold the sugar and rid ourselves of blood!" in the words of one initiate's chaperon. "We get rid of [men's] pollution and regain our strength. We outdo the men on the roof! We break the sugar into pieces until only a very small part of it is left." Breaking the pole to pieces reverses the finale of the Giant Penis myth when the infuriated heroine, acting on her own, cuts off the Giant and discards his huge severed length intact; and it recapitulates the finale of women's Python myth when the heroine's Mother *and her Brother* (in the usual version) not only decapitate the Snake and pull it out of the dead Girl but also cut up his enormous body. Like the succession of Dream Children appearing one after another in the doorway of Dream Man's tree-top house, the pieces of Python are a collection of severed "heads" that, in the substitute form of "head" payments (sections of pork or, in the past, marsupial meat), become a totemic meal for everyone. And like the "head" payments men 'force fed' women cannibals to liberate the man they supposedly devoured in secret and out of men's sight, the "sugar-pigs" presented to female initiates empty their bodies of a primal Father they consumed 'out of sight' before they were even born.

"Eating the Head of the Child:" Women's Myths Provide the 'Recipe' for the Totemic Meal Shared by All

The heroine of the Giant Penis myth cut the Giant down to size and heedlessly threw away the huge severed portion in a river. In the sequel Python myth, which corresponds to the latter part of female initiation ritual when the initiate's future affines climb onto the roof of her mother's house, tear open a hole in the thatch and insert a huge stem of sugarcane, the Giant *returns* as a vicious Python intent upon revenge. Performance of the myths in ritual remedies or reverses their tragic dénouements by switching the personnel. In myth, the Girl's Mother and Mother's Brother sever the Giant's head and cut up the rest of him. "They made a fire and cooked the pieces of the Snake with a pig.... They did not *eat* the Snake, of course!" a man named Goran exclaimed (alarmed at the inference I seemed to be making), "because the Snake is *the same* as menstrual blood!" The pig cooked "in the same fire" as the Snake replaces the Snake as incarnation of the decapitated and sectioned "first husband," the stillborn "first children," the menstrual blood, and converts him into *food consumable by all* – exactly as men used pigs or "wild" marsupial meat to replace the man's corpse as incarnation of the primal Father in cannibal rituals of the past (see pages 123–127 above).

In both female initiation and cannibal rites of the past, as in every Gimi rite of passage, the 'replacement pork' is called "the head of the child" which, *as only women's myths and rites reveal*, represents the decapitated and cut up primal Father. From this perspective, women's worldview provides *the* organizational premise for men's exchanges of wives and "head" payments in which women participate either as objects or recipients but never as donors in their own right. In the sense that Gimi men appropriate a 'female perspective' as the framework for exchange they do it to contradict women's narratives and undermine women themselves.

When the female initiate emerges from seclusion, she is equipped with a "second vagina" on her face, reborn as a 'two-holed' creature in the image of men's "secret" bamboo flutes. The ritual 'undoes' her grisly death depicted in myth and leaves her with a "beard" as evidence of her transformation into an exchangeable commodity. The newly-made "vagina" in her head shows that the Giant who has occupied her body (from one end to the other!) since before she was born – the mythic Snake/"first husband" who simultaneously invaded *both* the girl *and* her mother whenever he felt like it – has now "lost his head" definitively and been extracted from her body. The operation *exchanges* the mythic Giant – personified by the initiate's 'real-life' father and brothers – for her male affines who climb onto the roof and insert the sugarcane pole. The Giant who *re*invades and *re*occupies her house in ritual is *not* personified by the heroine-initiate's paternal kinsmen. The one the initiate and her chaperons break to pieces, whose many severed "heads" will be replaced with edible equivalents (pork or, in the past, "wild" marsupial meat, and other valuables) called "head" payments, is the body of the primal Father's look-alike. Men's exchanges that are 'modeled on' women's myths transform the Giant from a bloody catastrophe into a feast for everyone.

The decapitation and disassembly of the monolithic mythic Father, breaking the sugarcane pole into portion-size pieces, decapitating and cutting up the Python and then replacing pieces of his body with *other food* cooked in the same fire – *food the Giant cannot re-ingest* because it is no longer a former part of himself – means that he "loses his head" – who is also the girl herself – in a decisive way. When Gimi men slaughter, cut up, cook and distribute "head" pigs at the end of every rite of passage, they perform central episodes in *women's* myths, recapitulating the murder and partition of the primal Father – the Dream Man, Giant Penis, or Python – whose great length embodies all his unborn and *undifferentiated* Children, all the members of his Treetop Family murdered at the front door, the moment any one of them made an appearance at the exit in the attempt to become separate from his voracious "head." In women's "secret" myths, Gimi women and men *together* murder the primal Father, cut him into pieces and distribute portions to everybody. But in the public rites of distribution which carry out women's own mythic agenda, men exclude women *as donors*. In ritual exchanges that 'convert' the Dream Man and his family into "head" payments, women serve only *as recipients*.

Public exchanges of "head" payments, orchestrated by men, address the crimes of the primal Father according to Gimi women's "secret" myths and rites: as long as the Giant remains 'at home' inside Mother, he recycles his offspring as food and stays a Giant forever while "nothing but blood" fills her trap. To evict the Giant and rescue the child, the mother's husband (and his paternal kinsmen) must persuade the child's mother's father and brother, who are the Giant's usual ritual counterparts, to accept "head" payments, that is, to "eat the head of the child": public acceptance of edible replacements for what the Giant stole and devoured in the mythic past forces his heirs to let go of the original. Without 'other food,' different "heads," the Giant will not release the ones he devoured while they were still unborn, still inside the Mother, trapped inside the Treetop House or Cassowary's Belly, where he also resides and reclaims his offspring as lost parts of his gigantic, rapacious Self. A Gimi woman cannot be trusted to 'do business' with the Giant inside her by offering him enticing substitutes for the progeny he keeps accummulating "at his head." Like the women after a cannibal feast – unless forced or publicly humiliated – she holds on to the originals as parts of her body.

* * *

Freud identifies the primal father with a totem animal and says that eating the totem is the basis for kinship (Freud 1972 [1913]: 134). "[K]inship implies participation in a common substance," he says (*Ibid:* 135). "Not, however, for an unlimited time; strictly speaking, only so long as the food which has been eaten in common remains in the body" (*Ibid:* 134 citing Robertson-Smith 1894: 269–70). Through the exchange of "head" payments, which overcome incestuous attachments by substituting 'other food' for the primal father's body – a Father stuck inside Mother – Gimi invent kinship over and over again. The 'totem animal' – like the pig or marsupial "cooked in the same fire as the Snake" but which, of course, is *not* the Snake!" – replaces not just the primal Father as monopolist and ogre but also the world system he keeps recreating inside Mother. The Gimi rites of passage revive the era of incest in order to finish it in the same way food distributed at a feast disappears inside the recipients. But like any food and like hunger itself, the Father who is 'done away with' once and for all soon reappears and has to be decapitated, cut into pieces, replaced and distributed again and again, every time a man dies or a girl starts to menstruate or some other crisis occurs in a person's life.

Gimi rites of passage arrange the temporary rescue of otherwise-doomed *individuals*. In the conclusion, I argue that, interpreted as a primordial *couple*, the Chronos-like figure of the Dream Man and his various counterparts in women's myths, the Moon in everyday Gimi idiom, and the First Woman in men's Flute myth who plugs the Flute so no one else can play it may be usefully considered as condensations of the entire first part of Freud's narrative in Chapter IV of *Totem and Taboo*, "The Return of Totemism in Childhood" (Freud 1972 [1913]: 100–161). The Gimi mythic figures embody everything that happens until the fateful "one day" when the band of brothers *and sisters* conspire to murder the monster-Father, split up the Primordial Couple and distribute their conjoined Body – in substitute form, of course, using 'other meat' – as a totemic meal for all the members of the group.

Part II

Stories of Women – Stories of Men: Conversations with a Sister and Brother

Men's myths are *bidokaina*, "stories of the men's house," or *beheraisa kaina*, "daytime stories," (lit: *behe*, light or dawn + *rai*, 'toward' or 'of' + *sa*, poss + *kaina*, 'speech' or 'lore'). Some *bidokaina* tell of hunting exploits, wars, visits to other villages to receive pork at festivals, problems in interpersonal relations with wives, affines and age-mates – 'real experiences' – men recount for pleasure and then repeat in increasingly standarized or heightened ways as cautionary tales, lessons from example, pedagogic devices intended for initiates and other young men. Except to expedite the telling or emphasize the lesson, *bidokaina* tend not to contain supernatural elements. Men's lore concerns the important things in men's lives – kinship obligations, how to achieve prosperity, the best practices in horitculture and exchange relations and, in the past, warfare.

Women's myths (lit: *nene*, 'core' or 'moral' + *kaina*), are "stories of the night," "stories of the women's houses" mothers tell young children of both sexes. Women's myths provide scenarios for theatrical playlets complete with sets, props and costumes performed by women during female initiations and by women and men during the nighttime revels at marriages and male initiations (Gillison 1983b). Women's performances also memorialize or satirize real-life incidents or, during the secret portions of women's rites, are explicitly didactic, demonstrating proper behaviour for a wife in disposing of her menstrual blood or her husband's semen after sexual intercourse. But *nenekaina* tend to express painful, psychological truths from a highly stylized female perspective, using the stuff of dreams and the unconscious – the realm of the Dream Man and "the wild" – to reveal women's attitudes and perceptions of the world they inhabit and help to shape.

In July 1983, eight years after I first heard a version of the Python myth, I began to see that women's myths and rites were inextricably connected not only to each other but also to men's "secrets," the gist of which I knew before I arrived in the Eastern Highlands from the published literature on neighboring groups. Having started to converse with a few men, committed intellectuals and ritual experts, I decided to review with a man named Goran a version of the Python myth told to me by his lineage sister, Kamale, a woman whom I knew well (see Chap. 2). Here are some of Goran's remarks from an initial conversation.

> The Daughter bore a Child. The Snake was her Child. They cut off the Child's head and ate it. That is how they removed the huge Snake from her body and brought her back to life.... The head of the Snake was her first-born [her first menses]. They cut if off, cooked it, and ate it.

> The Girl died [she had her first period]. The Snake entered her [through one orifice] and came out of her [through another]! The Snake is her [first] Husband's penis going in [her vagina] and her [dead] Child coming out her mouth.... The Father took his Daughter and gave her to the Snake who

> is like a man from another place…. She sleeps and her fathers [men of her father's lineage] kill a pig…. She was pregnant and bore a Child. That is the meaning of pulling out the Snake.
>
> Afterwards the men kill a pig and cook it in the same fire with the Snake. They are making the feast for a newborn … but the Child is dead! … It is the *first* Child. The Moon killed her and they are celebrating. They kill a pig and initiate the Girl. That is the meaning of this story.

Only Goran and his mentor, a Big Man of about 60, provided such blunt exegeses and forthright interpretations of women's myths. Discussions about a myth or mythic episode with women over the course of a decade and, starting in 1983, with men, rarely elicted a point-black explanation that ended with "that is the meaning of this story." Instead, interlocutors went on to recitate other myths with related themes, showing me where to look for crucial connections rather than articulating them in other words of their own. Upon learning of my conversations with Goran about one of the myths she had told me, Kamale insisted on taking part. The following excerpts of conversations about the Python myth among Goran, Kamale and me in July 1983 are accompanied by my summaries, interpolations, background detail and digressions set inside square brackets or outside quotation marks. Goran began:

> "The Cassowary Trap is the Man who buys the Trap Setter's Wife … the Trap lies in wait for a Cassowary the way a father lies in wait for a wife [to give to his son]. When the Trap holds the Cassowary it is as if the father holds a wife[-to-be] by the hand. The Son is overjoyed! 'My father has bought me a wife and holds her …' So the Son has sex with her [i.e., he enters the Cassowary's anus].
>
> "Then the Wife follows the Trap-Setter into the forest … and he is *ashamed!* The Son is ashamed of having gone inside the anus of his Mother … his Wife [Goran corrected himself]. His Mother (sic) thinks, 'You go back up the passage you first came down! Shame on you! I am going to tell everybody … !' And so the Mother grabs his eyes and off she goes. She takes his *shame* away with her. He comes to look for [his eyes] but they are gone! … Women steal the shame of us men!"

I asked Goran about the relation between the Cassowary Trap and the Man who set it:

> "The Man who *sets* the Trap and waits for the Cassowary to enter it is *the Child* who hides and watches … [When the Man enters the Cassowary's anus] he climbs back into the place he came from! … The Man who sets the Trap takes his Father into the forest and leaves him on the path to lie in watch (sic). The Man who makes the Trap is the Child and the Trap is his Father … the Cassowary is a Woman. The Father holds the Woman he bought with brideprice…. [The Trap-Setter's] taking out his eyes and placing them on the ground is like taking off his fore-skirt…. When a man puts a fore-skirt over his penis he hides his shame!"

From Goran's remarks, one may surmise that the Man who enters the forest and sets the Cassowary Trap and then goes back and forth, in and out of the forest, to inspect it; and who, when his Trap ensnares a Cassowary, climbs into her anus and eats up her insides, is a Child who watches his parents' having sex *in utero* and then decides – after blinding himself – to participate in it. Tellingly, Goran glosses over the anti-hero's removing his own eyes *before* his "Mother … Wife" steals them, confiscating his "shame" – Goran's slip nicely illustrating the instability or telescoping of kinship relations in the primordial era – and puts all the blame for the Hunter's bad behaviour onto the Mother/Wife. When the Cassowary-Eater takes his Daughter into the forest, and places her on a distant ridge so *she can watch him* take out his eyes, place them on two fuzzy taro leaves, and enter his/her Mother, women's myth reduplicates the primal scene. The Cassowary is Mother to both the Hunter *and* his Daughter. Although the Daughter is stationed on a distant ridge – as far away as the Giant Penis is endlessly long – she also participates in parental intercourse: to get her hands on her Father's stolen eyes-in-bamboo, she has to retrieve them from the place where her Mother hid them – inside her "bed." To get hold of her Father's eyes – situated in his head – the heroine has to *go back* into Mother and repeat the fatal trip her Father made "back up the road he came down."

Goran:

> "The Man who comes home with no food is the man who brings no baby, no appetite for his Wife. He has nothing but 'empty skins' – a flaccid penis. He had sex with the Cassowary and he is *tired* of sex so he does not want to eat the food his Wife prepared! He ate all he wanted inside the Cassowary. He has no desire to 'eat' again so his Wife is enraged!"

Kamale:

> "She follows him and steals his eyes. She is furious because he has sex with another woman! She takes his fore-skirt – his eyes – and brings them back to the house. 'You want to have sex with another woman! Then you will be shamed!' And she hides the bamboo [with his eyes] in her bed. This is how she feels, 'You have sex with another woman and you think I do not *see* you .... But I have found out about you and now *you* have found shame!"

By stealing the Hunter's eyes and hiding them inside her bed/body/house, his Wife exposes his 'true identity' as the Giant Penis who crawls on the ground led by his nose – a big baby with an endless appetite! He is blind because his eyes lie inside his Mother while she is 'caught in a trap' having sex. Being inside her, unable to see but feeling and smelling her copulate, excites his lust so his Penis 'takes on a life of its own' while he stays blind and unaware (like the First Man in women's myth of the Giant Penis, alone and asleep in another house.) (See page 134 ff above.) But after his Daughter – out of *sympathy* for him – puts his eyes back in their sockets, the Giant goes into a rage and is out for revenge against her.

Goran:

> "The Man is ashamed now. The Woman said the things she did and brought shame upon him. So he gave his Daughter to the Snake! *It was his revenge* don't you see? ... The Snake is a sorcerer and the Girl dies. The Snake having sex with her is the same as the Moon killing her. The Snake is the same as the Moon. Her Father is ashamed to have sex with his own Child so he tells the Snake to do it! ... The Snake goes inside the Girl and the blood comes [out]. She menstruates and a pig is killed ... for the Girl's initiation. Pulling the Snake out of her vagina and cooking it in the fire dries up her blood and turns the blood to ashes! The next time the Moon will *not* have sex with her. Only her true husband will go inside her."

Goran insisted that the Wife who followed her Husband into the forest, watched him disappear into the Cassowary's anus, stole his eyes and put them inside a bamboo tube (to keep them moist) made her Husband terribly *ashamed* and so provoked his terrible revenge upon their Daughter. Kamale objected that the one wronged in women's Python myth was the Wife *not* her adulterous Husband!

Although men's "secret" Flute myth was not recited in mixed company, the narrative ran implicitly through our three-way conversations. Goran did not mention any of the obvious references to, or correspondences with, men's Flute myth, especially the resemblence of the Cassowary Hunter's thieving Wife and Daughter to the First Woman or Two Women who monopolized the Flute in men's myth. As Gimi women often said to me, before 'Masta Ben' arrived in the early 1960's, forbade the construction of menstrual huts and demanded that men remove the bamboo flutes from the rafters of men's houses, carry them outside and show them to the crowd of women and children he had assembled before conducting a mass baptism, "we never saw them, really *never*. We heard men's flutes and recognized the (distinctive clan-owned) tunes, but we never *saw* them! Men would have taken axes to our throats."

Men's Secret Myth of the Flutes

The thing Gimi women may never actually have *seen* they nevertheless fully understand and may even, by recounting their own myths to young sons, have helped to invent and sustain. According to men's "secret" myth, the First Woman or Two Women invented the flute and played it inside her/their "flute house," one of the terms for a menstrual hut. One night, the beautiful music woke her baby Brother asleep in another house. Drawn by the irresistable sounds, the baby crawled to his Sister's house and hid amid the tall grass growing outside her door. He waited there until she went to her garden, crept inside her house and stole the Flute from "the head of her bed" – the very place where the Cassowary-Hunter's Wife hid the bamboo tube in which she put the eyes she stole from him. When the Boy in men's myth tried to play the Flute for first time no sound came out. He *did not see* that his Sister had closed the blowing hole with a Plug of her pubic hair. When the Boy pulled out the Plug, he caused his Sister to menstruate for the first time. But before he unplugged the Flute – while he was 'blind' – he put his mouth on the plugged blowing hole, causing his Sister's pubic hair to grow on his face (Gillison 1993: 265–68; see Chap. 1).

Outside my conversations with Kamale and Goran, I learned other versions of the men's Flute myth told in later stages of male initiation – and intimated to me by Goran and other men after 1983 – which 'look inside' a magnified Plug of Sister's pubic hair in ways that bring men's myth closer to women's narratives. The Boy's wind could not enter the blowing hole on his first try, it turned out, because the Sister's pubic-hair Plug hid the "head" of their Father's erect penis. The Flute Plug condenses into a static impenetrable object the myth's entire opening sequence: the Boy seduced by the music of coitus, crawling toward his Sister's house, crouching *unseen* in the "tall grass" growing outside her door, precapitulate and 'blow up' the contents of her pubic-hair Plug. The closer look inside an enlarged Flute Plug reveals a portrait of the Boy hero *as/at* the "head" of their Father's penis. His Sister starts to bleed when he "pulls out the Plug" – which is his *very self* stuck inside her – because he severs *and is severed from* the Father's "head." In all innocence, the baby Boy wanders back inside his Sister and kills/is killed by the jealous Father he does not see lurking inside her: the Boy *becomes* his Sister's "firstborn child" who, as men are loathe to announce, incarnates their Father's severed head. This esoteric interpretation, more in keeping with women's portrayal of the Giant, and in which the First Woman is *not* all alone, nevertheless condemns her and serves men as added pretext for confiscating their sons from seductive, deceitful mothers – mothers who, if not actual killers, are ready to offer up their sons as food for the primal Father.

From women's perspective, of course, the Boy in men's flute myth is no innocent Babe but rather a Brother her own age, her partner in crime, who decapitates the Giant by himself – kills off a whole Dream species! – and, together with her, distributes the pieces as a cannibal meal for *everyone* (above page 127 ff.). But let us keep to *men's view* of this mythic episode: the Boy's wandering *back inside* his Sister's "house" is a heroic incest which costs him his life. For his sacrifice in ridding his Sister of their odious Father by making the terrible trip "back up the road he first came down," his ungrateful Sister plants her pubic hair on his face, exposing his shame for the world to see. "In revenge," men say, for the terrible thing his Sister did *in myth*, they tattoo a "beard" around the mouth of the bride before they send her to a husband. And they repeat the pattern of the bride's facial tattoos in the "female pubic hair" they etch around the blowing holes of the pair of flutes they hide inside the bride's net bag for her to transport "unknowingly" to her husband as part of the marriage transaction (Gillison 1993: 251ff.). The bride's fathers match the markings on the bride's face with those around the flutes' blowing holes as a "secret" visual code – a silent message to the groom and a warning – to save him from having to repeat the fatal head-on collision suffered by his counterpart in myth.

To avoid *any mention* of the Father-Son confrontation inside the First Woman, men's flute myth camouflages the Father's very presence in the Plug of "female pubic hair." The Flute myth blames the Sister for starting to menstruate, for using gorgeous music to "trick" her baby Brother into a suicide mission inside her body, providing men with justification for removing boys from their mothers' murderous care, secluding them inside the men's house and giving birth to them again as children of men. 'Look at what happens to the child *left alone* with mother!' men's myth proclaims. 'The First Woman is utterly capricious: sometimes she delivers a beautiful boy who cries irresistably and whom everyone wants to see; other times she turns the baby to blood between her thighs that falls to the ground and lies there deathly silent. Mothers are dangerously unpredictable and leave us no choice but to confiscate *all* our sons.'

* * *

Why, I wondered aloud during the present conversation among Goran, Kamale and me, do both sexes refer to a menstrual hut as a "flute house" (*kamidama*, lit: *kamiba*, giant fictitious bird and code word for men's sacred bamboo flute + *nama,* 'house')? Goran explained that the First Woman looked down at her vagina and made the Flute [in the image of what she saw] and blew into it and the Child cried. The *kamidama* is the place where children are born. Each menstrual period, each seclusion inside the *kamidama,* is like an assignation, Goran reminded me. It's as if another man, the Moon, who is the menstruator's "first husband" were copulating with her and making her blood run. To quote Goran: "It's as if another man goes inside the woman and we banish her from the settlement.... When the Moon is killing her another man is having sex with her! And the blood comes. This other man is the enemy of her [present] husband:

> "We celebrate [female initiation] before a girl leaves her father's house [when she marries].... We thrust the sugarcane and casuarina through the hole in the roof [in the tug of war with the initiates' chaperons]. It is as if the Moon's Penis were being broken, [as if] her [first] husband were having sex with her.... Really, we celebrate the birth of her first child. [We kill pigs ...] and eat the 'head' of her firstborn.... *I* would not eat the meat of a girl's initiation feast because it is the same as [the head of] a child whose *face* I did not see! 'I do not see the child's face so I throw away the meat!' The meat is the 'head' of a dead child not fit to be eaten."

But the flute! I insisted. Why do men say they ought to *kill* (and in the past sometimes actually did kill) a woman who so much as glimpses a flute when, according to men's own "secret" myth, a woman *invented* the Flute by *looking* down at her vagina and copying onto to a bamboo tube what she saw on her own body? Goran and Kamale agreed that the flute is the body of the First Woman. The flute has "two vaginas," they said again: the blowing hole surrounded by etched designs of insects and other animal motifs to represent the First Woman's Plug of pubic hair; and the open end of the bamboo tube where the music "flies out." The stream of the player's wind entering the blowing hole is his "penis" going into the "vagina" at one end of the instrument and pushing the "cries of his newborn" out the "vagina" at the other end. The meaning of flutes, as Goran often repeated, is copulation. Flutes are always played in pairs: two players coordinate their blowing and hand movements to produce syncopated rhythms. As each flute-player blows into the instrument's side hole, he closes the open end with a clump of muddy earth that contains tufts of grass like the hairy Flute Plug and like the "tall grass" where the Boy hid outside his Sister's house. Blowing into the flute while closing the open end is "the same as filling the womb," Goran added, and releasing the hand that holds the muddy 'plug' is "letting out the [cries of the] newborn."

Kamale and Goran agreed with me when I suggested that women's Python myth "joins together" male initiation and female initiation and rites of sister-exchange marriage. Although I was careful to avoid leading my interlocutors down interpretative paths of my own invention, I nevertheless ventured a summary of some of the foregoing to help me keep track of our discussion. When the 'story woman' in the Python myth saw the Man take out his eyes and enter the anus of the Cassowary, and then stole his eyes and put them into a bamboo tube "to keep them moist" and ran home to hide the bamboo "at the head of her bed," I offered, she "stole the flute." "Yes!" said Kamale. "No!" Goran objected. Kamale added: "It is the firstborn who dies." Goran: "The blood is *not* the woman's [blood]. It is her father's blood. 'Moon's blood' is the father's [murdered] semen."

Perhaps, I said, the menstrual hut is called "flute house" (*kamidama*) because the First Woman or Two Women possessed the Father's flute, his sex, his shame. "House of shame" (*keterama*, lit: *kete,* 'shame' + *nama*, 'house') is another term for a menstrual hut. The First Woman still has the Giant Penis inside her, I said. The Moon has not killed her – yet! "*Oooo*," said Kamale, "yes." But she is in her husband's village so she has to be moved to the outskirts, Kamale insisted, "so the enemy cannot come inside." The menstruating woman dallies with her father who is her husband's enemy. "What you are saying is true," Goran said to preface his firm objection, "the *kamiba* comes from the *kamidama* …" *but* the *kamiba* is *not* a penis! The *kamiba* is the body of a woman! he declared emphatically, and then repeated what I seemed not to understand: A man's blowing into the *kamiba* and withdrawing his breath are *coital* movements. Playing the flute is like inserting his "penis" into the First Woman and pushing his "child" out her *other end.* The music that emerges from the instrument's open end is his baby "crying," and flying away like a bird.

Heedlessly, I persisted that maybe, in some contexts, in some sense, the *kamiba* might *also* be a penis? … Goran humored me some more before repeating his explanation yet again. "Inside the *kamidama* the First Woman saw her own Vagina and made the Flute…" But I interrupted (wrongly, it would turn out): she saw *blood* inside her Vagina [which was] the Father's dead child. "Yes," Goran said but then – categorically – "No!" I still did not catch on. The First Woman who *made* the Flute did not menstruate. The *kamiba* she possessed was still plugged! Nowadays, the women who retreat to "flute houses," menstrual huts, find there is "only blood there" and feel utter "shame." That is why today (that is, before Masta Ben forbade their construction in the early 1960's), "flute houses" are also called "houses of shame" and "toilets" (*arega,* lit: *are,* 'feces' + *ga,* 'place' as word ending.)

Neither the First Woman nor the Primal Father Is What She or He Appears to Be

This was one of the moments, late in the day, when I began to realize that the flute Goran kept insisting was "the body of the First Woman" did *not* represent a single person or instrument, as I kept thinking, but was rather the *condensation of a sequence of events for which women remain entirely to blame*. Goran's repeated assertions about the flute and men's insistence in their myth that the First Woman was sublimely *alone* I now understood to mean that when she charmed her baby Brother to her door, he could only hear – that is, *misunderstand* – her coital rapture with her Father. The thing the Boy innocently stole away from his Sister but, at first, could not *see* was a 'primal scene' radically condensed into a seemingly-unitary object – the flute – *knowledge epitomized as a thing one may possess or lose but can never share*. The object the boy steals is the distillate of a complicated sequence of events he does not grasp and that turns out to have multiple and contradictory meanings: in men's Flute myth, the Sister's music draws him irresistably back to the hairy place between her thighs where he expires; in men's rites of initiation, the music of bamboo flutes heralds his rebirth. When men's myth of Woman's foul deed is converted to initiation ritual and manufactured in objects of exchange – brides, pairs of flutes, and "head" payments – the deed is 'undone,' at least for the present.

By revealing the presence of the monster-Father and describing his evil exploits, women's myths fill in the gruesome details of men's purposely cryptic and deceptive scenario: the Boy is 'fatally attracted' and has no choice but to return to his Sister's house because he has no life of his own. He is the still-attached "head" of their Father's Giant Penis so that when he dares to try *by himself* to re-enter her house, which is the Giant's exclusive territory, *the Giant* 'cuts him off.' (See Chap. 3 p. 115 ff.) Gimi women's and men's separate portraits of the primal Parent show that He – or She – is not a singular creature with multiple attributes but rather an *arrested primal scene*, the 'coagulate' of an incestuous pair congealed in perpetual coitus like the First Man whose Giant Penis coiled itself into an enormous bundle that protruded over his belly, giving him the profile of a pregnant woman (women's myth); or the Flute before the Boy removed the Plug of his Sister's pubic hair (men's myth). The primodial Gimi Father/Mother is a stuck-together pair – 'two *in* the same' – who may sometimes look like, or have the profile, of *only Mother* because she is his permanent address, his habitual place of residence that – according to women – *he* converts to a bloody prison. No baby escapes alive because his "head" blocks the exit, a gaping maw lying in wait to take back any offspring who so much as pokes its head out the door! The First Couple's *appearance* in the sexes' separate myths as a single object or mythic personage or kind of knowledge that can be "stolen" but never shared places the blame for death and misfortune entirely on one sex or the other.

Inside the *kamidama*, as Gimi men would have it, the First Woman looked down and saw the hair-covered crown of her baby's head "plugging" her vagina. She saw the birth of her Son/Brother coming out of her body with "no eyes." In men's view, 'coming out' of mother – "passing between her thighs" as a blind baby – is *the single event* that causes her son's and all men's insatiable, lifelong hunger; the desire of every boy and man "to go back up the road he first came down." Flute-playing is men's attempt to counter the self-destructive impulse their mothers "planted in their heads" – to depart from the Flute myth's catastrophic end – by putting their mouths on vagina-*facsimiles* men manufacture out of bamboo. Women's myths describe not only what the First Woman *saw* but also how she *experienced* both Father and Son "blindly" eating away at her insides: it was like being a huge, flightless Cassowary with *a grown man rapaciously* climbing in and out of her inert earth-bound body. In women's terms, the climbing up (coitus) and coming back down (parturition) are parts of the same loathsome itinerary. The Cassowary Hunter's entering the Cassowary's anus is the initial phase of his coming back down the fecal tract *and vice versa* – in-and-out, out-and-in movements as inseparable as breathing and flute playing. (See the 'Rape of the Python' above.)

Gimi men regard birth as the first time a man 'has sex' – "passes between a woman's thighs," as they say – and, therefore, as the singular cause of his need and addiction to the First Woman in his life who is his mother. That very first moment, when the baby *came out* of her body and *only she* – the First Woman – had eyes to see is an image Gimi men find intolerable because it instilled in them a lifelong desire for exclusive attachment. A baby boy who is blind at birth is *totally possessed by his mother*, a humiliation men do everything they can to reverse when they grow up. For the correspondingly opposite reason, Gimi women also consider parturition and copulation to be 'one and the same.' The baby's 'coming out' of her is inseparable from a man's 'going in' to her because the man is just as blind and selfish as a great big hungry baby crawling on all fours, eating up her insides and bringing her nothing to eat. The two are as one to her – a monolithic Giant Penis – because she sees father and son while both are without sight or awareness *of her*. Why? … because she is greedy for sex and *steals* men's awareness, in Goran's view; or rather, from women's perspective, because the Giant is both a rapist and a thief who steals all her children. For Gimi of both sexes, everything in life is either/or. Except for the tacit basis of discord, nothing is shared between the sexes, certainly not the capacities for seeing, knowing and possessing.

Myths and rites of both sexes *equate seeing with repossession or theft*: 'to see' means 'to have *again*' because in order to 'see' one has to have 'gone *back*' inside Mother – *re*entered the dark primeval forest – and tried to feed again upon the Giant Hunter-Penis coiled like a heavy rope of vine inside her belly (Gillison 1997). The one who 'sees' is greedily "eating the head" of a Father lost in esctasy inside Mother: the one who watches *devours* a Father who is blind and unaware (Gillison 1999: 170–185).

Flute-playing is "the same" as the Cassowary Hunter's trip inside the Cassowary, "a trip," Goran said, "back up the road he came *head first* into the world!" The Boy in men's Flute myth likewise tried to go back into his Sister head first when he put his mouth on her vagina without realizing that now, on the way *back* inside, something else was there blocking his re-entry into his Sister? or was it his Mother? – into the First Woman? or was it the first Two Women Flute-players? Men's deliberate confusion about the number and identity of the First Woman, whom women's myths and rites unequivocally show is the dual unity of Daughter-inside-Mother, is another device men use to hide the primal Father's vile habits. In men's Flute myth, the Boy causes his Sister to menstruate for the first time. Hence, the First Woman who made the Flute by "looking down" at her vagina inside her "flute house" – the name for a menstrual hut – did *not* see the blood of her "firstborn," as I tried unsuccessfully to make Goran agree with me that she did, because she had not *yet* menstruated: her baby Brother had not yet *returned* to die between her thighs.

The First Woman still possessed the Flute with its Hair-Plug intact: Father and Son were still united as one Giant Penis. In men's myth, it is the Boy who inadvertantly 'kills the Moon' and himself when he removes the Plug: he is a hungry child who still wants to eat up his Mother 'from the inside' as he did during gestation, except that now – as women's myths insist – he is no longer a blind foetus! *He sees that the food inside Mother is Father* so he removes his eyes before entering! The whiskers that appear on a boy's face at puberty testify to the *second incest* of his mythic counterpart, the attempt, knowingly say women, to "go back up the road he first came down." Men's retort is that the Boy did *not know*. Men's mythic baby Boy ate his Father's Penis *in utero* in the form of regular infusions of semen and then tried to go back as a newborn who could not see the hard impenetrable thing hidden inside his Sister's/Mother's pubic hair. His innocent 'mistake' is entirely *her fault*, in men's view, stemming from her ambivalence and insatiable desire to keep the Giant hidden inside her forever. The First Woman seduced her baby Brother and then became furious at his unwanted intrusion! In anger, she transferred her pubic hair onto his face to humiliate him and all men before the world.

In women's rendition of the Boy's return trip into Mother, he is no baby able to hide in "tall grass." His body has grown into an enormous thing, a Giant Penis, able to enter her Vagina, move all the way through her body and come out her Mouth! Whatever his age or size, the myths of women and men agree that the result of the male's 'second coming' is to endow his daughter/sister with a "second vagina" in her head – to make of her a two-holed instrument – fit to give away as a wife for a real-life husband who will never have to put his mouth on a plugged flute nor risk getting killed by going back up the road he first travelled down. No more two-way traffic through a single door! Until advanced age, Gimi men traditionally depilated one whisker at a time the beard they acquired at puberty as the result of their mythic 'collision' with the Father. The same crime left the Giant's bloody residues inside men's noses and their sisters' vaginas. But – because the sisters cannot 'excise' the blood like a beard nor transfer it like a flute – they have to hide every month inside "houses of shame."

Why the Secrecy?

As Goran explained, a man has to make sure his wife knows nothing about his mother's crimes, nothing of what she did to him in his prehistoric past. Men must keep secret from their wives what transpired between themselves and their mothers lest their wives, out of jealousy and feelings of exclusion in later life, seduce their sons. "A mother, as she grows older, saves herself from [the uneventfulness of her emotional life … the danger of being left unsatisfied] by putting herself in her children's place, by identifying herself with them; and this she does by making their emotional experiences her own" (Freud 1972 [1913]: 15). Keeping flutes a secret avoids the prospect of mother-son incest in the next generation, according to Goran. By a single tactic, a man both protects his son from the predations of an insatiably hungry mother and keeps his wife for himself. He prevents his son from being 'swallowed up' in the way he once was by keeping secret from both mother and uninitiated son the knowledge of exactly what occurred inside the belly of the beast.

Whereas his son's ignorance is temporary, his wife's is supposed to be permanent. Once the First Woman who made the Flute and saw everything – who had eyes while her Son and rapist-Father were blind with desire and she treated them as one and the same – once that *one* Woman died, according to most versions of men's Flute myth, all women ever after – sisters, wives and daughters – remain in the dark. Men's insistence upon women's ignorance is a sham, of course, the pretense they concoct anew in each generation: in each generation there is a mother who has "seen everything" and will die. But from her absolute "prior knowledge" and once-exclusive relation with her son comes all women's guilt and men's justification for punishing *all* women with retaliatory exclusion lest they repeat the mother's crime of making their own vaginas – and the kind of attachments they breed – irresistable.

To quote Goran:

> "What is the reason men have sex with women? Why do men go back up the road they first came down? Because women have taken away their shame.... If the woman had not stolen his eyes, that man would have been ashamed even to *look* at the thing for doing it [the hairy hole]... and he would not have gone up [into] her.... But women take men's shame and men go around asking women for sex! It's women's fault! If women did not do what they did [while men were babies], men would not have sex with them. Women would have no husbands! They would not be able to bear children! Women *trick* men into sex to get babies out of them.... Women wonder, 'How will we get babies? We must steal men's awareness so that, not realizing *where* they put their penes, they will put them into us.' Women take away men's shame so men will not know [the vagina] is the hole they came out of (lit: 'down from')."

Indeed, some women, especially as they get older, agree with Goran's harsh judgment that mothers seduce their sons and are inclined never to let them go, creating a habit for dyadic connection that is antithetical to adult social life. In one version of the myth of the Giant Penis, which I heard in a neighbouring village from several women well past child-bearing age, the virgin Girl inside her Mother's house, although "fast asleep," is able to offer the lost and bewildered Giant a little 'free advice' about how to find her vagina and penetrate it.

> The Woman lifted her skirt and said, "Look, the hole is here." "She showed it to me," the Penis thought so he ate open the Vagina. The Penis shot her [because] she said to him, "It is down below. It is here!" "She said, 'You are my Child and can see me,' and she *showed* me her Vagina.' She *showed* me where to go," the Penis said to himself, "... I saw it and thought, 'Yes'."

Note

1. Because of their close association, Gimi myths and rites are often discussed together. Mythic figures and artifacts are capitalized to distinguish them from their ritual counterparts. But pronouns that refer to mythic figures appear in lower case. Big Man and Big Woman, individuals recognized as important persons and leaders in the community, are also capitalized.

References

Berndt, Ronald M. 1962. *Excess and Restraint: Social Control Among a New Guinea Mountain People*. Chicago: University of Chicago Press.

Freud, Sigmund. 1972 [1913]. *Totem and Taboo. Some Points of Agreement Between the Mental Lives of Savages and Neurotics*. Trans. James Strachey [1950]. London: Routledge and Kegan Paul.

Gajdusek, D. Carleton. 1973. Kuru in the New Guinea Highlands. In *Tropical Neurology*, ed. John D. Spillane. New York: Oxford University Press.

Gillison, Gillian. 1983a. Cannibalism Among Women in the Eastern Highlands of Papua New Guinea. In *The Ethnography of Cannibalism*, ed. Paula Brown and Donald Tuzin. Washington, DC: Society for Psychological Anthropology.

———. 1983b. Living Theater in New Guinea's Highlands. *National Geographic Magazine* (August).

———. 1993. *Between Culture and Fantasy*. Chicago: University of Chicago Press.

———. 1997. To See or Not to See. Looking as an Object of Exchange in the New Guinea Highlands. In *Reading Visual Anthropology*, ed. Marcus Banks and Howard Morphy. London: Yale University Press.

———. 1999. Fieldwork and the Idea of the Unconscious. *Psychoanalytic Studies* 1 (i): 49–56.

Robertson-Smith, W. 1894. *Lectures on the Religion of the Semites*. New 2nd ed. London (1st edition, 1889).

5

"Eating the Head of the Child:" Ritual Exchange as Remedy for Crimes of the Mythic Past

The Conjoined Primal Parent

If Gimi women's separate myths and rites are not a permanent Trojan Horse, living at the heart of men's stories and jaded views on motherhood, then they counter Gimi men's narratives with precision and wit. In the Python myth, the Wife steals her Husband's eyes and removes his shame, as Goran insists, but the Husband has *already* established a routine of taking his Daughter into the forest as a witness, removing his eyes from their sockets himself, placing them on fuzzy taro leaves and climbing into the Cassoway's hairy anus, showing that he willingly colludes in the theft.[1] Men's vaunted secrecy hides nothing from women, whose myths and rites seem to expose and mock it, but the pretense allows men to blame women for their own longings without having to answer women's objections and accusations. By juxtaposing women's productions with those of men—backing up the 'camera lens' to get a panoramic view—we see the "flute house" during *female* initiation ritual (*haro*, lit: 'roof') in a frame that encompasses not only the doorway through which, in men's myth, the Boy crawls to steal his Sister's Flute, but also the roof

G. Gillison, *She Speaks Her Anger: Myths and Conversations of Gimi Women*, Culture, Mind, and Society, https://doi.org/10.1007/978-3-030-49352-3_5

of the house where the initate's future affines, who embody the Giant Penis, rip open the thatch and insert and withdraw a long sugarcane pole. Women's perspective creates a bigger picture that contradicts men's myth in which the First Woman is all alone inside her house and invents the Flute by "looking down" at her vagina: the men standing on the roof of the woman's "flute house" reveal the Giant raping his Daughter while she is still ensconced in Mother. (See Fig. 3.2.)

In the wide-angle view women's myths and rites provide, we watch men tear a hole in the thatch to open a 'second door' in the "flute house" where the initiate is sequestered and then lower the sugarcane edition of the Moon's Giant Penis: we see the Giant invading her premises from *on high*, through the roof, showing that the plugged Flute the Boy finds inside his Sister's house "at the head of her bed" was put there by the Giant. The First Woman's Flute which men insist is "the body of a woman" who deliberately closes it with a plug of her own pubic hair now appears to be occupied from one end to the other by the Giant Penis who shapes her body entirely in his image.

Women's Giant Penis and Python myths and their translations into the rites of female initiation reveal what men's Flute myth and male initiation rites try to hide: namely, that the First Woman did not invent the Flute all by herself. She 'got hold' of it in the first place while still inside her Mother's house, still an unborn babe nourished entirely on her Father's ejaculate. The First Woman possessed the Flute, according to women's myths, because her Father, the Moon, the Dream Man, the Python viciously raped her: the Flute got "inside her house" while she herself was still an unborn babe. Men's Flute myth cuts out the Giant as he enters through the roof and 'zooms in' for a close-up that enlarges the doorway so that all we see is the Boy hiding in "tall grass" waiting to make the trip "back up the road he first travelled down." Women's Python myth mocks this scene. Instead of an innocently curious baby Boy, women portray a man-size baby who fastidiously takes out his own eyes and climbs into his Cassowary-Mother to gobble up her insides, leaving her an 'empty skin' with nothing for anyone else to eat. The Cassowary Trap-Setter of women's Python myth is hardly a champion: he is a grown man, a Husband, who behaves like a big baby, *refuses to see*, and is shameless and a liar.

But at the tale's end—which corresponds to the penultimate moment in female initiation ritual when the girl emerges from seclusion inside the "sugar-bed" and receives crucial help from her lineage brothers to end her ordeal—it is the heroine's Mother's Brother who "laid in wait and ... shot her Python-Husband dead." Without the Brother's grown-up heroism, women's myths say, "our husbands would lie to us and bring home empty skins [flacid penes] for us to eat."

Taken together, men's and women's separate myths and rites create an oscillating vision of the primal crime and origin of sexual difference in which one sex presents itself as innocent child and the other as adult predator, the conjoined primal parent as baby-eater and child molester. But women's myths and rites provide many intimations of collusion between the sexes. Underlying both sexes' views is the shared premise that the baby Boy who steals the "head" of his father's Giant Penis will one day *exchange* it for another whereas the virgin Girl who evicts the Giant, or is helped to get rid of him by her Brother, will remain permanently *hollowed out.* The Father rapes and kills his Daughter—"sends her to the Snake"—in revenge for the Wife / Mother stealing his 'eyes-in-bamboo,' an item in women's myth which objectifies the Father's desire to eat from Mother's bounty at any time and to any extent he pleases. With crucial help from her Brother / Mother's Brother, the heroine-initiate is resurrected and sent off to marry: the Snake is decapitated, pulled out of her body, cut into pieces, cooked and eaten *in the substitute form* of pork or marsupial meat, a gift of food Gimi call "the head of the child." But once rescued, revived, married and the mother of living children, the female is still bereft, emptied out over and over again: the regular exchanges of "head" payments between affines—which I treat as the Gimi equivalent of the totemic meal Freud describes as the basis of kinship and social relations—are designed to 'eradicate' the mother and install her brother in her place (Freud 1972 [1913]; Gillison 2016).

Despite women's eloquent and ingenious counter-narratives, men's version—or revision—of the origin and cause of human existence carries the day and determines the organization of society, in part because women also collude in—or help to invent—the system that maligns and shuns them. In the recent past, women lived in separate houses alone with children of both sexes throughout their early formative years and spent much of daily life apart from men. As individuals, Gimi women are no less forceful, articulate, charismatic or violent than men. Yet when their voices are heard, they still seem to provide few clues about why women are relentlessly slandered and mistreated, why their sex is associated with everything contaminating and vile, or why Gimi and other Highlands men once imposed the *death penalty* for the mother's crime of *looking*.

Women collude in the system that excludes them partly because they mainly agree with men that the social project to separate children from their mothers requires emancipation not only of the children but also of their mothers from the 'childhood ties that bind'. This is one complicated truth upon which the sexes seem to agree. Once the early years of childhood are over, and even during the period when the child is singularly attached to mother, there needs to be concerted intervention—at first gradual and incremental and then radical—to separate mother and child and to destroy the early childhood 'habit' of dyadic attachment, especially in boys. The exchange of "head" payments between affines starts when a child is born and continues at every rite of passage thoughout the life of a boy and until the marriage of a girl. Gimi women seem to agree with men—and may even originate the conviction—that the drawn-out process of separation from mother crucial to a child's growth into healthy maturity is an immensely difficult task that a mother *by herself*—who is immersed most of her life in the mother-child realm—may not always be inclined nor equipped to carry out. In the terms of both sexes' myths, the one who "comes down" from mother and then succumbs to the wish to "travel back up that same road" will die.

In order to survive, the child who gets out of mother alive needs a lot of help to *stay* out. Nothing less than ongoing work by society as a whole in rite after rite is required to rescue *each person* from the original attachment to mother – and from an entire *style of being alone with her* that becomes obsolete and destructive—on the understanding that the task of extricating a girl from the mother-child morass is less urgent because, once liberated from her mother at adolescence, she will soon become a mother herself, re-ensconsed for most of the rest of her life in mother-child dyads.

Further Discussions with Goran and Kamale

With no prompting from me, and consistent with his interpretation of the Cassowary Trap in women's Python myth as both the Trap-Setter's Father and the brideprice he holds—the lure and payment for a bride—Goran offers a further interpretion of why the Man entered the Cassowary and devoured her entrails:

> This is why the Man ate the Cassowary's insides: sometimes a woman gets pregnant before her brother has a chance to "eat" her pay. He may have died before her husband finished making "head" payments [that are the continuation of brideprice]. In that case, she may tell her dead brother or father, "Go inside my vagina and enter my womb and eat the child that is there. The man who bought me did not pay up quickly so that you could 'eat the head' before you died." She speaks in anger because her husband did not make the "head" payments in time! "'It won't do for me to bear the child and make my husband a happy man. You must kill the child and eat it!'"
>
> The Man who comes home with no food is the Man who brings no baby, no sex for his Wife ...

So, I interjected, the "head" payments a man makes to his wife's brother and father are intended to compensate them—induce them to let go of—the residual "head" of her father's penis still inside her even after she is married and her brideprice is paid. In mythic terms, her every unborn child starts out attached to the Giant Penis *as* his "head," as her "firstborn" who is her own brother 'in a former life,' the life cancelled during his first initiation. A woman's 'next' unborn children are also conceived as her father's "head" and will *remain or revert* to that status until her father and brother "eat the head of her child," that is, accept *replacements for her brother's own unborn self*, her 'first' firstborn, so to speak, from whose flesh all her future children derive, and thus release them into the world outside her body (cf. Mimica In press: 60–61). Even after the woman's initiation, after her chaperons, assisted by her brothers, broke into baby-size pieces the sugarcane phallus her affines inserted through the roof of the menstrual hut, her unborn children still belong to—and easily revert to the custody of—the Moon. Goran expanded:

> The Moon's Penis comes down to have sex with all the young women. Then they seclude the girls [in menstrual huts]. And when it is time to bring them out [of seclusion] they break the Moon's Penis [so that] the Moon will not kill them anymore [and they will conceive the 'second' husband's living child].

So then, I interjected again, each segment of the sugar pole the women break off and leave to rot in adjacent shrubbery is a "firstborn child that falls down," born one after another after another on the Moon's monthly visits. The vibrating head of the Python crying "Daddy" inside the dead Girl's mouth before her Mother and Mother's Brother cut it off, pull the Snake out of the Girl's body and cut it into pieces; the Dream Man's offspring appearing one after another after another in the doorway of his Treetop House and dropping murdered to the ground with "a loud thud" after the Marsupial Hunter picks them off one by one ... all these are women's mythic images of the 'sugar-babies' they sever in the tug-of-war with men on the roof at the end of a girl's initiation. And, I threw in, the flow of affinal payments received by her father and brother after they give the girl away in marriage—the successive "heads" of each child she bears—compensate them for the loss of the daughter / sister they *impregnated before she was born*, a loss that is renewed and augmented every time she bears a child (cf. Gough 1955).

Listening to my myth-ritual interpolations with some alarm, Goran said, "It's like eating the head of the penis!" I added, "The head of the mother's father's penis who *is* the mother's brother." Goran provided a hypothetical example: "Let's say her husband has sex with her and she gets pregnant ... and she bears the child and her brother comes and gets the head [payment] ..." Unwisely, I interrupted again: "To cut off the head of the Snake is to seize the head of the [Girl's] Father's Penis." *This*, I thought to myself, must be the origin of the expression "to eat the head of the child" to describe the mother's brother accepting child payments from his sister's husband. Goran was now incensed: "Cutting off the head of the Snake is like cutting a man's penis! *This* we throw away! *This* men and women do not keep and eat!!" No one *eats* the Snake, Goran vehemently insisted, "because it is blood." But they *do* eat the pig cooked with it "in the same fire," he added. Pigs or, in the past, the "wild" meat of marsupials—"head" payments—are the edible replacements for the Snake's bloody severed head or the Moon's first Children born dead who appear one after the other, month after month. Goran continued, his patience with me stretched:

> If, when a child is born – when the Snake sticks his head out the Girl's mouth – if her Brother does *nothing* and all the women [all mothers] do *nothing*, do you think we would have children nowadays?! Of course not! A man could have sex with a woman, he could use his penis to go inside a woman's vagina ...

Now Kamale interrupted: "... her Brother *has* to cut off the Snake's head!" Too quickly, I jumped in again, "Then the pig is killed and cooked with the Snake to celebrate the birth of the *first* child, the first menses ..."

On another occasion, alone with Goran, I tried a different tack. The only way to get the Snake out of the Girl's body was to cut off its vibrating head. Then her Mother / Mother's Brother cut the rest of the Snake into pieces and cooked them in a fire with 'other meat' that *was* eaten: the other meat was *not* the Snake but also "the same" as the Snake. So, I went on, offering "head" payments to one's wife's brother and father (men who 'copulate' with her *in myth*, or during her own prenatal past, and leave actual 'residues' inside her which reappear monthly)—men whose acceptance of "head" payments is called "eating the head of the child"—is designed to *replace* what these men lost from "the head of the Father's Penis" in the primordial past, *while the two of them, as Giant and Firstborn, were still undifferentiated* and while the Wife / Sister was *herself* an unborn babe residing inside her Mother's "house" being repeatedly nourished / raped in the process of coming into being.

Hence, I concluded on my own while I was by myself, for a man to "give the head of his child" to his wife's brother and father is to induce him / them, with edible substitutes, to vacate her body and "get out of her house." "Head" payments are a man's attempts to 'buy off' his wife's "first husband," the Moon, and his "firstborn" Son—incarnated in her father and brother—and compel them to leave her body. The gift of the "head" is a *parting gift:* an inducement to quit the premises that has to be rendered over and over again because the "first husband" returns every month to engender and murder new progeny. In the absence or serious default of "head" payments, the child sickens and dies because it reverts to the 'custody' of its Primal Parents whom both sexes picture as a Pair still lethally 'stuck together' in copulation.

The Gift of the Head Part I: Exchange as 'Remedy' for the Myths of Both Sexes

The "head of the child" is one of three Gimi prototypes of a ritual payment, the other two being a wife and a pair of flutes. "Eating the head of a child" is the Gimi idiom for receiving obligatory "gifts" of pigs and money or, in the past, marsupials and other valuables (like marsupial fur, pearshells and Bird of Paradise plumages) from one's affines, the men with whom one has exchanged wives and remain in lifelong reciprocal debt (Fig. 5.1).

A man and his brothers offer the "heads" of each of his children to his wife's father and brothers, and other affines, on designated occasions in a

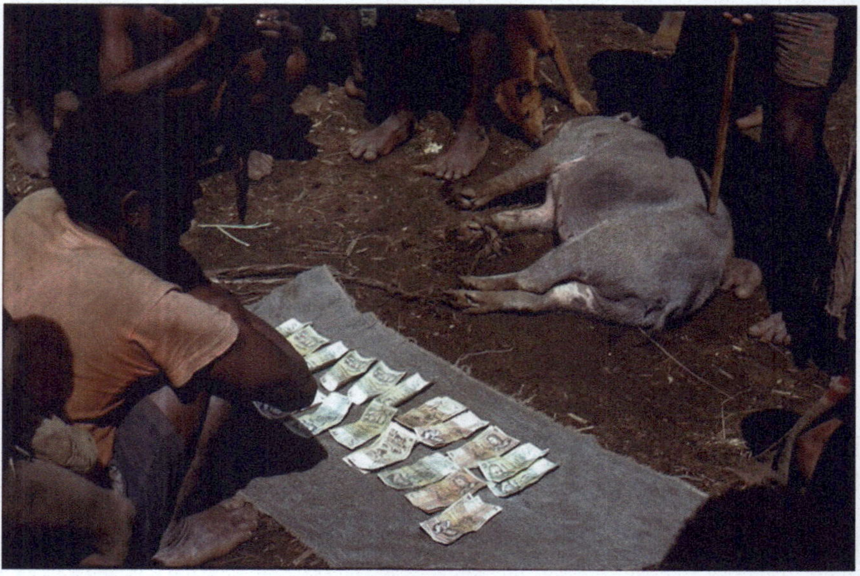

Fig. 5.1 Presentation of a "head" payment to the mother's brother and other affinal kinsmen. To receive such payments, in the Gimi idiom, is to "eat the head of the child." (© David Gillison)

child's life: at birth, when the child suffers any crisis or passes any milestone, when it cuts its first tooth, has its first haircut, is weaned, falls ill, is injured, gardens or hunts for the first time, is initiated or marries—in sum—whenever there is any new phase of growth or achievement or risk to well-being. (The mother's brother may also "eat the head" when *he* falls ill or suffers some misfortune, according to his needs of the moment rather than the child's, in recognition of his sister's husband's ongoing indebtedness.) On each occasion when the mother's brother or matrilateral kin receive these payments, Gimi say, they "eat the head of the child." The Gimi custom of exchanging "head" payments is similar to celebrations of *naven* among Iatmul peoples of the Sepik River described by Gregory Bateson (Bateson 1958 [1936]; Gillison 2016).

During the violent family dispute that erupted one night, an enraged Gimi father, with his eldest son sitting beside him, shouted to his married daughter, "My son and I will not eat the heads of your children!" To show his fury, the father lifted his fore-skirt to expose himself—an obscene reminder to his daughter of their original connection. Then the father spit, thus invoking the "curse of the mother's brother" (Chap. 2; cf. Wagner 1967). A child who is cursed by its mother's father and brother will not prosper, nor survive the rigours of childhood because, by refusing to accept "head" payments from the child's father and his lineage, figuratively speaking, the two men "eat the child" *instead*, reclaiming what is originally theirs. Such a child is re-attached *as* "the head" of the Giant Penis or Moon whose only offspring are "firstborn" and "the same" as menstrual blood. Without the remedy of ritual exchanges among affines, in other words, a child is doomed to live out in the reality of everyday life the tragedy of its mythic origins in the world before kinship when Mother was forever 'stuck together' with her Father.

Further Adventures of the Giant Penis and His Firstborn Son: Women's Myth of the Home Invaders

The myths of both sexes portray the primordial past by enlarging to cosmic proportion what happens *in utero*. The next tale in Gimi women's repertoire visualizes the conception of the two first children, a pair of boys, as a drama that takes place inside the womb and the territory immediately outside the mother's body visualized as the mountain landscape surrounding the village. The myth names familiar sites along two facing mountain ridges to trace the arrival of the Giant Penis in the valley between the First Woman's thighs. The Giant is now portrayed as a *pair* of Home Invaders—a Father and identical Firstborn Son—who descend in perfect unison from opposite mountain peaks, gaily singing and dancing as they raid the valley where an enticing pair of "boys have been left at home alone."

Like the Dream Man and his Marsupial Hunter Son, or the Cassowary Trapper and the Python he recruits as his surrogate, the two Home Invaders are both separate and identical. Both come to "play around" with unattended children in the same way as each Dream Child, when questioned by the Dream Mother, replied, "The one we have been eating has come back to eat me!" Once again, women's myth 'looks inside' and makes visible *the father-son relationship* that men's Flute myth conflates and conceals as a Plug of "female pubic hair." Whereas the Marsupial Hunter in women's myth of the Dream Man summarily shoots and kills every Dream Child who pokes its head out the door, the Pair of Home Invaders in this myth appear able to negotiate and to accept other "wild" meat—marsupials—in exchange for the Boys they hunger for.

In order downwards from the two opposing mountain peaks that dominate the settlement and its closest neighbour, women's myth of the Home Invaders names familiar landmarks, rainforest plantations of red and white pandanus trees, clan-owned hunting grounds, hamlets and outlying compounds, perched at parallel altitudes on the two facing mountain sides that enclose the place where each Invader, in sync with his opposite number, pauses before meeting in the valley where a pair of unborn Brothers have been left tantalizingly alone. The myth's landscape recreates on a vast scale the territory between a woman's thighs where a "child's head" enters the world outside mother for the first time. The narrator is Aramo, aged about 43 years in 1975, the mother of four grown children including Kamale and numerous grandchildren. Aramo is the second or four wives of the Big Man Situpe who, with his oldest son Fandi, cursed the two daughters of Kamale whom she named 'Fandi' and

'Situpe.' (See Chap. 2, Fig. 2.2.) As in the Dream Man myth, the Wild-Woman / Wife in this story is wholly allied with her Husband / Brother, contradicting men's portrayals of their wives as treacherously loyal to their own fathers and brothers.

hoEEEdada

Coming down from the peak of Mt. RakItI towards Miniabibi, One was singing, "*kirekireso ... mora' kinasoso doride...*" Coming down from the [opposite] peak of Mt. Abini, the Other One was singing, "*kirekireso asIdome* [lit: *kire*, 'a marsupial' *asIdome*, 'is born.'] ... *kirekire sasa dorire ...* Little boys were left at RuyIpi [the next-to-lowest-lying hamlet on the ridge of Mt. Abini].

"*kirekireso ...*" sang the One as he reached KuedabutaE [opposite Miniabibi]. "*doredore kinaso...*" sang the Other as he reached Biriari [opposite RuyIpi]. The One coming down Mt. Abini approached the children at RuyIpi. He arrived from FututaI crying, "*kirekireso ...*" The Other one, crying, "*doredo-reeee...*" came down Mt. RakItI, passed Biriari and arrived at HakoyIpi [the lowest-lying hamlet where the story-teller lives].

The One arrived at BinumIbipi [just above RuyIpi on the Abini side] crying, "*kirekireso ...*" The Other crying, "*doredore kinaso*" arrived at RuyIpi. The One singing "*kirekireso ...*" was at Badahiabipi [opposite BinumIbipi].

The Two of them came down [opposite mountainsides in unison]. One arrived to meet the Other at RuyIpi where the Two Boys were. The Two met up and asked the Boys, "Where are your Mother and Father? Why are the two of you here all alone?" One Boy answered, "Our Mother and Father have gone into the forest to hunt marsupials." And One of the Men said, "And when your Mother and Father bring home the marsupials they kill, what will you give us?" And the Boy said, "When they bring home the ones [they kill], you can eat the head." "But I don't like the head," the Men answered.

"Then you can eat the arm and shoulder," offered the Boy. "But I do not like the arm and shoulder." ... "Then you can eat the leg." ... "No, I do not like it." ... "You eat the rib cage." "No, I do not like it." ... "Then you eat the other leg." ... "No, I do not like it." ... "You eat the other arm and shoulder." ..."No, I do not like the other arm and shoulder." "You eat the belly." ... "No, I do not like the belly." The Boy mentioned the tail but the Man said he did not like it. The Two Men hit the Boys – hit them hard – and said, "We do not like *you*!" They beat the Boys and then took off in opposite directions. One went one way and the Other went the other way [back up the two facing mountain ridges].

The Two Boys were crying, mucous filling their noses and tears falling [from their eyes], when their Mother and Father came back from the forest. "Who beat you?" they asked, and the Boys answered, "A man who came down from there and another man who came down from there. The Two came inside here and hit us. Men we do not know. Men whose faces we did not see!" The Parents went to sleep and in the morning went off again into the forest [to hunt marsupials].

The One descending from Mt. Abini was singing, *"kirekireso asIidome."* And the One coming down from Mt. RakItI was singing, *"doredoreee kinaso horidoreme ..."* The One singing, *"kirekireso asIdome"* reached Nagiati and the Other singing, *"doredoreee kinaso..."* reached Biriari. The One reached FututI singing, *"kirekireso ..."* The Other got to HakoyIpi calling, *"doredoreee kinaso..."* Arriving at BinumIbipi ... *"kirekireso"* .... Arriving at RuyIpi ... *"doredoreee"* ...

The Two met up with each other and asked the Boys again, "Where did your Mother and Father go?" And the Two Boys answered, "Our Mother and Father have gone into the forest and left us here." "... and when they bring home the marsupials they killed what will you give us?"

"You eat the head."	"I don't like the head."
"You eat the shoulder."	"I don't like the shoulder."
"You eat the other shoulder."	"I don't like the other shoulder."
"You eat the leg."	"I don't like the leg."
"You eat the other leg."	"I don't like the other leg."
"You eat the tail."	"I don't like the tail."
"You eat the rib cage."	"I don't like the rib cage."
"You eat the liver."	"I don't like the liver."

"You eat the lungs." "I don't like the lungs."

"You eat the kidneys." "I don't like the kidneys."

... The Mother and Father came back from the forest and asked, "Did they come and beat you again?" "They did."

The Husband said, "I am angry [lit: 'my stomach is not right']!" And his Wife took up her digging stick and the Man took his bamboo spear. They said to the Children, "You two stay here," and they made the motions of going off into the forest again. "Whose Sons do they come to *play around* with?" the Boys' Father asked and went to lie in wait for them. The Two Parents laid in wait near the house [ready] to ambush [lit: 'trick'] the Two Men.

The One came down calling out [in his fashion] and the Other came down calling out [in his fashion] and they met each other. The Two asked the Boys ... and the Two Boys in reply offered the liver and the stomach ... and the Man said to his Wife, "I am going to kill them now. [Are you ready?]" She took hold of her digging stick and he grabbed his bamboo spear and off they went. He shot One man and his Wife broke open the head of the Other. The Two of them died.

We bear children and leave them alone in the house. But if we do not kill the Two [Men] and get rid of them they will come inside the house and *play around* with our children!

hoEEEdada!

Women's story reiterates the Gimi theory of conception advanced by both sexes according to which many acts of intercourse—many "feedings" by the father—are required to bring the embryo and foetus into being part by part, limb by limb, and organ by organ. The repeated foetus-forming contributions represent the father's successive ejaculations, each loss of vital substance a diminution of his limited life-time supply (cf. Kelly 1976). The unborn exist because the Giant 'loses his head' and 'falls to pieces' over and over again. And each "head" the Giant loses is a replica-in-miniature and mirror image of himself: just as the invading penis "shoots" nourishment out of the urethra, a "first mouth" on top of the penis' "head" (glans), so does the unborn "eat the head" of the penis through its open fontanelle, a hair-surrounded "first mouth" on top of the foetal head (see Chap. 4 pp. 143 ff.). The unborn of either sex replicate the Giant not only as a diminutive set of identical anatomical features but also as embodiments of *the entire story* of the Giant's adventures inside the forest and the First Woman's house, shooting marsupials asleep in trees by day and eating open the vaginas of sleeping Girls by night, thrusting his enormous length into the hairy 'ravine' between the First Woman's thighs.

In this primordial, prenatal state of existence from which there is no exit—*no 'second door'*—everything operates according to a parthenogenetic mode of reproduction, a kind of creativity in which 'like produces like' (Frazer 1963 [1922]). Discontinuity devolves easily into continuity: those 'shot' into existence inside the womb may be effortlessly reclaimed and reabsorbed by the shooter who merely rewinds his enormous length and remains intact. "The one we have been eating has come back to eat me!" as the Dream Children declare over and over again. In women's myth of the Home Invaders, the wandering Giant arrives in the person of two 'faceless' Men singing and dancing while the Parents are "away in the forest hunting marsupials," a standard expression for having sex or 'making babies' while oblivious to one's surroundings. During sex with her husband, the myth suggests, a woman feels "invaded" by her father and brother, figures of her own prehistory who continue to visit her "house" uninvited and to wreck havoc.

During the Parents' absence 'inside the forest,' "the Boys left at home alone" try desperately to placate the Invaders by offering them, part by part and organ by organ, the marsupials their parents are shooting at this very moment! When one of the Boys says, "You can eat the head," and recites a list of marsupial parts and organs, he speaks as the unborn child to his mother's "first husband" who penetrates her "house" *whenever he feels like it*, with gay abandon, dancing down the sides of her mountainous thighs singing a lip-smacking ditty like '*fi fy fo fum...*'—the discourse of ogrish "wild men" like the Moon who come back to "play around" and never stop trying to *take back* the ones they carelessly gave up. The Boys offer their parents' other 'babies'—wild meat of the forest—as delicious substitutes for each and every morsel of themselves.

The Giant Pair arrive repeatedly, moving up and down opposite mountain sides, because they are copulating, returning to gobble up the ones they "shot" inside Mother. Like the Boy in men's Flute myth waiting to steal his Sister's Flute, the Two Invaders wait until the house is empty to make entry and "put their mouths" on the 'furry creatures' she left unattended. To the anonymous Duo—so huge their faces are out of sight—the Boys plead, in effect, 'take other meat and leave behind your "heads," the stuff upon which we feed and which *are* the Two of Us. But the Invaders are too angry to negotiate. "We don't like you," they tell the boys. Inside the dark womb, the unborn cannot *see* the Invaders as they come and go but they can *feel* their "beatings." The mucous in their noses and tears in their eyes suggest they are pubescent, with seminal fluid in their penes, aroused and in pain as they undergo the torments of first stage male initiation.

Just like the Marsupial Hunter who kills the Dream Man and all his Ilk, the missing Parents who return from the forest to lie in wait and murder the Two child-molesters are a reduplication of them. Both pairs of adults go on marsupial-hunting expeditions and both 'still' have the penis—the Mother, her digging stick, and the Father, his bamboo spear. Both the weapon-wielding Wife and her passive counterpart, the Mother whose world-size womb is the scene of the action, are "wild women." They 'still possess the flute' in men's terms because, as women see it, the Giant constantly rapes them. To rid her "house" of her "first husband" and his identical "firstborn," and to guarantee the lives of her unborn sons, the mythic heroine joins forces with her 'second husband,' stick in hand. She has to do more than her counterpart who merely 'cut the Giant down to size' and angrily discarded his huge severed portion in a river. This heroine joins forces with a Husband to help her evict the two-headed colossus who keeps invading her womb.

The best way to save her Sons' lives is to engage in the kind of exchange the myth portrays in dramatic detail as the way to compel her father and brother to eat the children's "heads" instead of the children themselves. To a mother, however, no child is exchangeable for any other *nor, certainly, for some other kind of "meat"!* The heroine resorts to violence to guarantee the lives of her children: together with her Husband, she "breaks open the head" of the capricious Home Invaders who come to "play around" inside her body. The blood that keeps "appearing between her thighs" testifies to her own murderous inclinations—even, or especially, when the life-giving alternative of exchange is spelled out over and over again, organ by organ, limb by limb. But if women's own myths sometimes show a mother's 'unfitness' and help to make the case for her exclusion from men's transactions in "head" payments, they also expose the Father-Son Duo men 'airbrush' as the Plug of "female pubic hair." This exposure is an essential first step in liberating her Sons from the Pair's vicious grasp. Once the heroines' original consorts, her "first husband" and his no-longer "little boy," are split in two—once her brother is himself no longer attached to / at the mercy of their Giant Father—her 'second husband' can oppose him as a man of *equal size*. At the conclusion of boys' first-stage initiation—which women's story describes—a woman's husband exchanges "head" payments with her brother as a coequal.

Sister-exchange marriages and exchanges of children's "heads" are the ritual *alternative* to the ending of women's myth in which the Boys' Father and Mother together murder her "first husband" and "firstborn child" portrayed here as Home Invaders; in other women's myths, as the Dream Man and Marsupial Hunter; and in common parlance, as the Moon. Instead of having to 'kill the Moon' in cahoots with his wife as he does in women's myth, in ritual exchange, a man can ignore her altogether and come to terms with her brother instead (Gillison 1993: 59ff). Long before children are born, men put in place the strategy for replacing the mother with her brother as 'male mother' to her children, one who may be *open to negotiating their lives.* The rules of sister-exchange marriage mean that, structurally speaking, the moment a woman becomes a wife she is absented from the 'atom of kinship' (Lévi-Strauss 1967, 1969[1949]; Gillison 2016). Women's myth of the Home Invaders illustrates why she is excluded and therefore why brothers-in-law need leverage over each other. Each partner in the exchange excludes his own sister on account of her 'refusal to make amends' for her role in the Father's murder—leaving her to kill the Moon *all by herself* inside the "house of shame"—and comes to terms with her brother in her stead, each man prevailing on the other to accept "head" payments *in lieu of* the Boys and as recompense for their respective Fathers' irretrievable losses.

Gift of the Head Part II: Using Intrauterine 'Events' as the Model, Men's Rites of Exchange Remake the Child Outside Its Mother's Body

The "head" payments a man presents to his wife's brother on his child's behalf symbolize his obligation to return to his mythic predecessor—his wife's "first husband" and *still-attached* "firstborn child"—every single thing the two lost to create "the Boys left at home alone." The repeated recitation of body parts in women's myth echoes the Gimi theory of procreation according to which vital organs are created within the phallic-shaped foetal core and limbs and appendages emerge from inside it. But meticulous pronouncements in myth and ritual of exactly what it takes to bring a human being into existence *in utero* proclaim a quantity that is really uncountable because it represents the unlimited measure of a woman's attachment to her own father and brother as an immensity hidden inside her since her own conception. Despite—or because of—the fact that "head" payments are designed *quid pro quo* to substantiate each and every one of the mythic father's or "first husband's" contributions, a man's debt to his male affines is virtually in perpetuity (cf. Mauss 1967 [1925]).

Rites of exchange recapitulate events in myth in order to diverge from their mythic outcome or to elaborate upon myth's tersely-stated resolution: 'and that is why we do it differently today.' In myth, which is to say, *in utero,* the too-great affinity and identical structure of Giant Invaders and unborn Boys allow the Giant to *feed* the Boys *and feed upon* them at the same time—lets him "play around" with them—with gay abandon whenever he feels like it. In the imagery of women's and men's myths, the Giant *re*absorbs his own ejaculate—*all* the stuff his children are made of—into his oversize "head" so that he remains intact and undiminished, as big as the whole world. Brothers-in-law curtail the Giant's size and unpredicatable cruelty by using the same digestive-procreative method of parthenogenetic reproduction as the model for *reciprocal* exchanges of "head" payments. Men of equal dimension repeat *ex utero* the Giant's predatory connection to his offspring, each man possessing the leverage to compel the other Giant's ritual counterparts to accept *substitutes* for his own progeny and thereby release them, feature by feature, in rite after rite, to become viably separate individuals. By the same token, the mother's father's real-life rejection of "head" payments—and the rage that inspires his rejection—prevent or end the transformation of "the head of his penis" into a daughter's or sister's child. The 'curse of the mother's brother' "is truly a radical malignancy immanent in matrifilial kinship. ... and it alone ensures that the life payments due from the ZCh to the MB will be made by hook or by crook" (Mimica In press: 61).

The only way to create individuated, socially adjustable sons and daughters is to 'cut the Giant down to size'—not violently, *leaving blood everywhere*, the way the heroines of women's myths decapitate the Giant Penis or goad their Brother-Husbands to murder the Dream Man and help cut him up into a meal *with no replacement meat*; nor by abandoning "little boys at home alone" to plead helplessly with those far bigger than they are. 'The better way' is for two of the murdered Giant's *like-size sons* to exchange replacements for his "heads."

Transfers of "head" payments are analogous to, and modelled upon, the 'head-to-head' transfers of male substance that occur in the womb between father and offspring. Outside the womb, a pair of brothers-in-law—men of equal size—engage in a relation of reciprocity. Unlike "the Boys left at home alone" in women's myth, brothers-in-law are able to compel the substitution of delectable children for cooked marsupials or pork and other material goods. By replacing the Giant's 'ejaculate' with "head" payments—*edible substance that does not emanate from him*—the Giant cannot reabsorb and treat sadistically as mere playthings the children he installed in the Womb. Origin myths do not have to come true: they can be altered and disaster forestalled when transposed on a reciprocal basis into the realm of ritual objects. Ritual 'operates' on myth by breaking up the continuous flow of *one's own* primal narrative and transfoming the pieces of one's past into consumable objects of exchange. Packaging a piece of one's own prehistory, offering it as a gift in exchange for the corresponding package of someone else's prehistory, and then "eating" it, installs *someone else's past* as part of oneself and vice versa, thus neutralizing the poisonous return of one's own 'unwanted material' (See Chap. 2, endnote 3 [Douglas 1970 (1966): 147].)

In female initiation ritual, the "head" payment is the "sugar-pig"– a cooked and dismembered marsupial or piglet encased in 50 cm lengths of sugarcane and wrapped around and around with a continuous liana vine—the material objectification of the Giant Penis' evil adventures, offered to the initiate by her prospective fathers-in-law. The affines' gift of the "head" averts the outcome women's myths describe because, converted into female initiation ritual, the Giant Penis' deeds originate with men who are not the girl's own fathers.

The Primal Scene and the Primal Crime

Interpreting the regular rites of exchange between affines, which Gimi call "eating the head of the child," in terms of women's myths and rites suggests that social relations—whatever their result in creating bonds of affinity and solidarity—are designed to 'undo' ties of incest established before *one's mother's birth* in a primordial intrauterine world. The ties are extraordinarily difficult to undo not only because they involve one's mother's origins as well as one's own, but also because they originate with a Giant Penis *all* of whose offspring are identical in shape and structure to their *unique* source. Every child is the replica-in-miniature of a Giant who lost his head, broke apart and fell to pieces inside Mother. The Gimi theory of procreation is supremely phallic: it posits only one sex—the male—with the female serving as a phallic-shaped container like a flute or house to be hollowed out or broken open, shattered, remade, emptied and refilled *ad infinitum*. The relentless phallicism of both sexes' symbolic productions, as I see it, is one expression of the main work of Gimi culture to 'erase the female' in the post-neotenous phase—which is to say, most of a person's life.

Without the input of Gimi women's myths, the ritual project of erasure is hard to discern because the actors are related categorically, that is, as members of the same patrilineal kin group. From the perspective of ritual and daily life, the critical distinction between the mother's father and brother—between the Flute Plug and the Boy who removes it (which Gimi men conflate and obscure) and between the Dream Man and Marsupial Hunter who slays him (which Gimi women expose)—may be lost because both men stand to receive their daughter / sister's brideprice and regular payments for her children's "heads."

Without the scenarios of women's myths, in other words, Gimi exchanges of "head" payments seem to derive their entire meaning from the predominate male view expressed in the Flute myth and male initiation ritual in which the mother's brother—first as murdered infant and then as a young man reborn from men in "secret" rites of initiation—emerges as culture hero. The Brother in men's Flute myth is an innocent babe, roused from blameless sleep by the hypnotic sounds of copulation and drawn irresistibly to his Sister's "flute house," the term for a menstrual hut. But by looking at women's myths and rites, we know that the *two* Sisters who play the Flutes in some versions of men's myth are really Mother and Daughter, one ensconsed inside the other 'singing the same song' because the omnivorous Giant Penis is copulating with both of them at the same time. From women's perspective, the one who "crawls out of his house," makes his way in darkness to the "flute house," and eagerly puts his lips on the blowing hole, is no baby.

Seen through Gimi women's eyes, men's Flute myth 'airbrushes' what happens next: the plug of his Sister's pubic hair that closes the hole and transfers a beard onto the Boy's face—signalling his sudden puberty—camouflages the Boy's deadly encounter with their Father. Indeed, men's Flute myth conceals the Father's presence altogether, declaring that flutes were invented and owned solely by one or two First Women: "The Flute once belonged only to women," men say. "It wasn't ours! We men stole it!" (Gillison 1993: 266). But men's myth *pictures* the consequences of what it fails to mention: the "female pubic hair" planted on the Boy's face is proof of his journey *back* into the female interior and inevitable encounter with his Father's penis. Inside his Sister / Mother, the Boy "ate the head" of the Giant, killing him and causing his Sisters' first menstrual flow, the first time the primal Father lost his head *irretrievably*.

The metanarrative implicit in Gimi men's and women's separate "secret" myths and rites seems to combine or *superimpose* two of Freud's classic constructs: *the primal scene* in which the child witnesses its parents' copulation and *the primal crime* in which a 'band of brothers' murder and devour their ogre-father and then renounce marriage to the sisters on whose account they rebelled. "Thus the brothers had no alternative, if they were to live together, but – not, perhaps, until they had passed through many dangerous crises – to institute the law against incest, by which they all alike renounced the women whom they desired and who had been their chief motive for dispatching their father" (Freud 1972 [1913]: 144). Freud seems not to have considered that the primal father's utter monopoly of every female—in Gimi men's terms, the Moon sending his Giant Penis out of the night sky to penetrate every nubile girl—enraged not only Brothers denied access to their Sisters' "plugged flutes" but also the Sisters who were likewise trapped inside Mother and whom the Father came to 'play around with' whenever he felt like it! "[T]he tumultuous mob of brothers ... hated their father, who presented such a formidable obstacle to their craving for power and sexual desires;" Freud says, "but they loved and admired him too" (*Ibid*: 143). Gimi cannibal rites of the past, orchestrated by men, suggest that there was also a "tumultuous mob" of Sisters upon whom men could foist *all the blame* for the Father's murder because, although the Sisters "hated their father" as much or more than their Brothers and were also ambivalent, they stubbornly clung to his bloody remains.

* * *

By 'situating' the primal crime inside the Womb, the combined Gimi metanarrative unites the psychic origins of both the individual and society: the act of *seeing* father-inside-mother is tantamount to, or the essential preliminary for, killing him by cutting off his head and causing first menses. Given their intrauterine setting, Gimi myths further 'revise' Freud's account of the father's murder by replacing the 'band of brothers' with a "small boy" or a "virgin girl" or a brother-sister pair. But when Gimi enact their myths in exchanges of "head" payments, they perform the Father's murder as "an act *forbidden to the individual* and justifiable only through the participation of the whole clan; nor may anyone absent himself from the killing and the meal" (*Ibid*: 140, emphasis added). "Participation of the whole clan," in the terms of Gimi women's myths, included women as co-conspirators and cannibals. But in the funeral rites orchestrated by men, women are the *only cannibals;* and they are excluded as donors in the rites of exchange that served to expiate the Father's murder. Women's 'defect,' the sexes sometimes agree, is their 'refusal' unequivocally to renouce the thing that motivated their hatred of him.

Gimi women's myths portray the primordial murder and cannibalism upon which Gimi social order rests—the decapitation and cutting up of the Dream Man and distribution of his parts to the entire community—as the deeds of a *first couple,* a Brother and Sister / Husband and Wife who were united in rage, complicit in the crime and mutually responsible for it. The same cooperation seems to underlie the sexes' *show of conflict* in ritual, for instance, in the mutually-assured outcome of the tug of war staged at the climax of female initiation between men on the roof who teasingly insert a giant sugarcane phallus and women assembled inside the menstrual hut who reach up to grab it and break it to pieces; and, especially, in the charade of cannibal rites of the past when women supposedly "stole" a man's corpse and devoured it in secret. For the Gimi, myth is more than a blueprint for rituals that convert the heroism of solitary mythic figures into collective performance. Because 'crimes of the past' took place *inside the womb*, they manifest themselves as *defects in the anatomy and physiology* of both sexes that appear "suddenly" at puberty.

'Defects' of Adolescent Anatomy

Gimi of both sexes treat the "first appearance" of anatomical and physiological changes—menarche, a beard, nocturnal emissions—as if they were the unwanted consequences of a primordial deed—*a crime sister and brother committed together*—but for which only the female remains unwillling to atone and therefore primarily responsible. Gimi women disagree with men on which sex took the initiative and is still largely to blame for the Father's murder. But to disagree on this crucial issue women necessarily share with men the main narrative of prehistory. The markers of adolescence, anatomical features like whiskers and menstrual blood, are 'shameful residues' of the primal crime—a murderous *theft*—the sexes committed *together* in the primordial era but that now define the *differences* between them. One way to make amends for the primal crime is to try to 'undo' it by erasing its visible consequences: that is, to *send back* to its source in the other sex the features one's own sex acquired during joint commission of the crime—*attributes of the other sex*, "female public hair" on a boy's face and "blood of the penis" leaking out of a girl's vagina—thereby ridding one's own body of the crime's disfiguring traces.

Before sending a bride away in marriage, her fathers "take revenge" for her mythic crime by tattooing a "beard" around the bride's mouth, *giving back* the pubic hair her mythic counterpart implanted on the face of her Brother while he was a mere babe, crawling on all fours and *unable to see* where he put his mouth, while she was already grown and fully aware, engaged in ecstatic raptures with a Father she kept to herself. (See Chap. 1, Fig. 1.1.) In the same sudden way they first appeared, indecent proofs of the primal crime—menstrual blood and a beard—can be sent out of oneself back into the body of one's brother or sister where they originated and rightfully belong because it was *the other sex who knew*, whose eyes were open, while one's own sex was blind or oblivious and trusting, tricked and misled, as innocent as a babe in tall grass or a virgin girl asleep in her mother's house. In the shared narrative that inspires both sexes' "secret" songs, myths and rites, blame for human misery is manifest in the anatomical features that separate the sexes at adolescence and circulate between them afterwards like a poison gift. 'When the music stops' in the sexes' "secret" round of exchanges of beards and menstrual blood, only one sex—the male—manages to purify his body and escape blame for the Father's murder.

Zero Sum Game: Blame as an 'Object of Exchange' Between the Sexes

According to men's Flute myth, the Boy's acquiring a beard and his Sister's first menstruation are virtually simultaneous. As soon as the Boy's lips touch the Plug of his Sister's pubic hair, *her* hair starts to grow on *his* face. Unable to produce a sound, the Boy looks down and sees the Plug and pulls it out of his Sister, causing her to menstruate for the first time. The siblings intrauterine encounter—condensed and camoflauged in the Boy's crawling into his Sister's house and unplugging her Flute—is tantamount, in women's terms, to decapitating the Giant or, in ordinary parlance, "killing the Moon," *while he is ensconsed inside Mother.* Although left unsaid in men's myth, men enact the belief that unplugging his Sister's Flute has consequences for the Boy beyond the appearance of her pubic hair on his face that leave no doubt about his participation in the primal crime. In "secret" rites near the end of boys' first initiation, they are led to an icy forest stream in the forest where men bleed their noses: held by an older boy, each initiate stands shivering with his head bent forward. His initiators jab and sharply withdraw a plug of stinging nettles to induce a heavy flow, creating a "hot" blood-soaked wad like the tampon a woman uses when she menstruates (Gillison 1993: 183–84). Murdering the Father left bloody residues inside *both* sister *and* brother.

The siblings' new adolescent bodies reveal their joint crime in mythic prehistory. But the sudden way that a beard or menstrual blood appears suggests that the crime was fleeting, intended yet inadvertant, a mere touch that transferred the First Woman's pubic hair onto the face of her baby Brother, turning him into a man before his time; or that it was highly motivated and wholly justified, but impulsive, as the First Woman cut the Giant down to size and discarded his remains intact. If each sex acquired secondary sexual characteristics from the other sex during a momentary 'transaction,' then a boy's facial hair and a girl's menstrual blood can be made to disappear by sending each one *back to the other sex* and undoing the exchange. A Gimi boy who plays, handles or so much as touches a flute before his initiation, immediately sprouts a beard and, after cycling through life at warp speed, dies an early death. Not only do men give a boy's beard *back* to his sister by tattooing a beard around the bride's mouth before she marries, until advanced age, men traditionally extracted each whisker, using a tiny loop of bamboo string as a tweezer. But "female pubic hair"—however shameful, especially when it appears on a man's face!—is just camouflage, as men secretly admit when they bleed the initiates' noses. Like the pubic-hair Plug the Brother pulls out of his Sister, a man's beard hides something hard and bloodied—the severed "head" of the Giant Penis, "the firstborn child of the Moon." The "Moon's blood" men expel from the noses of adolescent initiates and from their own noses in self-administered purgings throughout most of adult life, first entered their bodies in the mythic past, during the fatal 'return trip' inside Mother to decapitate the Father and liberate their

Sisters. "When a man shoots [sharp grass up] his nose," one man told me, "he sends the blood of his sister *back* to his sister. The man wants to get this blood *out* of his body. 'Let the blood of my sister return to my sister!' we men say."

The "secret" blood songs Gimi women teach female initiates to end their periods seem to be the precise response—or provocation?—to men's "secret" blood-letting rites. To end her period, a woman sends her menstrual blood *back* to its "true source" in her brother's nose. "What the Moon kills," one woman told me, "is blood from our brothers' noses. Those boys give us their blood." In "blood songs," the menstruator addresses her blood in the intimate form of addresss as "you, my brother's nose-water." In separate verses, she names six or seven of her real and close classificatory brothers. Women's blood songs also name Papuan Lorikeets and other red birds. "We name [these birds] because they are red. We name them so the initiate will bear a healthy child. ... The blood of the bird – [inserting a brother's name] – refers to 'the nose blood of the boy who is inside me.' We get rid of this so that *now* 'the true child can sleep in my belly.'" Speaking in the voice of an initiate, her chaperon added: "'The Moon kills me so I recite these spells. I name my brothers. … The song gets rid of their blood.'" By no coincidence, the red birds women name in their "blood songs" are also men's "secret" names for the initiates whose noses they bleed in freezing forest streams and whom, in preparation for emergence from seclusion inside the men's house, they decorate in shining red pandanus oil and gorgeous red feather headdresses (Gillison 1993: 183–85).

Note

1. Because of their intimate connection, Gimi myths and rites are often discussed together. Mythic figures and artifacts are capitalized to distinguish them from their ritual counterparts. But pronouns that refer to mythic figures appear in lower case. Big Man and Big Woman, individuals recognized as important persons and leaders in the community, are also capitalized.

References

Bateson, Gregory. 1958 [1936]. *Naven. A Survey of the Problems Suggested by a Composite Picture of a Culture of a New Guinea Tribe Drawn from Three Points of View.* Stanford: Stanford University Press.

Douglas, Mary. 1970 [1966]. *Purity and Danger. An Analysis of Concepts of Pollution and Taboo.* London: Pelican Books.

Frazer, Sir James George. 1963 [1922]. *The Golden Bough: A Study in Magic and Religion.* Abridged ed. New York: Macmillan.

Freud, Sigmund. 1972 [1913]. *Totem and Taboo.* Translated by James Strachey [1950]. London: Routledge and Kegan Paul.

Gillison, Gillian. 1993. *Between Culture and Fantasy.* Chicago: University of Chicago Press.

———. 2016. Whatever Happened to the Mother? A New Look at the Old Problem of the Mother's Brother in Three New Guinea Societies: Gimi, Daribi and Iatmul. *Oceania* 86 (I): 2–24.

Gough, Kathleen E. 1955. Female Initiation on the Malabar Coast. *Journal of the Royal Anthropological Society of Great Britain and Ireland* 85 (1/2): 45–80.

Kelly, Raymond C. 1976. Witchcraft and Sexual Relations: An Exploration in the Social and Semantic Implications of the Structure of Belief. In *Man and Woman in the NewGuinea Highlands*, ed. Paula Brown and Georgeda Buchbinder . Washington, DC: American Anthropological Association. Special Publication no. 8.

Lévi-Strauss, Claude. 1967. "Structural Analysis in Linguistics and in Anthropology," Chapter II in *Structural Anthropology.* Translated by Claire Jacobson and Brooke Grundfest Schoepf. Garden City, N.Y.: Anchor Books.

———. 1969 [1949]. *The Elementary Structures of Kinship.* Boston: Beacon Press.

Mauss, Marcel. 1967 [1925]. *The Gift. Forms and Functions of Exchange in Archaic Societies.* New York: W. W. Norton & Company.

Mimica, Jadran. In press. *Of Humans, Pigs and Souls: An Essay on the Yagwoia 'Womba' (Cannibal) Complex.* Hau Malinowski Monograph Series. University of Chicago Press (forthcoming July 2020).

Wagner, Roy. 1967. *The Curse of Souw: Principles of Daribi Clan Definition and Alliances in New Guinea.* Chicago: University of Chicago Press.

6

The Problem with Women

'Tis grief that stops her utterance, and words sufficiently indignant fail her tongue …
Nor is there room for weeping. But she rushes onward …
And is wholly occupied in the contrivance of revenge.
Ovid. *The Metamorphoses.* Book VI: "Tereus, Procne, and Philomela."

Is Anatomy Destiny?

Unlike *Totem and Taboo*, where Freud ventures into anthropology, his observations about "the psychical consequences of the anatomical distinction between the sexes" are addressed to fellow psychoanalysts and mostly concern the childhoods of early twentieth Century European analysands (Freud 1974 [1925]). Freud outlines a "practical" method *for psychoanalysts* "slowly and laboriously [to drag] up from the depths … [and] accurately guage … the time of the early efflorescence of sexual life … [that is] remodeled and overlaid in adult life" (*Ibid*: 17–18). In the individual, the developmental process is multi-phased and non-linear. It

G. Gillison, *She Speaks Her Anger: Myths and Conversations of Gimi Women*, Culture, Mind, and Society, https://doi.org/10.1007/978-3-030-49352-3_6

begins "at a very early age [with the child's] listening to his parents copulating" (*Ibid*: 19), being awakened or sexually aroused but unable to grasp what he hears. Only in retrospect, "owing to its after-effects … may … that event act as the starting point for the child's whole sexual development" (*Ibid*). Only later on, in consequence of new experiences, especially around puberty, is the child able to attach *visual* and narrative meanings to what it *heard* or felt as a baby and young child.

The psychic mechanism of *nachtraglich* or *après-coup* means that infantile experiences, sensations and memory traces, such as listening to parental intercourse, observing the genitals of the opposite sex or performing masturbation, are always reworked and reexperienced. This includes the "momentous discovery which little girls are destined to make [when t]hey notice the penis of a brother or playmate, strikingly visible and of large proportions … and from that time forward fall a victim to envy for the penis." But in pointing out the girl's tragic discovery and judgment – "[s]he has seen it and knows that she is without it and wants to have it" (Freud 1974 [1925]: 21) – Freud includes the overlay of the life the analysande has lived since, her complex remodelling of infantile experiences according to her own personal history which is inseparable from her social and cultural milieu. Despite the fact that Freud summarizes individuals' clinical analyses in anatomical terms, his theory does *not* rest upon the simple fact that little boys have penises and little girls do not. Such a finding would contravene Freud's own conclusions about "the bisexual disposition [of] … all human individuals … [who] combine in themselves both masculine and feminine characteristics, so that pure masculinity and femininity remain theoretical constructions of uncertain content" (*Ibid*: 25).

For Gimi of both sexes, the vagina is first of all the site of menstrual bleeding, something no 'little girl' or 'little boy' is likely to observe at first sight of a playmate or sibling or even an adult woman. The interpretation of the bleeding vagina as residual evidence of a severed or 'decapitated' penis appears to be a very grown-up myth. The question for the Gimi and many others, then, is why a culture or world view would 'remodel' generic infantile experiences into dogmas of violent sexual polarity which fixate on genital difference and ignore the biological substrate of strong resemblance.

> Men and women are, of course, different. But they are not as different as day and night, earth and sky, yin and yang, life and death. In fact, from the standpoint of nature, men and women are closer to each other than either is to anything else. … [T]he idea that men and women are two mutually exclusive categories must arise out of something other than a nonexistent "natural" opposition. Far from being an expression of natural differences, exclusive gender identity is the suppression of natural similarities (Rubin 1975: 179-80.)

Gimi women's collaboration with men in the public resolution of their "secret" dispute makes women complicit in their own subjugation but hardly explains their motivations. The terms of the dispute – the separate and corresponding ways women and men refer to the Red Lorikeet, for instance – provide clues about the deep narrative upon which they agree to differ and why women acquiesce. To end her period and hasten pregnancy, Gimi women teach a female initiate secret songs to send her blood back where it came from, into the noses of the Red Lorikeets whom the songs identify in separate verses as her own real and close classificatory post-adolescent brothers (Gillison 1993: 184ff). In response, or as part of the cycle, men refer to the male initiates whose noses they bleed as Red Lorikeets. Men's purificatory ordeals send the boys' blood back inside their sisters' vaginas. In secret songs and rites, Gimi men and women engage in a clandestine 'dead-child exchange' in which the dead child, symbolized as either menstrual blood or nose blood, stands for the mythic Father's bloody severed head. (See Chap. 5.)

But when the exchange of children between the sexes is carried over into the public arena, in rites of passage and transfers of "head" payments, women are replaced by their husbands and brothers. In women's hands, the 'bloodied birds' – the Moon's children, the murdered "firstborns" – are transferred from one lethal site (the girl's menstruating vagina) to another (her adolescent brother's bleeding nose). When sisters rid their bodies of 'dead birds' by sending them *back* to their brothers, they show themselves to be unworthy partners in exchange, *unwilling to traffic in substitutes*, leaving men no choice but to bypass women and 'transact' the children among themselves. In "secret" rites, men purge the initiate of his sister's 'dead child' – *her* menstrual blood flooding *his* nose – but they also concoct a substitute called "the head of the child" – cooked pork or marsupial meat – to present to the mother's brother.

The only way to bring "firstborns" back to life is for a pair of brothers-in-law, men who stand as equals to one another in the exchange of sisters, to remove the children from their mothers' "hands" and exchange them with each other in the form of substitute meat or "head" payments. At the end of weeks of grueling initiation rites, men show off the results of removing 'dead' boys from their mothers, 'gestating' them inside the men's house, and carrying them back into daylight reborn as gorgeous Red Lokikeets perched on the shoulders of their mothers' brothers. Adorned with red feather headdresses, faces and bodies smeared in gleaming red pandanus oil, the boys sit astride the shoulders of their mothers' brothers who give out joyful war cries as they run out the door at one end of the long oval men's house, along an outer wall, back into the house through the opposite door, through the central corridor and out the first door again, each circuit representing movement out, back inside and all the way through a house-size Flute or two-holed Mother. After three or four noisy circuits back inside, through the central corridor and out the other door of the men's house, each brother-in-law and mother's brother sets down his charge beside a stack of cooked pork and other valuables his exchange partner, who is the boy's father, has assembled to "buy his head" (Gillison 1993: 278).

Everything relating to the young male bird-initiates, especially the flutes, called "birds," whose wind-made music is "cries of the newborn," emphasizes flight, untethered beauty wafting skyward, magnificent tail-feathers swaying in soft breezes. The imagery of men's songs and performances insist that a boy reborn in initiation is set free as a bird, launched into life as a *separate entity* unattached to the ground upon which his "firstborn" self fell from the womb "with a loud thud." Unlike a mother – except the one portrayed in certain women's myths (see below page 213 ff.) – a mother's *brother*, simply because he is a man, can be persuaded to accept *substitutes* for his sister's child. In exchanges of "head" payments, each brother-in-law "eats the head" of the other's child instead of the child itself, as if the Home Invaders in women's myth were made to relent and accept every limb and organ of the marsupials the Boys offer as substitutes for themselves. By "eating the head of the child," the initiate's mother's brother – in stark contrast to his own mother – *does not refuse* to release the child from its mythic origins and so does not impose a curse.

The men's reciprocal arrangment allows each child to escape its mother's clutches and, perhaps, its own inclinations, like those of the Hunter in women's Python myth who took out his own eyes before climbing into the Cassowary's anus, eager to retravel the "road he first came down," and devour everything he finds at his destination.

The explanation for why Gimi men mainly win the argument with women about which one is still to blame for the primal crime and likely to repeat it – which one not only killed and ate the father in the mythic past but also, to this day, 'refuses to make amends' by accepting a substitute and letting go of her father-begotten child – tends to affirm Freud's dictum, taken from Napoleon, that "anatomy is destiny" – *on condition*, as I argue, that possession of a vagina is interpreted as far more than a missing penis. As the site of menstrual bleeding that starts at puberty and continues throughout child-bearing years, a woman's vagina is the place where a child *dies* not only at first menses, and once a month thereafter, but also at the end of its long post-partum attachment to her as the condition of human neoteny.

The negative assessment of female anatomy as the primary site of death rather than of life derives, as I see it in Gimi terms, from radical condensation of the female role in sex and reproduction starting with menstruation, including detumescence after climax, a mother's capacity to watch a wholly-dependent infant emerge 'with eyes closed' "between her thighs" and, most important perhaps, the eventual imperative to separate not only from her as a person and the enclosed mother-child zone she dominates, but also from the 'habit of mind' that allows *no substitutes*. Years of breast feeding, close body-contact, a mother's murmurings, soothing nonsense sounds, sweet whisperings and other wordless communications and ceaseless care create a unique *dyadic* universe of psychological as well as physical intimacy. But the very same maternal tie crucial to the child's early survival and ability to thrive becomes, with the passage of time, the opposite of what it started out to be. As the child grows increasingly adept, able to sit, crawl, walk, feed itself, control the release of urine and feces, and communicate through language, an over-close tie to mother cripples the advance to self-sufficiency it originally fostered, threatening the child's capacity to mature and engage in a full range of *triadic* social relations upon which group life depends. Only with men's help and supervision, and by exclusion and wholesale denigration of their sex with which Gimi women seem often to agree, can the severance from mother essential to every child's success be assured. The vast cultural machinery put in place to end *each person's* 'childish ways' speaks to the crucial importance and immense difficulty of the task.

From this perspective, it is easy to understand what is otherwise perplexing, namely, why the onset of menstruation, a sign of robust health and readiness to propagate the species, is almost universally miscontrued as dangerous or deadly. When Gimi and other peoples interpret first menses as a stillbirth, the discharge of dead blood that otherwise "might have been cherished to make a child," they treat it as material proof of the *lethally ambivalent* nature of motherhood (Mead 1970: 248). So connected is a mother to the child no longer an actual part of her body or attached to it like an appendage that her inclination is to kill it rather than let it go by *accepting a substitute*. The very essence of Gimi magic and sorcery is the attempt to redeploy the supreme power for good or ill inherent in the *dyadic maternal condition*; to perpetuate outside the womb the kind of union established at the moment of birth when the child "passes between her thighs" into the visible world. In gardening, pig-rearing, hunting and love, the spell-sayer aims to merge her or his own animating life force with that of the nurtured or manipulated object so that their two spirits – *the one all-knowing, the other unaware* – are joined in perfect union. A mother or spell-sayer uses the wiles of seduction to lure her charge into a state of seamless oneness with her so that her wish becomes an irresistable command and virtual *fait accompli*. Such connection may have a miraculous effect on plants, pigs, babies and other things, such as Karapmene's charmed cigarettes or a female initiate's co-wife-beating baton (see Chap. 3), but it is hellish for a grown child, impeding its capacity for independent volition and wider social relations, especially men's organization for war.

The over-kill Gimi use to break the mother's spell indicate just how difficult a task both sexes deem it to be. A great deal of the work of Gimi culture – which women help to create, participate in and protest against – consists in attempts to erase the female sex "through violence against women (including female infanticide), residential and other kinds of segregation, and especially vilification and symbolic abolition of female attributes and existence" (Gillison 2016: 4). According to the ever-operative law of talion, these anti-female institutions are held to be mainly defensive and *preemptory*, the life-saving response to those who would eventually kill and devour all they bring to life and cultivate. No matter how lovingly she applies it at the start, a mother's uninterrupted embrace turns out to be malignant.

What is the source of ambivalence in a mother's devotion? Nothing in Gimi culture *just is* – everything has a mythic prehistory and *raison d'etre*. There is no notion of a maternal 'instinct' born at the moment of conception or parturition, nor the sense that motherhood is a dedication so demanding and prolonged that it becomes habitual and cannot die nor be diverted. Gimi myths and rites of both sexes show that a mother's ferocious attachment to her child is a 'reincarnation' of her longing for her father's Giant Penis, recalling Freud's profound insight about women's "penis envy" (Freud 1937). But Gimi women's productions also suggest that the father's mythic penis is an object of deep hatred – the invader she decapitates, precipitating her own scandalous menstrual flow. When Gimi women first explained to me that their mythology was the "true source" of garden and pig magic, that "only those of us who understand [the myths] know how to speak to food," I could not reconcile the exquisite tenderness and intimacy of 'food talk,' filled with sweet nonsense and images of resplendent wildlife, with the incest, murder, and cannibalism that were themes of women's myths (Gillison 1993: 169–172). Gradually I realized that the things a woman nurtures like plants and pigs she identifies not only with the babies she cherishes but also with the Son the Wild Woman murdered and cooked like a suckling pig and then presented to her "first husband" as a meal of revenge served piping hot.

The Myth of the Torrent Lark

In women's myth of the Torrent Lark,[1] the heroine is a beauty whom every man wanted to marry, the very kind whom Karapmene described as her young self (see Chap. 3). And, like most heroines in women's myths, she is accompanied by her Mother.

Fig. 6.1 A performance of ritual theatre reprising a theme of women's myths in which an Ugly Old Man acquires a beautiful wife and child with foul tricks instead of brideprice (© David Gillison)

hoEEE dada

A Woman bore and raised a beautiful Daughter. Men far and wide wanted to marry her. "Marry me!" said one. "Marry me!" said another. "Marry me!" said another. "I want her!" they all cried. The Daughter was a real beauty – one of a kind.

She lived in a house in the forest where a Trouble-Maker (*koreda*, lit: *kore*, 'wild' or 'spirit' + *ba*, 'man') followed her. He saw a ringtailed possum (*maboni*) go up a tree. He killed it, emptied the intestines and stuffed the feces into a tiny bamboo tube that he hid inside his hair [behind his ear]. "Soon it will be dark," he said, although darkness was not close.

The Two Women ate the possum and went to sleep in a bush house [a lean-to with a roof of dried sugarcane leaves used as a hunting lodge and for assignations] without a care. Mother and Daughter went to sleep facing each other. The Trouble-Maker lay down in a corner of the house. Then he got up and looked at the Girl. She had taken off her bark-string skirts, uncovering her vagina and her anus. He smeared the possum feces over his face and lay back down with his face in the Girl's buttocks.

The Mother awoke and looked at him. "Oh!" she gasped. "He sleeps with his head in her anus!" She blew on the embers and saw the Trouble-Maker asleep. Then she poked her Daughter awake with the fire tongs.... "You have put something [defecated] into the eyes of the Old Man sleeping near you!" The Girl sat up beside her Mother and the two of them wept.

At dawn the Mother said to her Daughter, "You must marry him." The Daughter, who was a Story-Woman (*nenebadaha*, lit: *nene* 'moral [of the story]' + *badaha*, 'woman'), quickly became pregnant. The Child lying inside her closed her body.... Being a Story-Woman, she bore the Child quickly. "Let us make a garden," her Husband said....

The Two were married and made a garden and planted taro. One day ... the Old Woman arrived to help them weed.... As her Son-in-Law was heating the stones [for an earth oven], he quietly began to sing [to the baby]

> *maboni kauro ponikauro kiagia*
> *[possum-child taro-leaf trala trala trala trala]*

Hearing the song, the Old Woman realized that the Son her Daughter bore was the Child of a trick! "You used a possum's feces to trick us!" she thought.

She told her Daughter. "I am enraged and sick at heart (lit: 'my insides are bad'), her Daughter said. I have married a rotten Man!" The young Wife took her Baby from its net bag and laid him on the ground. She went down to the lower reaches of the river and gathered leaves of a ficus tree – leaves that were black on top and red underneath. She tied them to herself like tailfeathers and they fit perfectly. She got more ficus leaves and put them on her chest, first on one side, then on the other. And they were like the feathers of a bird. Without a hitch, she flew down to the estuary and back up to the source of the river high in the mountains.

Sure that she was well and truly able to fly, the Story-Woman killed her Son [striking him on the head with a stone] and prepared a *magaru* [an oven made from a large hollowed-out tree stump]. She placed the [heated] stones inside the oven. She peeled taros and bananas and tied leafy greens into bundles and piled them high [inside the oven]. Then she placed the Child on top, lying him on his side [in the foetal position] together with his arm bands and knee bands, and covered him with more food. Then she closed the oven. That is how it is told.

When the cooking time was over, her Husband arrived and said, "Why don't you empty the oven?" "You do it!" she said to him. "I worked hard to *fill* the oven. So now you – you ugly Old Man – *you* empty it!" And so he did. He went down deeper and deeper through the layers of food and took a bite. "This does not taste right [lit: sweet] to me," he said. "Ah! What is this?" he cried. "An upper arm band!" "Oh," said his Wife, "I carried the vegetables from the garden in the net bag I use for the Baby. It must have gotten mixed in."

Her Husband continued to unload the oven. He went down and down and down. "I see the Child's knee bands!" he exclaimed. But again his Wife said, "Never mind! I used the Child's net bag to carry the vegetables …" And so the Old Man went deeper and deeper into the oven until he saw a wrist band. He unloaded some more and saw the other wrist band but said, "You must have used the Child's net bag …" "Yes," said his Wife. "Now you eat!" At last the Old Man saw his Son [cooked like a suckling pig], his bare wrist bones piercing the shrunken skin of his tightly-curled hands and bare ankle bones piercing the shrunken skin of his tightly-curled feet.

The Old Man went into his house to tighten his bow. "What are you looking for?" his Wife asked him. She had placed the ficus leaves on her hips and with a long sharp stick she jabbed a ripe pandanus fruit. The red oil gushed out noisily and covered her body. She sat on a fence … [hopped] on top of a nearby stand of sugarcane … [lept] up onto the roof of the house … alit again on the sugarcane [back and forth, back and forth she went trying to take off …].

Giving out a cry of "*netere netere netere netere*," the Wife flew to the lower reaches of the river. Her Husband tried to shoot her but she had flown away.

You, Woman, you are the *netere* bird [Torrent Lark] who lives on the shore.

hoEEE dada

The Story Woman (*nenebadaha*) is a Wild Woman (*korebadaha*). She kills and cooks her Child, presents it to her Husband to eat and then escapes as a Torrent Lark. In other versions of women's myth, the heroine and her Mother escape together to dwell as a pair of Torrent Larks on the banks of rivers at lower elevations, paralleling women's initiation rites in which the First Woman is a *dual figure* of Daughter ensconsed in Mother and the many versions of men's Flute myth with two First Women instead of one. In the dead of night as part of the 24-hour cycle of activities during the combined celebrations for marriages and first-stage male initiations, women perform duets in playlets of their own invention that bring to vivid life these figures of myth (Fig. 6.2).

In the Torrent Lark dance, two women – the beautiful Daughter and her Mother who escapes with her into the forest or two gorgeous Sisters – decorate their bodies with white clay and poinsettias and other leaves to resemble the Torrent Lark. "The bird sings, 'I go down to the water's edge but I will fly back to see you!'" one female spectator remarked. The pair of birds "fly up" from the river basin to "waken" the sleepy revelers inside the stifling women's houses and communal men's houses where brides and male initiates are separately secluded. "The dancers [are] the Torrent Larks who fly down to the river! They do not marry (lit: 'go to men'). They have no [true] children. They are like birds. They are free."

Fig. 6.2 During all night revels to celebrate upcoming marriages, when those inside the crowded, stifling women's house begin to doze, a pair of Wild Women 'fly up' from their forest home on the banks of a river to wake the revelers and show off their Wild Child (© David Gillison)

The Dance of the Torrent Lark

The Torrent Lark playlet is a duet of two ravishing Wild Women – a Mother and Daughter or two Sisters – who come "inside" to celebrate their freedom and show off their Wild Child, a bamboo tube decorated with poinsettias which the pair toss back and forth between them as they prance on the spot, giving out the Torrent Lark's cry, "*terere terere terere terere*" and singing in separate verses, "Torrrent Lark … Papuan Lory, I am one of your kind come up from the riverbank …. Tiny Kingfisher … Pygmy Parakeet, I am one of your kind come up from the riverbank …" The song of the Torrent Lark names other species because, like most birds, the Torrent Lark is one of a pair that combines large and small members, one being the child or younger sibling of the other. The Torrent Lark (*neterebuda*) is senior to the Kingfisher; the "big" Papuan Lory is the elder of the Pygmy Parakeet.

In the Torrent Lark playlet, the two dancers identify themselves first as Torrent Lark and Kingfisher – a dazzling pair of "wild" mother-daughter or two-sister incarnations – who have flown up from the banks of two rushing torrents that border the settlement to "look at you" revelers and rejoice in their "wild child," the bamboo prop they toss back and forth between them. Referring to the Torrent Lark myth, one female spectator commented:

> The Woman killed her Child and became a Torrent Lark and flew down to the river's edge. Now the two Wild Women – they have no husbands! – bring their Wild Child and sing, "We two Torrent Larks carry the Wild Child' up here." … The Child has died and rotted away but the Two hold his spirit (lit: *kore*). They bring him up here to show him off to everyone: "We two Torrent Larks bring the Child inside [the settlement (lit: 'house')]."

The paired birds in many of women's theatrical productions represent the 'doubled lives' not only of mythic Mother and Daughter, or of the two Sisters who serve as the First Women in many versions of men's Flute myth; but also of the "firstborn child" (lit: *maru arak*), who is "the same as menstrual blood," and the "second" child born alive who suckles at the breast. A surviving eldest child is also *maru arak* (on account of which he

Fig. 6.3 In a performance of ritual theatre during the nightime revels to celebrate marriages, a duet of Wild Women – a Mother and Daughter or two Sisters – pay a visit to the settlement from their home on the banks of a river to proclaim their freedom as unmarried creatures of the forest and to show off their Wild Child, a bamboo tube decorated with red leaves which the pair toss back and forth between them as they sing and prance on the spot. (© David Gillison)

or she[2] was never eaten in cannibal rites of the past); but a living *maru arak* also has a predeceased 'alter-ego' embodied in the umbilicus and placenta which women dispose of with scrupulous care (see Chap. 3). Just like menstrual blood or a stillborn child, the afterbirth of a child born alive has a lasting spirit that, improperly discarded, may grow to monstrous proportion in the wild.

The bamboo tube women decorate with leaves and toss back and forth between them during the nighttime performance represents the Wild Child or Story Child. It is called *kaiba ridi* (lit: *kaiba* + *ridi*, 'bamboo'), a name similar to *kamiba ridi* (lit: *kamiba*, 'fictitious bird' + *ridi*), the term men use to refer to their sacred bamboo flutes when speaking to women and the uninitiated. The bamboo child the Wild Women display in their dances for all to see "has died and rotted away" and its spirit now lives with the two Women inside the forest. The "bird" men hide from women in the rafters of the men's house and play in haunting duets is a Child they *rescue* from the forest and make "cry" with syncopated life. Goran explained how men use the *kamiba* as a ruse:

> … [We] men blow flutes to fool women. The *kamiba* (lit: fictitious bird) lives in the bush and we capture it and make it cry. It is our child. We men capture the bird in the forest and look after it as though it were a *real child* … Men look after this thing…. We play the flutes (lit: *ridi,* 'bamboos') for a long while and then we [deliberately] mess up … make the notes go awry [lit: 'explode']. We put a dog near [the men's house so when] it barks women will think the dog bit the bird! … The bird lets out a terrific scream and men shout that the dog bit the bird's leg! The women hear this and think, "The men are telling the truth." That is how we trick women.
>
> … Playing the flute is [like] having sex and making a child. The sounds [that emerge from] the flute's open end are the baby's cries…. the baby is coming outside! … Men look at women's vaginas and create the mouth of the flute. We etch (lit: 'cut') "pubic hair" around it. Blowing into the flute makes the child come out the [other] end. Then we take a blade of grass (lit: 'parsley') [hold it between the little fingers of cupped hands] and blow on it to make the [high-pitched vibrating] '*whahee whahee whahee*' cries of a baby being born.

Two Bamboo Babies

The bamboo prop or *kaiba ridi* the two Wild Women dancers toss back and forth makes a rattley noise: the Wild Child women rear without husbands inside forest sounds very unlike the music of flutes. Like many items in the paired and polarized Gimi universe, the *kaiba ridi* evokes the thing it is not: the *kamiba ridi*, a seductively-crying "child" men bring *out of the forest* – not to show off before a sleepy audience during a few nights of revelry – but to live with them permanently inside the men's house where no woman or uninitiated boy ever lays eyes on him. The two bamboo babies – one a rattling phantom, the other "crying" and alive – condense into ritual objects women's and men's opposing myths of who seduced/raped whom and whose body still possesses traces of the primal Father's severed "head."

Gimi men find ways to deny that the primal Father even existed let alone that their own bodies hide his murdered blood: the blood they discharge in self-inflicted nose- and penis-bleeding rites of purification is blood that originates in their *mothers* – that is in the Child *she* killed – who is their very resurrected selves. According to men's Flute myth, the baby Boy had no choice but to put his lips on his Sister's vagina because she plugged the blowing hole with her own pubic hair. He started to grow a beard after just *once*, innocently, touching her Flute Plug because his much older, sexually-aware Sister maliciously "planted" her pubic hair on his face! The "beards" men tattoo around the mouths of sisters before they exchange them in marriage, and the pair of flutes whose blowing holes they etch with "female pubic hair" in designs that match the brides' tattoos and send to their husbands inside the brides' own net bags supposedly without their knowing it, are tokens of revenge. As one Gimi man remarked in 1983:

> Men look at woman's vagina and make the hole in the flute. A man had no whiskers until he played the flute! It was because he put his head down [and touched] a woman's vagina that he got a beard. That made men *furious*. Women have no beards? … So we tattoo them.

But men's myth cryptically suggests what men vehemently deny: namely, that the transfer of pubic hair from grown-up Sister's vagina onto baby Brother's face – in the moment before he saw the plug and pulled it out of his Sister causing her first menses – camouflages the transfer of Moon's blood *from him to her*. Men's Flute myth pictures but does not put into words equivalences between the baby Boy hiding in tall grass, the impenetrable plug of Sister's pubic hair, and the Father's huge erect Penis 'stuck' inside the Sister. Men's myth says that the Boy's pulling out the pubic hair Plug caused his Sister to menstruate for the first time and therefore to lose possession of the Flute she "invented and kept for herself alone." But when men's myth is compared to women's alternative accounts of the same scene, "pulling out the plug" and "causing the first menstruation" look like air-brushed images of the Boy – a.k.a. Marsupial Hunter or Python's Brother-in-law – decapitating the Giant *in flagrante delicto*. The Baby-thief ends up *without a trace of Giant's blood on him* not because he is blind and innocent, nor because his Sister *was all alone*, or alone with her Mother, as men's myths insist, but rather because men take violent measures to remove the Giant-Moon's blood from male initiates in "secret" nose-bleeding rites. Just as the Sister's extracted Plug of pubic hair concealed the Giant's bloody severed "head" so did the transfer of hair onto the boy's face. As women sing in songs to end their menstual flow, Moon's blood floods their brothers' noses, too. Men are able to keep it 'out of sight' by secretly bleeding initiates' noses inside the forest and meticulously depilitating facial hair.

Women's myths propose a different origin for the blood in men's noses and for the 'black stains' on their faces. They are not "female pubic hair" transferred from a seductive Sister onto her baby Brother but rather feces, foul-smelling like menstrual blood, transferred *from* the face of the dirty Old Man Trouble-Maker *onto* the anus of the Virgin Girl after he *blinded himself* with lust. Women's Torrent Lark myth 'unpacks' the euphemisms and condensations of men's Flute myth, in which the Sister *looks* as though she makes music all by herself, or with another Woman, and reveals the presence of a rotten Trickster who comes to "play around" with her inside her Mother's house. One of the three terms for a menstrual hut, besides "flute house," and "house of shame," is 'toilet' (*arega* lit: *are* 'feces' + *ga* 'place'). The Old Man fools the Heroine and her Mother by using marsupial feces to make it *look* as though *she shamed him* by defecating onto his face in her sleep. For the Old Man's crime against her, the heroine takes terrible revenge, killing her "firstborn," feeding him to her "first husband" and escaping permanently into the forest as a Torrent Lark.

The evil Trickster, Old Man Trouble-Maker in the Torrent Lark myth is another version of the Cassowary Hunter in women's Python myth who took out his eyes before climbing into the Cassowary's anus and then, because his Wife stole his eyes while he was blissfully dining, slithered along the ground like a giant Snake, his eye sockets filled with mud and worms and other dark debris. The humiliated Hunter makes a pact with his wild counterpart, the Python, to take revenge against his Wife by raping their Daughter: the Python enters her vagina and comes out her mouth, killing her in orgasmic fury at both ends of her body while tearing open a "second vagina" in her head. In the Python myth, and in the rite of female initiation it narrates, the only way for the heroine to get the Giant out of her body is for her Brother or Mother's Brother to cut off the Giant's head while it is still furiously vibrating inside her mouth, transforming her mouth into a "second vagina." The Giant's bloody severed head is her "firstborn child." According to Gimi women, a woman acquires a "second vagina" on her face not as 'just deserts' – revenge for what her mythic counterpart did to her baby Brother – but rather because the Giant raped her, traversed her entire body and stuck his head out her mouth, shaking in orgasmic fury until her Mother's Brother – or, in one savant version, her Mother acting alone – cut him off (see Chap. 4). In the Torrent Lark myth the heroine acts alone, killing her infant Son and escaping into the forest as a bird, banished forever from life inside the settlement yet unrepentant, occasionally returning during the rites of marriage to celebrate the eerie fruit of the mythic crime she plotted and carried out with her Mother's help but without a man.

* * *

Women elaborate on the Torrent Lark theme in other theatrical performances. In the 'dance of the monster-child' (lit: 'stillborn'), two performers exchange a large doll made of wild bamboo, its upper body covered in huge black burrs, the very portrait of women's rage. "It's not right to let the stillborn die," women explained. "'We Wild Women care for the child and now that he is grown [we] bring him into the house to show him to you.'" (Fig. 6.4)

> The two Wild Women have no chidren. They live [in the forest] while other women bear children [inside the house (i.e., settlement)]. When a married woman bears a child who is "no good" [i.e., stillborn; or the dis-

Fig. 6.4 In a performance of ritual theatre, two women portray Wild Women who rear their Wild Child inside the forest and show him off during the nighttime revels of marriage celebrations. "It's not right to let the stillborn die," women spectators remarked. The dancers exchange a huge doll made of wild bamboo with large black burrs covering the upper body and adhering to parts of the lower limbs, a celebration of women's anger and alienation (© David Gillison)

carded afterbirth] the two Wild Women find it and look after it and it grows up big! Now the Two of Them rejoice in their Child, "Ahhh, this is our First Child!" … It is big and clever and silent. The second-born drinks at the breast. [The second one] is small, not very smart and conceited. The firstborn is the blood-child. The second one is the milk-child made from semen. 'The Moon killed you,' the Wild Women sing, 'but we reared you out of [the Moon's] blood!'"

So while men possess glorious-sounding flutes, always played in pairs, and give birth to beautiful males who, by extracting each whisker and regularly purging their noses, successfully remove the 'black stain' the primal crime left on their faces, women, whose crime was *the same* as men's, bare guilty residues that are *impossible to eradicate* and that women sometimes embrace in joyful rebellion! Even after sending menstrual blood back into "the noses of our brothers," it returns a month later. For a woman to succeed in 'giving back' to her "first husband" the dead part of himself he planted inside her using foul "tricks," she has to flee or be banished from civilization, left to rear monster-children alone inside the forest. Although women are defiant in their art, embrace the role of vengeful baby-killer in myth and celebrate the stillborn in theatrical performance, their myths also place most – but not all – of the blame for the Mother's crime on the ugly Old Man who seduced her. The Trouble-Maker, the forest-dwelling Ogre who obtains a virgin bride and her baby with dirty tricks, is a standard character in women's myths. But their myths also show that the heroine and, usually, her Mother too are complicit in his crimes because they cooperate with him despite clear warnings: "'Soon it will be dark,' the Old Man said, although darkness was not close."

The Myth of 'Eros and Psyche'

I dub the women's myth that follows 'Eros and Psyche' because, like the Greek goddess, the Gimi heroine disobeys her husband's order not to look. Her renegade deeds contradict the dominant male narrative that a mother by herself cannot let go of her offspring nor launch them fully into life as "birds" and is therefore unfit to be a partner with men in the exchange of "head" payments that guarantee her children's survival and success in a world without her. The Giant Penis, or Wild Man-Trickster, reappears here as the heroine's Father who has just died and stalks the nearby forest as his ruthless ghost (lit: *kore*, 'wild'). Like the heroine of the Torrent Lark myth and her Mother, 'Psyche' and her Mother have reason to know who the Old Man really is yet they enable and participate in his deeds most foul. The following narrative is a composite of several versions of 'Eros and Psyche' with some of the repetition condensed and details of some variants omittted.

hoEEE bada

'thus speaks [the Wild] Woman'

Once there was a Widow. Her Husband died leaving her with a Daughter [ten or twelve years old] and an infant Son. She left them alone in the house and went to gather wild ferns in the place where their Father had been sharpening planks for a fence and the garden was half-cleared. "I am going to gather wild ferns for his *behedabada* (lit: *beheda*, 'fern' + *dabada*, 'spine'; the name of the rite celebrated about a year after a man's death to commemorate the cannibal meal in which the dried spines of wild fern fronds used to wrap the human meat are burned and the ashes dispersed)." The Mother left her two Children with a warning: "Watch the banana plant. If men kill me, bunches of fruit will come crashing to the gound, *'ororo ororo, ororo ororo, ororo ororo.'"*

The Widow followed the river to its source and began to gather ferns and wild yams. Up and up and up she climbed, catching frogs along the course of the river, wrapping them in leaves and putting them inside her net bag. At the source of the river, she uprooted wild yams. [Meanwhile] at the mouth of river, the Old Man was tending his stand of sugarcane. The hot sun made him thirsty. He took his bamboo [water container] and went to the river for a drink. But the water was dirty and clouded, dirty and clouded, dirty and clouded *'nudu'a nudu'a, nudu'a nudu'a, nudu'a nudu'a'* (onomatopoeia of a debris-laden torrent), so he followed the river upstream looking for clean water to fill his bamboo.

Up and up and up he climbed until he saw the Widow uprooting yams. "Your digging is dirtying the water below you," he told her. "I am gathering yams," she said, "and I have dirtied the water below me."

"I saw a rat making a burrow over there," the Old Man said to her. "Why don't you dig up the rat and kill it?" The Widow laid down her net bag and began to break up the earth. "The way to dig up a rat burrow," the Old Man advised, "is to put your head to the ground and lift your buttocks." So the Widow [bent over straight-kneed and] raised her buttocks and contin-

> ued to dig. The Old Man thrust his long sharp stick into her anus, burying it deep inside her until it came out her mouth and pierced the ground. Her whole body shook violently and she died in a spasm.
>
> The Old Man pulled her out of the rat burrow, pulled his stick out of her body and licked it clean. He took the Widow's beads from one arm and tried them on. They fit him well. He took the Widow's beads from her other arm and tried them on. They fit him well. He took the white Widow's beads from one leg … and from the other leg … he took the beads from her head … from her neck … and tried them on himself and they all fit him perfectly well. He took the ragged net bags (*agesagena,* 'mourning raiments,' lit *age* or *hake,* 'pork belly fat' + *sa,* 'of' + *[ge]na,* 'thing') she wore over her buttocks and her vulva and put them on himself. They too fit him just fine.
>
> … He cut off her breasts and put them on himself. They fit him *just right* so that he became like a woman! He cut off her hands and feet and fitted them to himself and they too fit him well…. he cut off her head at the neck and tried it on…. The whole change-over went off without a hitch.
>
> When he had taken from the Widow everything he needed, he ate her. He ate and ate and ate until not a trace of her was left! The bananas came crashing down, *'ororo ororo, ororo ororo, ororo ororo'* and the two Children cried, '*oooo iiiii oooo iiiii*' our Mother is killed! [Men] have killed her!"

Disgused as the Widow, the Old Man set out for her house to trick the Children she left at home alone:

> He slung the Widow's net bag across his forehead [i.e., as only women do] and set out for her house. Inside the Widow's net bag were the rat she killed and the yams, ferns and greens she gathered. "Dear one!" 'she' called out to the Daughter upon entering the house, "I'm hoooome!" "Mother?" uttered the Girl. "The banana cried '*ororo ororo, ororo ororo, ororo ororo*' and bunches of fruit came crashing to the ground …" "But I have come baaaaack," the Old Man replied. "It [the bananas' falling] must mean that *my brother* is dead!" So the children thought their Mother's Brother was killed.
>
> "I'm thristy," the Old Man said to the Daughter, who was already a young woman. "Give me the Baby and go fetch some water for me to drink." The Girl handed over her baby Brother and took the bamboo to go to the river. "I will not drink the water from the river close by," the Old Man said to

her. "… nor from the river beyond it … nor from the one beyond that. I will drink only water from Papua drawn from the base of a red-fruitted pandanus tree. You must cross one ridge, then another, and another and another … [eight or nine in all] and fill the bamboo with water from Papua and bring it to me!"

As he was saying this, the Old Man broke the bottom of the bamboo. "You've given me a broken bamboo!" the Girl cried. "If it won't hold water," the Old Man told her, "just say to it:

> *I'll eat, you'll eat, so fillllll yourself up!*
> [interspersed with rhythmic onomatopoeic sounds like the 'glug glug glug' of water filling a bamboo tube].
> *You, bamboo, better eat [take in] water otherwise I will eat you! So fillllll yourself up!"*

The Daughter repeated the Old Man's spell many times but water still leaked out of the bamboo. [And while she was far, far away detained further by the leaky bamboo …] her 'Mother' heated stones in the fire. "Open your mouth," 'she' said to the baby Boy. "I want to feed you a rat's liver." The Old Man tossed hot stones into the Boy's mouth. Down, down, down they went deep inside him and he died. The Old Man wrapped his body in bark cloth and placed him on the [overhead] rack [for drying firewood, i.e., the place inside the men's house where men hide bamboo flutes wrapped in the bark cloth mothers use to swaddle infants]. His Sister returned from the river far, far, far away and asked, "Where is my Brother?" The Old Man replied, "*iri 'orepisana,*" (lit: 'let [what is hidden] inside the net bag [stay hidden].' Idiomatically: 'Never disturb a sleeping baby!'). Then he fell fast asleep [gorged on his huge meal of the Widow].

The Girl sat down beside the fire and started to roll string across her thigh. A drop of fluid dripped from her Brother's nose onto her thigh and she wiped it away. Another drop [of her Brother's nose-water] fell onto her thigh and again she wiped it away. Another drop fell onto her thigh and she picked it up with the tip of her finger and smelled it. It smelled like death. She looked up and saw her dead Brother wrapped in barkcloth and stashed on the rack for drying firewood. She pulled him down, [unwrapped the barkcloth], looked at him and then covered him up again.

> The Girl stoked the fire to get a [good] look at the Old Man [as he lay sleeping]. She saw his penis under the Widow's weeds and said to herself, "I thought you were my Mother but you are a *man!* You tricked me! You killed my Mother and ate her and came here and killed my Brother."

The heroine placed her Brother's corpse, wrapped in barkcloth, inside her net bag and added the string she made by rolling bark fibres across her thigh. While the Old Man slept, she went out the door and sealed it shut in the traditional manner by stacking planks horizontally across the opening and lashing them together with vine rope. Then she set the house on fire. Using the intimate form of address of a magic spell, she commanded the fire to consume the Old Man limb by limb and organ by organ. The list of his body parts echoes the many mountain ridges she crossed to "fill his bamboo" and is about to cross again now in search of a "true" husband.

> Into her net bag, she loaded her pandanus mat and the string she made and the dead Child wrapped in barkcloth. She took a lighted faggot from the ashes and went out the door of the house. She laid the Child and the faggot on the ground while she stacked the planks [one on top of the other] across the doorway and lashed them together with vine, singing:
>
> > *kore arere dusa arere kore arere dusa arere*
> > [lit: *kore*, 'wild' + *arere*, 'close' + *dusa*, 'domestic,' 'civilized' or 'human' + 'close.' To make the planks stack seamlessly, the heroine addressed each one alternatively as 'wild' or 'civilized' – father or husband.]
>
> She sealed the house completely and set it on fire.... flames engulfed the whole house and fell on the Old Man. He woke up screaming, "*heeh! heeh! heeh! heeh!* What is happening to me?" Hearing his cries the Girl shouted, "I have *seen* you! I have *seen* you! I have *seen* you! You came to trick me and I am going to burn you [alive]!" And the Old Man called out, "Orphan! Orphan!"
>
> "As I cross the first ridge," the Girl ordered the blaze, "explode one of his testicles. As I cross the next ridge, explode his other testicle. As I cross the next ridge, explode his penis. As I cross the next ridge, explode his head. As I cross the next ridge, explode both his eyes. As I cross the next ridge, explode one of his legs. As I cross the next ridge, explode his other leg. As I cross the next ridge, explode one of his hands.... As I cross the next ridge,

explode his belly …" As she went on her way, she instructed the fire to destroy each and every one of the Old Man's limbs and organs.

Her little Dog was with her and the two came upon a sugarcane garden where she saw a lean-to [with a roof] of dried sugarcane leaves [a place for assignations]. She said to her Dog, "If my Husband[-to-be] is there, come back to me wagging your tail. If you see another man, come back growling." The Dog returned wagging its tail but she sent him back again to make sure it was not another trick! The Dog came back a second time wagging its tail and this time she followed [her Dog] and saw the Man who would pay her brideprice.

When she arrived, her Husband asked, "Why have you come?" "An Old Man killed my Mother and ate her all up. He tricked me and I thought *he was my Mother!* He sent me to the river [with a broken bamboo to fetch water] and he killed my Brother and hid him away. So I brought my Brother with me and came here." … Her Husband said to her, "Make knee bands, a foreskirt, a waistband and a net bag. And I will make armbands, anklets and a belt [with the string you have brought]." …

The Man went away and cut the top (lit: 'head') off a hoop pine and hollowed out the trunk, digging deeper and deeper and deeper. He went back up to the top of the tree and dropped a stone inside it. '*nudu nudu nudu nudu nudu nudu'* echoed the stone as it fell, letting him gauge the depth. "I have finished," he said to himself and went to fetch his Wife.

The Newlyweds threw all the body decorations they made together into the "head" of the hollowed-out tree. Then the Husband threw in his Wife's dead baby Brother and sealed the tree shut. He forbid his Wife to touch the tree or to go anywhere near it while he was gone. Then he went away.

The Pair threw all the decorations they made into the hollow tree. The Husband threw in the dead Baby and closed the top of the tree and went away. Before he left he said to [the Boy's] Sister, "Sweet, sweet sounds will come out of the tree where I have put the Child. But you must not go near it nor strike it with a stick!" He said this to his Wife and left her. But she did not listen to her Husband! She went over to the tree and heard such sounds, such *beautiful* sounds! So she hit the tree with her stick!

Out of the treetop flew the Hornbill, the *kidoba* Parrot, Pesquet's parrot, the Raggiana Bird of Paradise crying "*o o o,"* and the Cockatoo, the Crow, the Parakeet, the *nora* Parrot, crying "*aa aa aa.*" She watched them fly down to the lower reaches of the river. Out the head of the tree flew the King of Saxony Bird of Paradise, crying "*burepure burepure, burepure,*" the Blue Bird of Paradise, the Princess Stephanie and the Sicklebill, the Papuan Lory, the Superb Bird of Paradise, and Belford's Honeyeater. And she watched as they all flew up to the headwaters.

And so it came to pass. Once all the birds gathered on the branches of hoop pines and sang. They did not know how to fly. But that Woman hit the tree and all the birds flew out! Because of what that one Woman did, all birds can fly. Some fly up and some fly down. And we women and men are as we are in this world today.

hoee dada netepolete

In the same way as a dream is the output of a single dreamer, a Gimi myth, which is invented and refined by learned adults over generations, is designed to express the attitude and understanding of a *single iconic individual*, a hero or heroine undergoing a rite of passage – birth, initiation, marriage, or death – from whose perspective everything in the myth transpires. Creation of fully aware individuals *is* the social project. The myths of Gimi women and men that parallel the rites of passage trace the mythic ego's awareness as it develops from childhood to adolescence, adulthood and death, tracing his or her consciousness of denial and complicity in the primal Father's murder as *the* condition of separation from Mother.

Gimi women have a more nuanced view than do men of how the primal crime took place. The heroine I call 'Psyche' was no babe-in-arms. But neither did she realize until much too late that the Old Man was not her Mother. Women's myth clearly signals that both the herione and her Mother ought to have known the Old Man's true identity from the start. By the time he arrived at the Widow's house in hideous disguise, 'Psyche' and her Brother had already heard the *'ororo ororo'* sound of the bananas crashing to the ground, exactly as their Mother warned them would happen when "men have killed me." After the heroine nevertheless accepted the Old Man as her Mother, he gave her another dramatic indication of who he really was: *while she watched,* he "broke the bottom" of the bamboo container he gave her to fetch water, repeating before her very eyes what he just did to her Mother. Yet the Girl continued to take him at his word and do his bidding.

The story opens with a Widow leaving her children "at home alone" and going into the forest to gather wild ferns, the accompaniment for human meat whose inedible spines were saved and stored to celebrate the first anniversary of a cannibal meal. The Widow in the myth was in full mourning regalia. In the rites of mourning, a Gimi widow wore many necklaces of white Job's Tears and used the dead man's torn and shredded clothing and net bags, soaked in the belly fat of pigs slaughtered at his funeral feast, to make head coverings, fore- and rear-skirts and knee bands. In the past, when cannibalism was still practiced, a widow might also wear around her neck her husband's jaw encased in netted threads made with marsupial fur and amulets containing his hair and teeth. A widow's face, like the faces of all female mourners, past and present, was covered in a glistening mixture of soot and pig fat that, especially in the sun's glare, 'erased' her features so that she was nearly unrecognizable, literally, a "nothing woman" (see Chap. 4; Gillison 1993: 136–37). Like the deceased's other close female relations, the widow's whole body was caked in whitish clay to add to her ghostly appearance: the heavy layers of light-colored clay gave her body the pale cast of a corpse just as her barely recognizable face mimicked the anonymity that gradually overtakes the dead. A widow who in the past shared in the consumption of her husband and still, in the ethnographic present, covered herself in his body-relics, blackened her face and lightened her body like a corpse, became in a material sense the hideous vessel of his demise.

The 'Psyche' myth opens with the phrase, "Once there was a Widow," which I ascribe to the heroine as a narrative device to get her Father out of the way – to kill him off at the very start – in order to deny her wish to possess him. Father is dead yet everpresent still wreaking havoc. His death provides his ghost with the motive for brutal revenge against his cannibal Widow, another device to disguise the heroine's wish to get close to her Father by getting rid of her Mother. Instead of disappearing, Mother turns into a 'cover up' for the vile Old Man who hides himself inside her by stealing every item of her elaborate mourning garb, hacking her to pieces, attaching the parts of her anatomy – including her head – seamlessly to himself, and eating up the rest. By *'hiding Father inside Mother,'* women's myth speaks to – or inspires – men's Flute myth in which the Father seems to be missing altogether but is *camouflaged* inside the Plug of Sister's Pubic Hair that her baby Brother "cannot see." Once again, women's myth 'zooms in' on the Sister's Pubic Hair Plug in men's myth to expose the simultaneous rapes of Mother and Daughter that it conceals.

Like the Pair of Marsupial Hunters in women's myth of the Home Invaders, the Widow left her Children "at home alone" and set out for the forest, a way to announce conjugal intercourse. She headed for a part of the forest on the margins of the settlement that was half cleared, the fence only partly built, where her dead husband "sharpened posts," an explicit reference to his erections. She went there to gather ferns to celebrate the anniversary of his death and was met by his enraged ghost who pursued her, wanting sex. Ferns were the main "wild greens" once used to wrap human meat for cooking. (No cultivated foods accompanied human flesh.) The cannibal women set aside the central spines to dry out, tied them into bundles and, about a year later, carried them into the forest to the source of a clan-owned river, "the river of our [husband's] fathers." There the women set fire to a large pile of the bundles and, when the ashes cooled into a silky powder, they rubbed some of it over their thighs and discarded the rest into the rushing torrent (Gillison 1993: 144).

The Widow "followed the river to its source," a high, forested mountain crevice which, according to narrative convention and echoing again the myth of the Home Invaders, is a colossal version of the valley between the First Woman's thighs. The Widow's activity there – digging for yams with her stick – dirtied the water "beneath her" because she was menstruating, copulating with the Moon who is her "first husband". The enraged Old Man is a portrait both of the Moon and of his Firstborn who starts off *down below* and finds the water contaminated by a predecessor who is 'higher up.' The Old Man / Firstborn started out at the mouth of the river, below the Widow, in the position of a child beneath its 'mountain' of a mother. The child was hungry for her water, her milk, and angry when he found it undrinkable, "dirty and clouded, dirty and clouded," because she was already in use by someone far above him he did not see.

In this version of women's 'Psyche' myth, the Widow's digging up wild yams makes the mountain torrent run noisily downstream, laden with dirt and debris. A yam is like a vagina, Gimi men say, because, eaten raw, it makes the lips pucker like engorged labia. Men also associate the yam's skin, covered in radicels, with a woman's hairy anus and heavy buttocks.

To his lazy wife, a Gimi man may remark, "Your ass turned into a yam?" But to a woman digging in her garden or the forest, each tuber she unearths is like her unborn "child:" it has a rudamentary "nose," an "anus," and "skin covered with tiny hairs" (*Ibid:* 169). In the densely-impacted gem-like imagery of women's myth, the Widow with her head to the ground and buttocks raised high as she digs for yams with her long stick is an image both of her congress with the Moon – what she is *already* doing to make the water beneath her "dirty" – *and* of what awaits her when the Old Man, a smaller "first husband" who is "the same as the Moon," plunges his stick into her uplifted anus and out her mouth, skewering her to the spot on the ground where she dies in convulsive spasms.

The Old Man withdrew his stick and "licked it clean." "The Old Man downed every morsel of blood and feces [on his stick] and then cut the Widow to pieces." Some women remarked that the Old Man's stick was *already* blackened and encrusted with the innards of many other women: "There is a lot of filth (lit: *firirina*) at the end of that stick. [The head] is covered with the dried blood and guts of the other women he killed. He is a Man who *tricks* women, kills them and eats them! *That* is the kind of man the Old Man is!"

In other versions of women's 'Psyche' myth, it is the Old Man who pollutes the water in the river. As the Widow follows its course *up*stream, she sees – and hears – the debris from a rotten log being carried downstream:

> The Old Woman followed the river upstream. '*nudu'a nudu'a nudu'a nudu'a,*' dirty and clouded, dirty and clouded, the water was dirty and clouded…. She climbed up and up and up until she came upon the Old Man searching for grubs, banging his forehead [from which an axe blade protruded] into a rotten log infested with grubs. "Father!" she called out, "What are you doing?" "I am looking for grubs," he said. "And you?" "My children are hungry for rats and frogs. I have come to find some," she said…. "Do you know how to unearth yams?" he asked her. "I am a yam-gathering woman," she answered. "Then take the yams I have planted [dig them up] and bring them [to your Children]."
>
> The Old Man followed the Widow as she went to dig up [his] yams and instructed her: "When you dig yams, lift your buttocks to the sky." …

The Widow and her dead Husband's ghost are *both* polluters: she, by digging for yams; he, by slashing open a rotten tree trunk to get the delicious juicy grubs inside it. Each one is tunneling down for 'unborn babes' to eat: light-colored yam tubers with "noses" and "anuses" and fuzzy-hair covered "skins," and fat, juicy whitish embryo-like grubs. Rats in a burrow provide another image of trapped foetal food. The Old Man pulled the Widow out of the rat burrow before he pulled his stick out of her and "licked it clean," leaving no doubt about the goulish unborn child-devouring habits of the primordial Pair who remain stuck together. Trapped inside her burrow, Gimi point out, a frantic mother rat eats her own young. Desperate to escape, she hesitates, thinking of the 'little ones' she leaves behind: "'How can I leave them?' she says to herself.... She picks up one child in her mouth ... 'You are a beautiful child so I will eat you first'" (Gillison 1993: 304).

The yam-digging, rat-hunting Widow and her Spirit-Spouse who slashes open her dead-log of a body to hunt for delectable squirming grubs and then 'withdraws his stick' to relish what he murders inside her are Gimi women's 'quick sketches' of the primordial Parent – male *and* female – combined in action. Their similar food-finding methods suggest they are perpetually copulating, a pair coalesced from whom no child can escape: the world inside Mother is a tunnel-like charnel house where Parents impale and cannibalize any life that manages to separate itself, however fleetingly or incompletely, from their violent all-consuming embrace. Like the Parents of the "Boys left alone at home" when the Pair of Home Invaders arrive in the valley between the First Woman's thighs, these Parents are both equipped with phallic weapons. Each one is still in possession of the Giant Penis' "stick."

Gimi Men Portray the Conjoined Primal Parents Differently than do Women

Men's stories also portray the primordial couple's habit of taking back whatever is lost during copulation. But in men's version of primal parenthood the 'retriever' is neither a serial-killer nor vicious fornicator like the

Old Man in women's myths but rather, once again, a static and distant father-figure camouflaged by the heroic baby Brother ensconsed at his "head." After the original theft of her Flute, according to one erudite Gimi elder, the Sister closed up her Vagina again. To reopen it the Boy had to go to great lengths – or rather heights:

> A woman knows more. The Woman who made the Flute [by looking down at her Vagina] knew more but she did not tell other women. She did not say that she lost her Flute and was looking for it .... She searched and searched but could not find it! Her Brother stole her Flute and thought, "This Flute must cry inside a *good* house!" ... He told other men to build the [men's] house and they built it and [made a second Flute and] blew the Flutes inside it. His Sister heard the cries and knew [her Flute] was stolen! But she did not say, "I miss my Flute!" She said, "The men have taken it. That is alright. It can stay with men."

But the Sister's apparent equanimity hid deep resentment, the elder continued:

> Her Brother stole the Flute and hid it. "You make me angry," she thought, and would not show her Vagina to men. She closed it up [again]! She just kept it hidden and did not tell other women that her Brother had taken the thing away. "Ah!" she thought, "my Brother has stolen it but never mind. It can stay with him." She ... hid her Vagina saying, "Because you have stolen something of mine, you will not have it." She ... closed herself up. Her passage became very small and she had no room for sex. By and by the Boy realized [what the matter was] and dragged [his Sister] to a stagnant pool [on a mountain top] and laid her down beside it.
>
> He took a stone and climbed to the top (lit: "head") of a huge tree and threw the stone [into the pool]. The water splashed onto the Woman and she shivered and opened both her legs (sic). The water went inside her Vagina and made it cold. It killed the fire raging inside her and opened her Vagina.... Her Brother threw down the stone and opened [her up] a little. And [so] the Moon killed her.... The hot thing inside her Vagina went cold. Afterwards men could have sex with her.

> … [The Boy] loaded the stone into his net bag and climbed [the tall tree] and threw it down…. he did not throw the stone away altogether! He put it inside the very, very long net bag [he wore around his neck] and threw it *inside* the bag. So after the stone splashed into the stagnant pool, he pulled up the net bag and got back the stone! The Boy is the same as the Moon. The Moon threw down his Giant Penis and had sex with the Woman [while she lay beside the mountain-top pool]. He opened her up a little, cooled the fire [between her legs] and withdrew into the sky. He took back the stone!
>
> The Moon says, "I am the one who opens her Vagina." The Moon is the first one to have sex with her. We do it *afterwards*. That is the real meaning of this story…. This is still our custom [despite the disappearance of menstrual huts]. When a man goes to ask a woman and she says, "No. The Moon is killing me …" then we do not do it because it is *the law*. It's as if she is with another man…. [To do] that – a man would die! If he went into her … and *that blood entered his body* and if he held it in his hand and ate it … he would cough and cough and when he wanted to climb a mountain or lift something heavy, he could collapse and die…. Because he gets the *germ* of another man. I do not want *another man's germ*! So when the Moon kills a woman, I do *not* have sex with her! …

Interpreting lectures from *docta bois* about Western hygiene, my male interlocutor uses the Melanesian Pidgin word "jem" to refer to menstrual blood as fatal pollution that derives from "another man" who is "the same as the Moon" and his offspring/surrogate "little Boy." When Gimi men attribute the lethality of menstrual blood to the priority of the Moon – a primal father figure – as every woman's "first husband," they refer in different terms to what Gimi women call the "filth at the head" (lit: *firirina*) of the Old Man's "stick," the accummulated residues of the rotted insides of the countless other women he already "tricked and ate." In the imagery of Gimi women's myths, "another man's germ" is the contaminating remains of *other women* whom the Old Man raped, generic predecessers of the heroic 'Psyche' who *include her own Mother*. In 1983, eight years after I first heard women's myth of the Giant Penis, Kamale confided that *firirina* was the real reason the First Woman cut the Giant down to size, provoking the first menstrual period. Kamale:

> [The Giant Penis] entered her body but the Man was asleep inside his own house. He coiled his Penis – that *huge* penis of his! – into a little net bag and slung it over his shoulder or around his neck [when he went into the forest to hunt marsupials] or hung it up inside the inner room (*umusaraE*, lit: *umusa*, 'pregnant' or 'inside space' + *raE*, 'there') of his house. When he felt like having sex, *he* stayed asleep while his Penis uncoiled itself and slid out of the bag. He [the Penis] thought, "I want to have sex." And his Penis crawled out of the net bag and out of the Man's house.
>
> The Man stayed asleep inside his house while his Penis entered the Woman's house and had sex with her while *she* slept. It went up inside her and then [slunk] back to the Man's house and [coiled itself up] back inside that little net bag of his. The Woman thought, "I am fed up with what you do to me," and she cut the Penis. She cut it with an axe. She cut it and that's why men's penes are short nowadays!
>
> But in the beginning, when the Penis was very, very long, going back and forth, back and forth, back and forth in and out of women's bodies, there was filth (lit: *firirina*) inside the little net bag and filth inside the Woman. So she got fed up and cut the Penis. That is why she did it!

When the heroine of women's Giant Penis myth is compared to her ritual counterpart, the female initiate secluded inside a cage-like "sugar bed," festooned with red flowers and foliage, specially erected inside her mother's house, the woman's house in both myth and ritual take on the character of a giant Womb, placing the heroine/initiate in the position of the unborn who feeds upon the "head" of her father's Giant Penis *after it is already inside her Mother* and therefore polluted. The marauding Penis enters both females at once because, in the images of women's myths and rites, they are combined like a nested pair of phallic-shaped Russian dolls. The girl imprisoned inside her mother during the "sleep" of gestation is entered repeatedly by her father's "head" (glans) on his many sorties into her mother, the many ejaculations required to bring her into existence: she is raped repeatedly by a father whose nourishment is contaminated with the remains of other women he already killed. Although she is unborn, trapped inside her mother and unable to see clearly, she is not utterly blind like her brother. Nowadays, on account of that First Woman's heroism, men's penes have been 'cut short,' and a man abstains from sex during the middle of his wife's pregnancy. But he returns at the end to "awaken" and "finish the child" by providing a final emission that *closes* – *"plugs up"* – the girl's open fontanelle, the urethra-like "first mouth" atop the foetal head.

In the mythic past, intrauterine development was never complete because the Giant was unwilling to give up any part of his enormous Self in order to "finish the child:" every time he "lost his head" inside the First Woman he yanked it back again. He was like the tree in men's myth with the small Boy perched at the top pulling back the net bag around his neck with the stone – the dead baby – inside it. The Giant comes back over and over again and, while making fresh deposits – splashing out the fire inside the First Woman's Vagina – also *retrieves* what he left on his last penetration, cannibalizing his own ejaculate, feeding on the blood of his own offspring, so that he remains huge and undiminished, with the "filth" of countless unborn stone-dead babies forever accumulating at his "head." The "head" the Giant Penis uses to feed his unborn Daughter is polluted by the rotted contents of the innumerable "other women" whom he has already 'tricked and eaten,' as Kamale mentioned, and who include her Mother last of all.

Notes

1. Because of their intimate connection, Gimi myths and rites are often discussed together. Mythic figures and artifacts are capitalized to distinguish them from their ritual counterparts. But pronouns that refer to mythic figures appear in lower case. Big Man and Big Woman, individuals recognized as important persons and leaders in the community, are also capitalized.
2. On rare occasions in the past, in recognition of her unusual stature and importance, a Big Woman was eaten.

References

Freud, Sigmund. 1974 [1925]. Some Psychical Consequences of the Anatomical Distinction Between the Sexes. In *Women and Aaalysis: Dialogues on Psychoanalytic Views of Femininity*, ed. Jean Strouse. New York: Grossman.

———. 1937. Analysis Terminable and Interminable. *International Journal of Psychoanalysis* 18: 373–405.

Gillison, Gillian. 1993. *Between Culture and Fantasy. A New Guinea Highlands Mythology*. Chicago: University of Chicago Press.

———. 2016. Whatever Happened to the Mother? A New Look at the Old Problem of the Mother's Brother in Three New Guinea Societies: Gimi, Daribi and Iatmul. *Oceania* 86 (I): 2–24.

Mead, Margaret. 1970. *The Mountain Arapesh. Volume II: Arts and Supernaturalism*. Garden City, NY: Natural History Press.

Ovid. *The Metamorphoses*. Book VI: "Tereus, Procne, and Philomela." Project Gutenberg. https://www.gutenberg.org/files/21765/21765-h/files/Met_IV_VII.html#bookVI

Rubin, Gayle. 1975. The Traffic in Women: Notes on the 'Political Economy' of Sex. In *Toward an Anthropology of Women*, ed. Rayna Reiter. New York: Monthly Review Press.

7

The Mother's Crime and the Cycle of Blame

Women's myth of 'Eros and Psyche' presented in Chapter Six provides a detailed look inside the "filth" that clings to the head of the Giant Penis and that, according to a woman named Kamale, drove the First Woman to cut him off in a fury.[1] The Giant in the 'Psyche' myth is the heroine's dead Father whose evil spirit haunts the forest. He murders the Widow, the heroine's Mother, because she pollutes the river with her menstrual blood – a stream choked with rotted flotsam and jetsam. The Widow's adolescent Daughter kills – or, rather, has her Father kill – her Mother at the time she herself starts to menstruate, the moment foul-smelling fluid from her dead brother's nose drops onto her thigh alerting her to the Old Man's tricks and to her own complicated desires. The heroine's wish to possess her Father entails getting rid of her Mother: a desire that comes wrapped in a dead package she discovers overhead and has to undo by herself and carry away with her.

At the very outset, the myth announces the heroine's wish to distance herself from the wish to possess her Father: when the story starts, he is

G. Gillison, *She Speaks Her Anger: Myths and Conversations of Gimi Women*, Culture, Mind, and Society, https://doi.org/10.1007/978-3-030-49352-3_7

already a ghost. As one Gimi elder, a ritual expert and savant, interpreted women's myth:

> This is the story of [female initiation ritual]. This is the story of the initiate. Her dead Brother she spies on the shelf overhead is her Father's penis inside her Mother. It is his "water" dripping down on her thigh, making her pregnant with his Child. She carries this part of her Father to her Husband and he helps her to convert these dead, red things into living children.... [In the ritual] the women [the initiate's chaperons] break up the sugar pole [the men insert through the roof] to get rid of the blood and replace it with a "true child." (See Chap. 3, Fig. 3.2).

Women's Interpretations of Cannibalism: On 'Being Eaten from the Inside'

Women's 'coming of age' story of starting to menstruate, finding a husband, and conceiving a child begins with the death of the Father and cannibalism (See Chap. 6, p. 213ff.). Gimi women told me that love and pity, and the urgent need to spare the deceased the agony and humiliation of decomposition, motivated their cannibalism in the past. But women's portrayal of the Spirit-Husband's brutal revenge against his Widow in their myth of 'Eros and Psyche' suggests that women also believed cannibalism was inspired by rage. The Old Man carries out a vile travesty of the historic rites when men supposedly discovered women's "secret crime" after the deed was already done. Transformation of the cannibals' appearance revealed their crime to the world: to mourn the man they ate, the women had to cover their bodies with caked layers of whitish clay; 'black out' their faces with a mixture of pig fat and soot; put on heavy layers of necklaces made of white Job's Tears; replace fore- and rear-skirts with shredded, fat-soaked remnants of the dead man's garments and net bags; wear amulets of his teeth and hair; and, in the case of his mother or wife, hang his jaw encased in marsupial fur around her neck and his skull inside a small net bag at the back of her head (Gillison 1993: 135ff). Women's cannibal "crime," as men constructed it, required the women to 'disappear' in various ways: by assuming the deathly aspect of the man they ate; by losing their names and kinship status so they became "nothing" (see Chap. 4); by remaining out of sight, secluded inside their houses and forbidden to enter their gardens; and by being forced to collect and consume only "wild foods" at the semi-cultivated margins of the settlement.

Just as a cannibal widow ingested her husband after she cut him into pieces and decorated her body 'in him' by wearing his shredded clothing and adornments made of his disassembled head – teeth, hair, jaw, skull; so, in women's myth, did his dead Spirit, exiled to the forest, take revenge by eating her up and decorating himself 'in her.' The man his widow ate in cannibal rites of the past – whose body she consumed in death and whose penis she "ate" in life – takes revenge, according to women' myth, by impaling her with his vicious "stick," relishing her tasty innards, putting on her Widow's garb and cutting her body into parts that fit his body seamlessly. Just as in past rituals, orchestrated by men, a widow helped to dismember her husband after he was installed on a platform outside the settlement, and made her body the hideous container of his dead self, so does his ghost in women's myth, exiled into the forest afterlife, cut her up and use the pieces to transform himself into a monstrous version of her.

Like every Gimi myth, the myth of 'Eros and Psyche' refers to other myths in the repertoires of both sexes and to rites of passage, in this case, female initiation and funerary cannibalism of the past. In some versions of the 'Psyche' myth the Old Man starts out at the mouth of the river, below the Widow, in the position of a child unable to see what lies above him. As he climbs the mountain ridge, he becomes bigger and stronger than 'the one he cannot see:' like the Husband who removes his eyes before he enters the anus of the Cassowary caught in his trap, gorges on her insides, and leaves her an emptied skin, the Old Man penetrates the Widow's anus, gets 'inside her skin' and eats up every morsel of her insides. Women's mythic images of a grown man who devours a woman *from the inside* – a rapist/monster-foetus whose penetration, gestation and birth leave her emptied – express women's view of sexual intercourse and child-bearing as a combined ordeal that leave her with nothing. The penis that invades a woman's body during sex seems to *remain* there, filling every part of her body (from one end to the other!) with repeated ejaculations that *eat away* at her insides until she is reduced to a hollowed-out covering of skin, a lifeless earthbound "house" for the huge male/s active inside her. As the Giant gets even bigger and *bifurcates into father-and-firstborn son*, she "dies." She is "killed by the Moon," left holding his stillborn issue, while he retreats into the night sky to strike her soon again.

Before the Widow departs, she warns her Children that if/when 'men have killed me' there will be a sure sign: bunches of bananas hanging from the plant just outside the door will come crashing noisily to the ground. Like her Daughter later on, the Widow knows what the Old Man will do to her *before* she sets out on her journey into the forest yet she departs nevertheless. When the Old Man breaks open the bottom of the bamboo container he gives the Daughter to 'fetch his water,' he repeats before her very eyes what he just did to the Mother inside the forest: the Daughter denies what she sees and does the Old Man's bidding because his demands fulfill her desires, too. Traversing mountain after mountain, going off alone to fill the Old Man's 'leaky bamboo,' pictures the heroine *all by herself* on a lonely journey yet accompanied by the 'man of her dreams:' perhaps she is masturbating while her 'real father' lies far away and fast asleep inside a different house.

The heroine is alone when she starts to menstruate, twisting shredded bark into string across her thigh. While she was absent, the Old Man murdered her Brother, wrapped his corpse in the barkcloth men used to wrap bamboo flutes and shoved it onto the overhead rack for drying firewood. He hid the dead Baby in the rafters, the place where men hid flutes inside the men's house. And just like the empty bamboo container whose bottom the Old Man broke and the heroine carried with her over many mountains, the corpse leaked: "water from her Brother's nose" dripped onto her thigh where she was twisting shredded bark into string. The first appearance of menstrual blood, her budding sexuality, caused her to look up and finally to see the killer beneath her mother's skirts. "I have *seen* you! I have *seen* you! I have *seen* you!" she cried. She now despises the Giant she once desired – the man of her dreams – and decides to burn him to nothingness while he lies asleep inside her Mother's house.

But before 'Psyche' destroys the Old Man hiding inside her Mother and sets out in search of a man who will not rape her – a Husband who will pay her brideprice – she places her Brother's corpse, wrapped in barkcloth like a pair of flutes, inside her net bag. The episode in women's myth refers to men's "secret" rite of marriage in which the bride's father and brother make a pair of flutes in her image (etching the same designs around the flutes' blowing holes as the "beard" they tattoo around her mouth), stuff them with chunks of salted pork with the hairy hide adhering, disguise them as containers of salt and place them inside the bride's net bag for her to transport "unknowlingly" to her husband. Women's myth identifies the *pair* of men's sacred flutes as the heroine's "firstborn child" – her menstrual blood – as the amalgam of *both* her dead baby Brother *and* the Father who murdered him and stashed him inside her body while *all three of them* were trapped inside Mother. The heroine's dead Brother is the 'dirty thing' (*firirina*) the Giant dropped from his "head" into her lap while she was 'twisting string' inside her Mother's house. Her "firstborn" is the dead issue of the many times her father raped her before she herself was even born!

Women's myth explicitly equates Moon-killed blood with the pair of flutes a woman's father and brother stuff with "hairy" meat and send to her husband inside her net bag for him to unpack as part of a transaction the men supposedly keep secret from the bride. Both 'Psyche's' murdered Brother and the pair of flutes a Gimi bride delivers "unknowlingly" to the groom symbolize the perfectly-united spirit Couple who look like one monster Parent 'plugged shut' (cf. Newman and Boyd 1982: 259). Until 'Psyche' decides to rescue her murdered Brother and to murder their seamlessly-combined Parents, the two devour every one of their tender, unformed, delectable and indistinguishable progeny – yam, fern, rat, frog, grub or foetus.

With the Old Man hidden inside the murdered Widow now asleep inside her house, the heroine uses a magic spell to seal the house shut and then sets it on fire. She instructs the fire to "explode" the Old Man's every limb and organ, starting with his testicles, as she crosses one mountain after another after another, getting closer to a real-life husband 'in step' with her violent destruction of the Giant Penis. The heroine carries with her the Baby the Old Man murdered 'in her absence' and hands the corpse over to her Husband who places it inside a hollowed tree – a giant rendering of both her body and a flute. This time, instead of leaking bloody "nose-water" silently onto her thigh, the corpse 'flies apart' – flame- and smoke-colored – transformed into the raucous lives of countless birds who fly off in every direction. Unlike the heroine of the Torrent Lark myth who murders her Child, cooks him inside a hollowed tree stump used as an oven, and feeds him 'back' to her "first husband" in an act of unmitigated rage, 'Psyche' annihilates her Father limb by limb and organ by organ, leaves him far behind her and, still acting alone, gives soaring new life to the carnage he left inside her body.

Women's various portrayals of the primal Father in myth – as Dream Man, Giant Penis, Python, Trickster and evil Old Man haunting the dark forest – show that he only *appears* to be a solitary figure. He dwells inside two women simultaneously, the unborn heroine and her Mother, both of whom collude with him unknowingly-yet-knowingly. Hearing the bananas crash to the ground and watching the Old Man 'break her bottom' make the heroine complicit in his murders of her Mother and Baby Brother. No matter how far she travels, she carries the dead issue of Father-inside-Mother as part of herself.

The Old Man kills her Brother while the heroine is far, far away fetching the Old Man's water inside a leaky bamboo; and then she lets it "leak" onto her thigh as she rolls her hand across it. Her menstrual blood is shameful proof of the *crimes she commits with* her Father and then, after she sees his Penis beneath her Mother's skirts, *against* him. Given her prehistory, the Girl cannot undo her crimes alone. So – *deliberately* according to women's myths, *unknowingly* according to men's rites – she hands over to a husband the baby she (at the very least) allowed her Father to kill and install inside her. The Husband lops off the top of a hoop pine and hollows out the trunk (a common Gimi burial practice), going deeper and deeper like the penis' many incursions needed to make a woman pregnant. The stone he throws into the trunk to gauge the depth replicates the hot stone the Old Man threw down the Boy's throat to kill him. This time, instead of leaking "nose-water" silently onto her thigh, the corpse she rescues and transports to her husband explodes into birds rising skyward, gorgeously smoke- and flame-colored like the fire she lit to consume her Father.

"Beautiful sounds will come out of the tree where I put the Child," her Husband says to her. "Do not go near it or hit it with a stick. Just listen!" he warns her, and then *leaves*. 'Psyche's' new Husband goes off to 'have sex' *by himself* like the Cassowary Hunter who left his Wife at home, removed both his eyes, placed them on leaves of wild taro, climbed into the anus of the Cassowary caught in his trap and devoured her insides! (See Chap. 4, p. 139ff). Her Husband's hasty departure also recalls *her own* behaviour when she went off by herself to fill the Old Man's leaky bamboo, allowing him to do as he pleased in her absence.

Women's myth affirms that the heroine needs a Husband to transform her shameful deeds, the "dead things" she brings to her marriage, into children born alive. But it also proclaims, spectacularly, that to launch her children fully into life, a mother has to disobey her husband and act without him when he goes away and leaves her alone with the children, as Gimi husbands so often did in the past and still do. Hitting the tree to release all the birds is the Gimi heroine's signature deed. "Because of what that *one woman* did," a story-teller proclaimed, "we are the women and men we are today."

Exchanges Outside the Mother's Body Between Her First and Second Husbands

The transformation that Gimi women picture in myth as occurring *inside* the mother's body, symbolized by the tree her husband hollows out and then refills together with his wife, in Gimi men's view, can only be achieved *outside* her body, when her husband and brother (and their respective patrilineal kin) exchange the child's "head," edible substitutes for its every limb and organ, between themselves. To possess a child 'of woman born' – to unplug the pair of flutes a bride "secretly" delivers to her husband from her father and brother and to *keep* them unplugged – her husband has to affirm *publicly*, over and over again, the relation to his wife's father and brother that converts her into an empty conduit or 'sterile vessel.' In public rites of exchange with his wife's father and brother—conducted right under her nose but without her active participation or, supposedly, even knowledge 'through' a pair of flutes she never sees – a man can gain access to his child's sordid prehistory, *which lies in his wife's own conception*, and try to rectify the damage. "Head" payments are ritual facsimiles of the mythical "heads" the Old Man/Giant Penis sacrificed repeatedly to engender and kill – *to make and unmake* – both his Daughter and her Firstborn Child. Men's exchanges of "head" payments rescue the child from the Giant – not by lying in wait, murdering him and his firstborn-sidekick, nor by running away with his dead babies into the forest! – but rather by providing his ritual surrogates (the mother's father and brother) with 'other meat' for them to devour *instead.* Once his heirs eat the 'other meat,' the Old Man can no longer "play around" and make a meal of his Daughter's children – no longer *re*absorb his own emissions – because they no longer originate inside his own "head."

Men's exchanges are designed to reverse the wife's tangled prehistory of copulation and murder in such a way that she is stripped of her role: by the time her children reach adolescence, motherhood is transferred to her brother – the one whose death the Father's evil ghost convinces 'Psyche' and her Brother to identify in place of their Mother as having caused the bananas to come crashing noisily to the ground (see Chap. 6, p. 215). "Head" payments effectively 'rederive' the child from its mother's brother and husband and cast the mother aside – to use the Gimi idiom – like an eggshell that breaks to pieces when the bird hatches or like a bamboo tube that shatters when the food inside it is cooked.

The Cycle of Blame

The universe of meaning in which Gimi describe how life begins resembles a cycle of revenge in which the sex of the wrong-doer depends upon which one is telling the story. The hero is always a virgin, babe or adolescent, and the villain is the one who *sees* while the other cannot and acts as a predator. In women's 'Psyche' myth, the heroine is a Girl just starting to menstruate who does not recognize her Father as a rapist. Once she sees him, sees his Penis beneath her Mother's skirts, she salvages her Brother's remains – her "firstborn" – and finds a Husband to help her transform his corpse to soaring life. In the sequel to men's Flute myth, the First Woman closes herself up again after losing her Flute. To open her a second time, the Boy climbs a high forest tree and drops a stone into a stagnant pool, splashing out the fire between her legs and causing blood as-red-as-fire to appear (see Chap. 6, p. 223ff). Goran:

> The Boy … is like the Moon throwing his Penis out of the sky to open the passage. Afterwards, men can have sex with her.… Before the Flute was stolen, the Penis was very powerful! It did not know how to have sex and was incredibly strong!

Like the Giant Penis, I remarked, to Goran's annoyance. He rebuked me for switching idioms. He was referring to a story from the *men's house*, he protested … but since I brought it up, yes! … the marsupial the Giant Penis kills is the same [thing] the Moon kills. When the Penis kills the marsupial and it rots *with the Penis' head still inside it*, it is the same as the Moon's killing a woman and her stinking [from it].

Goran moved quickly past my interruption and returned to the Flute myth:

> The flute is the Mother's body. She etched her own Vagina [on the Flute]. And the Woman who did that they *killed!* And the women who came after the Flute was stolen were forbidden to see it lest they get angry and say, "Ah! You men put your mouths on our vaginas and blew into the bamboo." …

I asked Goran: 'What is the origin of men's shame?'

> The flute is the Mother's body [as I told you]. If a woman were to *see* men's flute she would tell her son that men are blowing into holes like vaginas! Women must not say such things [to their sons]!

Referring to an episode in women's Python myth, I paraphrased Goran's remarks in a shorter version of the following: 'Our wives must not see us entering Cassowaries' anuses!/having sex with our Mothers! lest they tell our sons what they have seen *us* do. Our wives must not *see* us lest they repeat with our sons the seduction/siren-calling/Flute-playing our mothers used on us – that made us addicted to them, filled us with desire to "go back up the road we first came down." We killed the seductress-Mother and stole her Flute so that she cannot pass on to our wives the 'instrument' for seducing our sons as she seduced us while we were blind! … mere babes lurking in the tall grass outside her door.'

Fig. 7.1 Two men play bamboo flutes men once kept secret from women on pain of death. "The flute is the Mother's body," Gimi men say. "If a woman were to see men's flutes she would tell other women and her son that men are blowing into holes like vaginas! Women must not say such things [to their sons]!"(© David Gillison)

Goran:

At the time her Brother stole the [First] Woman's Flute men had *never seen* women's vaginas. They looked at the hole in the Flute and realized that women had the same kind of opening. That is how men *found out* how to have sex! Before the Brother stole the Flute, women were like men and could not have babies. They had vaginas but men *did not know it* so who was there to have sex with women? …

… Playing flutes is like having sex … when we hold one hand [over the end of the flute] and blow … [we put the baby] into the mother's belly and when we open our hand [we push] the baby out [the other end]…. Men play the flutes … but their sons must not know it and tell their mothers … so that their mothers know. The child must not *look* at his mother's vagina!

Then women would realize, "You men put your mouths on our vaginas." Men are ashamed and do not show [the flutes] to women!

Again I compared men's Flute myth with women's Python myth. Goran tempered his annoyance with me and riffed on the comparison:

> [The story of the *kamidama* ("flute house" or menstrul hut), of the First Woman's making and owning the Flute at a time when men were unaware is "the same" as the Cassowary Hunter's] entering the Cassowary *without his eyes* while his [Mother and Daughter] *watched*.... In revenge the Man takes his Daughter and sends her to the Snake [which is] the Moon's Penis. If the Mother did not *steal* the Father's eyes, then the Moon would not kill women! But the Wife (sic) *stole* the Father's eyes and enraged him so he took his Daughter and gave her to the Snake! The Snake went inside the Daughter's vagina [and came out her mouth].
>
> Before the Moon kills her, a woman's vagina is hot as fire. A penis that enters a vagina before the Moon would burn and break .... They remove the Snake from the Woman's body and cut it up and throw [the pieces] into the fire.

The *kamidama* is the place where the First Woman looked down at herself and made the *kamiba* in the image of what she saw between her thighs amid her pubic hair. According to women's myths, what she saw was the huge penis of a rapaciously oblivious father *going in* and the hair-covered head of a newborn 'without eyes' *coming out* – two insensible big hard hairy things moving as one in and out of her body! The Cassowary, an enormous bird who can 'no longer' fly, is women's version of the Flute-owning First Woman.

> As I told you [Goran continued, now referring to the Python myth], the road we men have come down we want to travel up again! But to do that, the man has to remove his shame. If he were to *see* with his own eyes what he wants to do he would be ashamed [to do it so] he removes his eyes and enters the Cassowary's vagina (sic).....

The Gimi law of talion is omnipresent and infinitely regressive which means that everything in myth that happens for "the very first time" is also the *response in kind* to a prior deed. From a male perspective, women's 'Psyche' myth begs the question of *why* the Old Man murdered the Widow, cut her to pieces, ate her up, raped her Daughter and murdered her Son. Why was the Old Man, the Giant Penis, the Python – or the Moon in regular parlance – so insanely angry? Men begin with the First Woman *alone* inside her "flute house" looking *down* at her vagina. She *sees herself* having sex with the Moon: "When the Moon has sex with a woman she is holding the *kamiba*," Goran repeated. "Holding the *kamiba*," in *women's* view, is a scene of perpetual rape: like being a lonely earth-bound Cassowary caught in a trap, watching a grown man climb into her hairy anus/vagina, feeling him eat up her insides and come back out again "head" first. Gimi women's 'First Woman' gazes at a *blind twosome* – her Father transported in lust, his Child's huge hairy head 'without eyes' – moving in and out between her thighs and making her cry rapturously some of the time. But no one who enters or exits her body – grown man, newborn, or corpse – is *aware of her*, leaving her alone to observe the comings and goings between her thighs as one continuous in-and-out/out-and-in invade-and-destroy operation. That is hardly men's view, however. Instead of a giant Cassowary invaded by a blind man who eats up her insides, men envisage the First Woman as supremely in control because she alone had eyes to see. Men's portrait of the Mother is of one who inflicts humiliation upon her *uncomprehending* son. Once the Cassowary Hunter realizes what his Mother/Wife *did to him*, Goran said again, he takes his Daughter to the Snake in revenge:

> If the Mother had not stolen the Father's eyes, then the Moon would not kill women. But the Wife (sic) stole the Father's eyes and enraged him so he took his Daughter and gave her to the Snake.

The Mother's Crime

According to Gimi men, the mother's crime is *seeing while alone.* Menstruation – and the isolation it requires – are her punishment to fit the crime. In men's portrayal of the First Woman, she sees coitus and birth as reciprocal aspects of the *same activity*, as inseparable as the 'in' and 'out' of breathing, flute-playing and sexual intercourse, which is why men say: "the road we have come down we want to travel up again!" In men's view, their compulsive and insatiable desire to make the 'round-trip' back inside their mothers is entirely their mothers' fault: it was the mother *in the first place* – while her son was blind – who saw his birth as just another "passage between her thighs," another tryst *all alone* with the Giant. A man's habitual desire to 'crawl back' inside his mother is the result of *her having seen him come out of her* while she was all by herself imagining another, much bigger "head." The siren sounds of her coital raptures drew him irresistably to her because, as a baby, he thought, "Your bamboo is empty."

The Boy in men's Flute myth was oblivious to the presence of the thing that blocked her passage – the plug that *looked like* her pubic hair but that hid his Father's erect penis. He wandered *back* inside her in all innocence, like the insatiable babe he was, to gobble up the endless supply of food she concealed. Unknowingly, the Boy fed upon – *and enraged* – somebody much bigger than he who was already making beautiful music inside her: *blindly*, he devoured the Father his Mother hid and acquired a beard to mark him ever after as a killer and a cannibal. When boys grow up – that is, once they have undergone the rites of initiation and been *reborn* as children of mothers' brothers instead of mothers – they redress the mother's crime by shifting blame for the father's "losing his head" onto *all* women, making women alone forever guilty of the primal crime. Until the recent past, as part of cannibal rites for a men of stature killed in war or by sorcery, Gimi men compelled the deceased's kinswomen to *act* as an unruly mob, "steal" and devour his corpse and then, by "forcing" the women to accept "head" payments in exchange for the dead man's bones, staged a public demonstration of women's criminality. Without men's civilizing interventions, the funeral rites showed, women would devour the whole man without remorse and then refuse to make amends or offer any compensation. By making women the *only* cannibals in the past and excluding them as *donors* of "head" payments in other rites of passage – as though, unlike their brothers in crime, women refused to let go of what they stole from the Father or accept any substitute – men shifted the entire blame for the Father's murder onto women. Primordial guilt forced Gimi women to retreat every month into "houses of shame." But women also *insist* on cohabiting with the Moon and bearing his dead offspring month after month. Men, however, take great pains to rid themselves of "Moon's blood," not only by scrupulously bleeding their noses and sending the blood "back to their sisters' vaginas" in "secret" transactions during male initiation, but also by making public payments called "the head of the child" to replace and ressurect the Moon's murdered progeny. Nothing is ever created or destroyed: to *get rid* of the primal crime's indelible bodily traces, men *transfer* them from men to women by depilating their own "female pubic hair" and tattooing "beards" onto brides' faces.

To See is to Dispossess – To Dispossess is to Humiliate

Men's Flute myth pictures the Mother or First Woman as supremely alone, or with another woman, and makes no mention of the primal Father, camouflaging his presence in the sounds of the music and the image of the Flute Plug made entirely of "female pubic hair." Without Father's *visible* presence, Mother gets all the blame for hiding him and tricking her Son into *re*entering her vagina to evict the Father from her body, something she fervently wishes but cannot accomplish by herself because, as women's own myths show, she is profoundly ambivalent. But because she is *the one who sees while the other does not see*, in men's view, she is entirely responsible for what the other feels and does. As the 'lone looker,' Mother creates *magical fusion* between herself and the unseeing object of her gaze. The one who is aware while the other is oblivious takes possession of the other as an integral part of herself – or himself in the case of sorcery – and exerts a control that is tantamount to appropriation by theft (Gillison 1999).

As lone witness to the moment of birth, mother attaches her child utterly: she and it become a dual entity who *appear* – like a plugged flute – to be a seamless whole. In men's scenario, the music stops because the First Flute Owner simply refuses to unplug herself – to let go of what is inside her. In men's Flute myth, the Boy-hero does the unplugging: he empties his Sister and opens her passage for others to follow – but at what cost to himself! The Plug-Baby extricates himself by becoming his Sister's menstrual flow: the moment *her* pubic hair is planted on *his* face, *his* whole body runs thick and red out of *her* vagina. The Plug/Unplugger is the "firstborn child," the severed "head" of the Moon whom, according to men, the First Woman was determined to keep unsevered and hidden inside herself forever. In death rites of the past, Gimi men turned their "secret" Flute myth into public spectacle by compelling women to enact the role of the First Woman: women devoured the dead man "in secret" – but really at men's invitation and insistance – and were publicly exposed and punished when men presented them with anatomically-matched "head" payments of 'other meat' as substitutes for the man they ate *as if* the cannibals would otherwise refuse to let him go. Men's gift of substitutes for the dead man's "head" was an accusation cannibal women were forced publicly to accept and never allowed to return or rectify by acting as donors.

According to men's myth, the Boy hero sacrifices his life to unplug the Flute and cause his Sister to menstruate so that afterwards a second child, installed by a different father, can be born alive. Unplugging the Flute released the first, primal Father-derived Child from his Sister's relentless embrace. In men's terms, menstrual blood is not simply 'the blood of the father' or the killed "firstborn" child but also the consequence of the mother's *refusal to let go of either one*. Woman's crime, in men's view, is that by "looking down" at her vagina she *attached two men to herself as if they were one and the same – one endless continuity*. She garnered excessive power from being *alone* as she watched her Father-going-in lost in rapture *and* her Son-coming-out with eyes shut. Simply by *looking* at what was happening within the precincts of her own body, the First Woman transformed the blind Father-Son duo between her thighs into one fabulous Giant Penis like a rope of liana vine, its vast length coiled into a heavy bundle hiding a dead baby at the center. The lone First Woman inside the "flute house" transforms a *threesome into a twosome*, attaching one male seamlessly to the other and both of them to herself. She creates the stifling *dyadic* connection to her that precludes any other and to which she 'holds on' unto death. Left to her own devices, men insist and women sometimes agree, no woman would relinquish the Child her Father sired, the one he keeps coming back to engender month after month. Rather than give up the Father-Baby, she turns it to blood between her thighs, emblem of her lethal talent for dyadic attachment.

Gimi women protest this portrait of motherhood: the Giant Penis women concoct in their myths and masturbatory fantasies is perfectly autonomous, venturing *by itself* into the forest to shoot marsupials by day and into virgins' houses to "eat open" their vaginas by night while the Old Man stays far away fast asleep inside a different house. In female initiation ritual, the initiate and her chaperons break to pieces – separate into offspring – the 'sugar daddy' men insert through a hole in the roof of the menstrual hut (see Fig. 3.2 above). "Women break up the pole and throw away the pieces to *get rid* of the blood and replace it with the 'real child,'" women say. In women's myths, the heroine decapitates the Giant Penis. She cuts the Giant down to size *all by herself* and sets out with her little Dog to hunt for a real-life Husband. Once she finds him she brazenly disobeys his instructions. Women's heroine strikes the tree he closes shut – a giant version of her body as a plugged Flute – and releases all the bird-babies to soar into the sky and make beautiful music. (See Chap. 6, p. 213ff.)

* * *

A deeper layer of agreement nevertheless exists beneath the 'tit for tat' that is Gimi cosmology. Men's non-esoteric version of the primordial Father, the Moon, is a solitary figure who throws his giant penis out of the night sky to copulate with every nubile girl and make her blood run. The First Woman alone in her "flute house" is also a supreme isolate, like the Moon, able to *see* those who cannot look back. The Moon strikes at night while virgin girls are asleep inside their mothers' houses. And just like a menstruating woman, the Moon *refuses to let go*. The Boy climbs to the "head" of the tall tree, casts the stone inside his very, very long net bag into the stagnant pool below, splashing the First Woman and extinguishing the fire in her Vagina; then he *pulls back* the stone-dead baby inside the net bag – a portrait of himself in miniature. The small Boy is the part of himself the Moon 'shoots' into the Woman lying beside the pool and then retrieves – eating it back up, turning it to blood – so that the Moon remains solitary and undiminshed (Gillison 1993: 204).

The First Woman in her "flute house" and the man in the Moon, both figures of men's invention, are very much alike. And each one also ressembles the death-dealing primordial Couple in women's myths: the Dream Man, Dream Mother and their proto-Dream Children; the Trickster, gorgeous Girl and her Mother in the myth of the Torrent Lark; the Widow and the Old Man in 'Eros and Psyche.' The original Parents in men's and women's competing narratives are nearly the same – 'one *in* the same' – as Father ensconsed in Mother, a pair locked together in perpetual coitus from which no life issues until "one day" when a baby Boy or nubile Girl pulls off the heroic feat of castration, leaving one parent with a drastically shortened penis and the other with a bleeding hole. But there is a crucial difference, too. Women's myths and rites reveal what men try to hide, which is the overwhelming presence of a cruel Father whom the sexes destroyed together and whose murder disfigures them both with tell-tale traces of their crime.

Note

1. Because of their intimate connection, Gimi myths and rites are often discussed together. Mythic figures and artifacts are capitalized to distinguish them from their ritual counterparts. But pronouns that refer to mythic figures appear in lower case. Big Man and Big Woman, individuals recognized as important persons and leaders in the community, are also capitalized.

References

Gillison, Gillian. 1993. *Between Culture and Fantasy. A New Guinea Highlands Mythology*. Chicago: University of Chicago Press.

———. 1999. Fieldwork and the Idea of the Unconsious. *Psychoanalytic Studies* 1 (i): 49–56.

Newman, Philip L., and David J. Boyd. 1982. The Making of Men: Ritual and Meaning in Awa Male Initiation. In *Rituals of Manhood*, ed. Gilbert H. Herdt. Berkeley: University of California Press.

8

Conclusion: *Totem and Taboo* Revisited

Totem and Taboo Revisited

Gimi women's myths and rites invite a revision of Freud's account about the murder of the primal father by a band of brothers in Chapter IV of *Totem and Taboo*. Together with Gimi men's usages, they create a meta-narrative that 'reads' like an adaptation of Freud's widely-misunderstood and discredited work. For one thing, daughters and sisters become part of the rebellious mob of offspring. If sons were enraged by a primal father who denied them access to their sisters because, in the imagery of Gimi men's Flute myth, the primal father was already inside all the sisters blocking the brothers' entry, leaving them as eternal infants mesmerized by the music of copulation but unable to participate, then the sisters the father raped in perpetuity – whose bodies he invaded and occupied in an orgy of sex and murder, making them sing like sirens or lie deadly silent – were just as angry and as determined to act as their brothers, or even angrier and more determined, and prepared to join with them or to take matters in their own "hand."

G. Gillison, *She Speaks Her Anger: Myths and Conversations of Gimi Women*, Culture, Mind, and Society, https://doi.org/10.1007/978-3-030-49352-3_8

In Gimi women's myths about the primodial era, the heroine is the one who spurs her male counterpart – a husband who is also her brother because they are the first couple – to murder the father. In women's myth of the Dream Man,[1] the heroine left at the base of the tree urges her Marsupial Hunter-Husband to murder the Dream Man and every member of his tree-top family and to send the "delicious food" down to her. Some of women's heroines, like the First Woman who cuts the Giant Penis down to size, are ready to kill the Father on their own. In women's myth of 'Eros and Psyche,' the heroine seals the Old Man disguised as her Mother inside her Mother's house and sets them both alight, instructing the fire to explode the Old Man's every limb and organ, starting with his testicles (See Chaps. 6 and 7).

Seen through the lens of Gimi myths and rites of both sexes, the primal father in *Totem and Taboo* becomes a *composite figure*: a seamlessly united pair who imprison and destroy everyone else. Freud's father also morphs into *an arrested primal scene*, the coagulate of an incestuous couple engaged in permanent coitus who appear to their offspring to be a single object like the plugged Flute in men's myth or a single person like the Old Man disguised as the Widow in women's myth of 'Eros and Psyche.' In both sexes' imagery Father is 'covered up' inside Mother. In myth, Gimi men obscure his very presence inside the "the plug of female pubic hair" the First Woman uses to close her Flute; and in death rites of the past, men forced women to assume the role of outlaw cannibal thieves and to cut up and consume a man completely "out of men's sight." The expanded context of Gimi women's myths reveals that men attempt to conceal their role in the primal Father's murder and consumption often by making him disappear altogether. In women's narratives the father is no mere "plug" in a Flute nor cannibal victim hidden inside women's bellies. He emerges as a full-fledged creature on the rampage like the Dream Man, Giant Penis, Cassowary Hunter, Python, or Old Man, exactly the kind of vicious monopolist Freud envisaged – his person augmented by the Mother he rapes incessantly and whose *whole body* he shapes as the perfect fit for his Giant Penis.

Seen in the context of Gimi women's myths, the primal father whom men try to conceal as an inert plug of "female pubic hair" emerges as a marauding Old Man who 'takes up residence' inside Mother and, after devouring her insides, reduces her to the hideous outer covering and inert disguise for his murdering body-size "stick." The primal father consumes his every progeny, taking back inside the "head" of his mythical Penis everything that "flies out" when he ejaculates so that, while Mother is repeatedly emptied, he is never diminished nor forced to leave the confines of her tailor-made phallic-shaped body. As Father's "house" and permanent setting for his cruel exploits, Mother often appears to be missing from the scene altogether.

Viewing Freud's portrait of the primal father in the light of Gimi women's and men's myths and rites expands him into the figure of a voracious, perpetually-copulating *pair*, an alteration of the father's identity which makes the primal crime part of a primal scene. As a corollary, simple murder becomes the far more complicated task of separating the primordial pair to allow their offspring to escape into the world outside their viciously-united bodies. In the terms of a Gimi-inspired revision of *Totem and Taboo*, the "one day" when Freud famously says "the band of brothers" came together to murder the Father translates into the moment when the Pair's stunted brood of incipient brothers *and* sisters united to remove Father from Mother by devouring his "head" – the *part of him* that made the two appear as 'one *inside* the same.' Throughout the primoridal Gimi era, it is impossible to know which parent has the penis because, until that fateful "one day," both do. Once the original Couple are rent violently asunder – after, for instance, the Mother's Brother in women's Python myth decapitates the Python still cockily "shaking his head" inside his Sister's Daughter's mouth – the two sexes come into existence: the male keeps a shortened version of the Giant Penis that once made the Pair inseparable; and the female is left holding the Giant's severed head "between her thighs." During commission of the primal crime, Father's blood enters the bodies of *all* his children, flooding the noses of adolescent boys and the vaginas of adolescent girls.

According to my interpretations of the Gimi life-world, the primal crime occurs in a past that is both primordial and *prenatal*. The Gimi metanarrative implicit in the "secret" songs, myths and rites of both sexes' brings together Freud's propositions about the murder of the father in *Totem and Taboo* and his insights about the formative trauma of a child's witnessing its parents' copulation, an association that may explain why Gimi invariably connect watching, or seeing, with killing and culpability. Introduction of active and passive female characters – sisters as part of the angry mob and mother's body as scene of the action – expands the primal father into a dual creature whom no one can escape and everyone exactly resembles. The trapped proto-children are *undifferentiated* and *incomplete,* each one condemned to *watch* the primal Couple from inside the womb, which is their only vantage point, until the "one day" when they come together to commit the primal crime. At this mythic moment, the Gimi sexes secretly agree, the unborn "eat the head" of the father's Giant Penis, a decapitation and *theft* that severs him from Mother and allows all the children to escape her charnel house. This is the moment when 'all of a sudden' adolescent bodies fill up with Giant's blood and boys acquire whiskers – shameful residues of the brothers' and sisters' common crime which paradoxically establishes the crucial differences between them.

Until the sexes emerge as distinct creatures, rampant sameness and contagious resemblence are the law of the universe. In the primordial era, reproduction is strictly *parthenogenetic*: it occurs "without concourse of opposite sexes or union of sexual elements" (The Oxford Universal Dictionary 1955: 1438). Frazer's unsurpassed description of "contagious magic," according to which *part of a person*, some leaving or *exuvia* such as a tooth, saliva, remnants of a meal, blood, and most especially faeces and seminal fluid, may substitute for *the entire person*, as in sorcery, also applies to the Gimi reproductive process (Frazer 1963 [1922]). Like the Dream Man and his family, or the First Woman and her Flute, characters in Gimi myths possess an *over-affinity:* after merely being lopped off or extracted one from inside the other, they fit back together too easily. The myths and rites of both sexes portray the Giant Penis' capacity to reabsorb his ejaculate, to take back his 'little ones,' and to stay ensconsed inside his custom-made "house." In the plugged Flute and Giant Penis – images of the First Couple as a 'perfect fit' unwilling to release any offspring – Gimi picture the confluence of interests and mutual desires of adjacent generations and opposing sexes.

When the heroine cuts off the Giant, or the hero unplugs the Flute, each one brings male and female into being as have and have-not: each one expels Father from Mother's "house" – a passive version of the mythic heroine herself – in such a way that *he* keeps a radically-shortened penis and *she* is left holding the severed "head" that once joined them so they were indistinguishable, the portrait of inexhaustible desire and rage, issuing and retracting unborn life in silent, unseen and continuous acts of violence. The capacity of the Giant Penis to reabsorb his ejaculate expresses the situation of compounded incest in which everyone is blissed out and furious – paralyzed with contentment and anger in equal measure. Ambivalence is universal: the child no less than its original parent/s wish to reunite and become one again. Uninterrupted, the dyadic bliss achieved in myth and magic evolves into horror and death: whatever one ejects, extrudes, ejaculates, puts forth into the world from one's own inner being – whether plant, pig or person – and continues to nurture through additional infusions of self, one wishes to recoup by eating the fruits of one's labor and investment.

The markers of sexual difference that erupt at puberty put an end, at least for now, to the primal era shaped by the Father's monster habit of reabsorption and assimilation. The "female pubic hair" that sprouts on a boy's face and the "blood of the penis" that leaks out of a girl's vagina reveal the exact nature of the epoch-making crime that ended his vile reign. So revolutionary and unwanted are the changes in adolescent bodies that – given the way things *used to be*, the easy affinity shared by all and sundry in the primordial past – it may still be possible to *reverse the mythic deed* which caused their "first appearance." Gimi women and men design separate "secret" rites to make the contagiously-acquired attributes of the other sex that now mar adolescent bodies 'disappear' by *sending them back* to their original and rightful place in the body of the other sex. After all, it was the other sex *who knew*, whose eyes were open, while one's own sex was blind or oblivious and trusting, tricked and misled, as innocent as a babe in tall grass or a virgin girl sound asleep inside her mother's house.

In order to disagree on the crucial issue of who took the initiative and is primarily responsible for the Father's demise and eviction from Mother's house, Gimi women and men necessarily share the main narrative of prehistory. When the music stops in their "secret" game of exchange in secondary sexual characteristics, only the male – the one able to *transfer* both the beard on his face and the blood in his nose to his sister – escapes eternal blame.

Unlike a man, a woman *retains* the piece of the Father-Mother she stole to create a discontinuous and recognizable world. Unlike a man, a woman *refuses* to let go of her prehistoric inheritance by converting it into an object of exchange. Both Gimi sexes seem to arrive at the judgment of women as unwilling or unfit to engage in exchange as full partners with men based upon their interpretations of human anatomy, reproductive physiology and early child development especially, as I emphasize, the prolongation of infancy or state of extreme unreadiness for independent life in each individual known as "neoteny" or "premature birth;" an immaturity which requires a kind of attachment between mother or primary care-giver and child that is extraordinarily difficult to interrupt or terminate as the child matures and even after it physically separates from the actual mother. Gimi systems of kinship and marriage treat women and their mythical antecedents as those who *chose perversely* to menstruate, suckle and nurture wholly dependent beings; as if, without men's connivance and violent interference in the relation of mother and child at puberty, the female would remain a "one-holed" phallic creature indistinguishable from the cannibal Dream Man she hides inside her 'one-door' house.

The Hatred of Women

When the First Woman "looked down at her vagina," according to Gimi men, she took possession of the man-child she saw going-in and coming-out of her, infecting all males with the unrelenting desire to "travel the road we first came down." In revenge, according to women's interpretation of male rage, her Father "sends her to the Snake." He rapes her and "kills," or converts to menstrual blood, the "head" of the Penis she tries to keep hidden inside her "at the head of her bed." The problem with men's solution to their lingering attachment to mother, in women's view, is that the Father/Giant Penis/Moon they send to do their dirty work closely ressembles the Mother they abhor! Men's portraits of the Moon and of the Small Boy who climbs to the top of a huge tree, throws a stone into a fetid pool, splashes out the fire in the First Woman's Vagina and then pulls back the stone inside the very long net bag he wears around his neck – a miniature version of his stone-dead self – seem hardly different from the devouring phallic Mother. So when men send the Moon or the Snake to "punish" the First Woman, the two profoundly-similar colossi *stick together*, recreating the problem of over-affinity men say they try to solve.

By introducing as full participants in the primal crime the female characters Freud omits – both as the silent 'scene of the crime' *and* as guilty accomplices who, like their brothers, are plagued with remorse – we see that the "band of brothers," whom Freud credits with inventing the social order, do more than merely 'exchange away' the sisters they covet and on whose account they murdered the primal father. In the Gimi scheme of things, the brothers *also* shift onto their sisters and co-conspirators – symbolized as a parting gift for the bride – *all* the blame for the Father's murder. Men's myth of the First Woman or Two Women as *sole* inventor[s] and possessor[s] of the Flutes and therefore all-powerful in an era when women had no husbands and all men were babies "hiding in tall grass," corresponds to the experience of infants and young children (Bamberger 1974). By removing or concealing the Father – treating him as 'silencer' and 'unseen presence' (the flute plug) instead of as a marauding Giant – men's myth leaves no one to blame but Mother.

Every society of the elementary type, as Freud emphasizes, places a premium on "the band of brothers" whose cooperation is essential in warfare and subsistence tasks like hunting and clearing the forest. Small-scale societies may be geared to the development of *individuals*, especially males, because a poorly-adapted or under-performing adult may significantly impede endeavours essential to collective life. For society's sake, a man needs to resolve his rivalry with his father and other men but has far less or no need at all to resolve hostility to his mother and to women in general (Spiro 1968). As I argue, Gimi culture promotes hatred of women as a dull instrument for the exquisitely *specific* job of undoing a grown child's – especially a son's – lingering attachment to his mother or mother-substitute (Gillison 2016). Once early childhood is past, especially for a boy, Gimi consider continuation of the bond to mother to be as harmful to the individual's further development and social integration as it was crucial to his early survival and well being. A woman's vagina reveals not simply that she 'lost her penis' (the stick she wielded as a lethal weapon alongside her mythic Husband in the primal past) but also that she *remains attached to a part of herself she cannot keep*, a part that *left* "in her hand" or "between her thighs" turns to blood as the final outcome of her care. For Gimi of both sexes, menstrual blood symbolizes the termination of a child's prolonged attachment to mother as if it were a death she herself may have caused rather than let her child live a life apart from her.

The suggestion that women accept some responsibility for menstruation as a punishment men inflict appears in 'Eros and Psyche,' women's tale of female heroism *par excellence*. In that myth and the myth of the Giant Penis, one source of the heroine's rage is the filth accumulated at the "head" of the Old Man's "stick," residues of the blackened innards of the countless women he raped, murdered and ate, including especially his last victim who was the heroine's own Mother. "He was a man who tricked women, killed them and ate them. That is the kind of man he was!" *And* the kind of man the Daughter-heroine desired: a man willing to go 'all the way through' her Mother – up her anus and out her mouth – in order to get to *her*. The heroine's collaboration in the Old Man's crimes is signaled repeatedly, first of all, by her Mother's warning about the bananas' noisily hitting the ground; and later, by her watching the Old Man "break the bottom of the bamboo" to demonstrate before her very eyes what he just did to her Mother inside the forest. Still, she follows his instructions to fill his bamboo at the end of a journey as endlessly long as her desire for his Penis.

Women's myths describe the heroine's ambivalence toward the Father. The parricidal 'Psyche' was at first in the Old Man's thrall – travelling over mountains to do his bidding. In that way, she resembles her Mother, his food-gathering Widow who, after warning her children that 'men may kill me,' ventures into the forest to team up with her evil ghost of a Husband to collect the delicious morsels – frogs, rats, wild yams, tender shoots of new ferns, fat white grubs – who symbolize their unformed progeny. To the extent that she resembles her widowed Mother, the myth's heroine is also a cause of the Pair's sealed-together condition, part of the reason why no baby escapes them nor exists for more than a moment as a separate being.

The Magic of Motherhood

The separate myths of Gimi women and men suggest that the sexes share similar problems of over-attachment to mother for which *she* is entirely to blame: her menstrual blood represents premature death for both sexes as the outcome of a mother's uninterrupted devotion. Like the Boy perched in the Treetop with the stone inside the very long net bag around his neck, a mother's intention is *never to let go* but rather to pull back inside herself the lives she releases and cares for during periods of exclusive attachment. A mother's plan for all her babies – porcine, vegetable and human – is to terminate their lives when they begin to ripen by fulfilling the promises she makes to them every day of their young lives, the irresistable invitations she issued – often in a language made *just for two* – to 'come inside and grow big.' To seduce her charges into blooming and flourishing, a mother articulates and then makes good on their dearest wish to rejoin her in complete intimacy. The reward for thriving under a mother's care is that she will take you back – eat you – while you are still tender and delicious: the reappearance of menstrual blood month after month is proof that she very often carries out her cannibal promises.

Garden and pig magic are ritual expressions of the ambivalent nature of a mother's love – life-giving but eventually fatal. The remedy, in the case of children of both sexes, is gradually to undo the tie to mother by replacing her with her brother – someone willing to carry out what she refuses to do: end the *uniqueness* she works hard to create and sustain between herself and each of her charges. The "secret source" of women's garden magic and talent as nurturers, according to both sexes, lies in women's understanding of their myths: "Those who know the meaning of the myths," women remark, "know how to speak to their plants." For years, the connection was not obvious to me because the two sets of knowledge are radically different in mood, length and format. One is tender, inventively intimate, playful, elliptical, rhythmically patterned, usually sung or chanted, and filled with spontaneous non-word verbalizations and caresses. The other – although bracketed with phrases and peppered with ditties and onomatopaeic repetitions in the whimsical language of "wild women" – is violent, discursory, obscene, affectively flat, without insignificant detail or much idiosyncratic flourish. Yet the two bodies of knowledge are inseparably connected, as Gimi women insist: myths reveal a woman's own traumatic origins as the wellspring of the intimate I-thou connection she offers her nurtured objects.

The 'magic of motherhood' derives from the mother's prehistory as the prisoner of a conjoined pair from whom no child escaped until *she* alone, or together with her brother, arranged a harrowing getaway and became a parent-killer in the process. The heroine of Gimi women's myths, like her ritual counterpart during initiation and marriage, is the one mainly responsible for her emergence from her mother's house: she cuts the Giant down to normal size although, significantly, the female initiate receives indispensable help from her brothers. Yet Gimi women's heroine /initiate/ bride is still the main agent of her rebirth into maturity, a feat women's myths describe as her "singlehandedly" creating a recognizable husband out of a huge marauding Penis: in essence, she is the one who transforms the chaos of her adolescent desires into a socially-recognized marriage.

Gimi women say that a woman who understands myth knows not only how to *speak* to food but also how to *apportion* it – another one of women's remarks about myth that mystified me until I realized how life-changing is woman's mythic deed. A married woman who undergones the ordeals of initiation, who makes *the* iconic separation described in myth between the Old Man and her Husband, between "wild man" and "domestic man," understands how to make other kinds of disconnections. She knows how to discriminate, to perceive with subtlety both the distinctiveness of individuals and their relations with one another, and to help calculate allotments of food accordingly. A woman who grasps the stories' deep meanings, which are to civilize her own fantasies and desires, also knows how to make practical decisions that engender good relations among the people around her.

Cycle of Blame: 'The Gift' as Accusation

The accusations and counter-accusations, thefts and counter-thefts, in Gimi men's and women's usages alternate the sex of the culture hero and create a cycle of blame. Underlying their opposition, men's and women's myths share a vision of the world as it was before the primal Father's decapitation, the onset of menstrual bleeding and "first appearance" of a beard, the era when no Child emerged alive from the monster-Father, Dream Man or Giant Penis who remained ensconsed in Mother, his immense length coiled around the rotting 'furry ones' he shot out of treetops. The Giant's wound-up bulk inhabited a First Woman who was forever pregnant because no piece of the Giant ever escaped her body. She served as the not-unwilling outer shell of a Conjoined Pair who *looked like* a single entity that was sometimes stilled and silent, at other times seductively "crying."

The only way to exit the myth – to break apart the primal Couple and allow their stunted offspring to escape, in men's view – is to manufacture *facsimiles* of the First Couple's unholy union, *especially as women depict it in myth*, and to exchange these ritual objects among themselves, bypassing the women. To 'save the child' and separate it from the mother requires that men undo *the mother's own* childish connections, a task for which she herself – who is stuck mostly in the dyadic domain – is ill-equipped. Men exclude mothers as organizers of the transactions that liberate their children by appropriating women's own narratives of their primordial origins and converting them to ritual acts. Men transpose women's words and ideas into ritual objects – which include the women themselves as brides – and, by transferring these objects to other men, *alter* the female scenarios from which they derive. In this way men's public exchanges of "head" payments at the conclusion of rites of passage settle in men's favor, if only for the time being, the argument the sexes wage inside separate houses out of each other's sight.

The objects of affinal exchange men manufacture – the "sugar pig" in female initiation ritual, the tattooed bride, the 'matching' pair of sacred bamboo flutes "plugged" with hairy chunks of pork, and "the head of the child" – condense both sexes' mythic narratives. "Head" payments, like the "sugar pig" men present to a female initiate to "buy her vagina," convert the mythic Giant of women's myths into edible substitutes, thus recapitulating the primal Father's decapitation and dismemberment in terms that change the myth's dénouement in which the Girl and her Firstborn die. To the extent that the mother's brother's "eating the head of the child" corresponds to women's "secret" narratives, it *alters* them by reallocating blame for the primal crime from donor to recipient. What is more – by a brilliant stoke of cultural logic – "head" payments that recapitulate the mythic crime transfer blame from donor to recipient by the very act of compensating the recipient for losses suffered during the crime's commission. In this sense, the gift is an *accusation* which women never get to bestow. Women embody the gift publicly as brides and "secretly" as a pair of flutes; and they receive it alongside their husbands as the "heads" of their husbands' sisters' children; and, in the past, in the transaction that defined them, women were forced to accept "head" payments in exchange for the man they supposedly stole and ate as public testimony of their crime.

Women's mythic prehistory, which is to say, women's and men's various interpretations of female anatomy and reproductive physiology as *faits accomplis*, disqualifies them as gift *givers*. Left entirely to her own devices, women concede, a woman may take the Giant Penis out of circulation by discarding his huge severed length in a river and keeping his bloody severed head "between her thighs." Women avidly desire the "delicious stuff" men continually "throw down" to them but, once consumed, they deliver a product *unfit for exchange*. Menstrual blood and infants 'stuck' in prolonged attachment to mother, Gimi women themselves often agree, are living testimony to women's participation in the primal crime and to their unwillingness to make amends by accepting substitutes that would require them to *let go* of what they "stole and ate." Despite the fact that some women's myths picture the heroine alone taking the initiative to emancipate her children by cutting off the Giant or by disobeying her Husband's command "not to look," they also show that she has no means to convert the dead stuff inside her into a living child until the Giant returns to "kill" her – raping her *again* to tear open a second "vagina" in her head – or until her Husband "cuts the top" off a tree used for burial and hollows it out.

"Why Can't a Woman Be Just Like a Man?"

Freud says men's renunciation of their own sisters and marriage to other men's sisters represent repentent self-denial: "they all alike renounced the women whom they desired and who had been their chief motive for dispatching their father. In this way they rescued the organization which had made them strong – which may have been based on homosexual feelings and acts" (1972 [1913]: 144). Freud's band of brothers murdered their father but felt remorse afterwards because they also loved him. Out of remorse, they renounced the 'parts' of the father they most coveted while he was alive – their sisters whom he monopolized and held captive. In the Gimi situation as I interpret it, men's enduring love for the father moved them not only to repudiate the sisters they liberated from his reign of terror but also to saddle the sisters with the entire blame for his murder as a kind of secret 'parting gift.' The premises of Gimi kinship are designed to exonerate men not only through renunciation and exchange of their sisters as wives for other men but also through the wholesale condemnation of women for what they did in partnership with their brothers in the mythic past but are now, in the ritual present, unwilling to undo by accepting substitutes for their children and surrendering them to others – as if that were a 'reasonable expectation' on a par with men's renouncing marriage to their own sisters. Gimi men's ambivalence towards the primal father gives rise not only to the incest taboo, as Freud convincingly demonstrates, but also to a hatred of women as those who do, and incite men to do, all the bad things, beginning with the primal crime – the original death and wound to narcissism – and who refuse to make amends as men do by giving up the ones whom they "stole" from the father and cherish most.

As long as Gimi women *keep* what they killed or "cut off," installing it between their thighs, inside their bodies and at the breast, the incest and murder are all theirs: the post-cannibal rites of the past in which men publicly forced women to accept 'other meat' as substitute for the man they ate as the condition of re-entry into human society was only a temporary remedy, as any meal is a temporary remedy for hunger. According to Gimi women's version of the primal crime, 'Psyche' annihilates the First Couple – the vile Old Man concealed inside her Mother – but not before she rescues and carries away with her a 'dead piece' of their vicious union. In a Gimi revision of *Totem and Taboo*, brothers and sisters collude to destroy and devour the primordial Father/Mother. But in keeping with Freud's scenario, and according to the Gimi rites of exchange that recapitulate both Gimi men's and women's mythic narratives, only brothers "allay their burning sense of guilt, to bring about a kind of reconciliation with their father" through sacrifice, and emerge as culture heroes (*Ibid*). "The sense of guilt," Freud says, "can only be allayed by the solidarity of *all* the participants" (*Ibid*: 147, emphasis added). To vindicate themselves and achieve solidarity, Gimi men do more than renounce marriage to their own sisters and exchange them with the sisters of other men. In homage to the father they murdered but still revere, they force their sisters to devour him as part of a ritual farce *as if* the sisters had conspired behind men's backs and *acted alone*.

Condemnation for the primal crime, which Gimi of both sexes dramatized in cannibal rituals of the past, placed the female sex temporarily outside the human race. As part of the ritual scenario men designed, the act of consuming a male cadaver de-personned the cannibals so that they lost their names and became literally "nothing" (*faba badaha*; *faba*, 'nothing + *badaha*, 'women'). To regain their humanity and individual identities, the cannibal women had to be 'force fed' "head" payments to replace with utmost precision the dead man's every limb and organ, enacting in public not only proof of women's hidden crime but also their reluctance *after the fact* to accept a substitute and let go of what they stole. By shifting all the blame for the primal crime onto their sisters – making them the *only* cannibals, defacing them with tattooed stigmata, forcing them to retreat into "houses of shame" and denigrating women as a species – men arrange their own exoneration.

As résumé of the mythic dispute, the "gift of the head" is an accusation and a proof of wrong-doing which women accept and embody but never expunge by exchanging it away. Gimi women serve as objects of exchange and as recipients but never as *donors* which means they never get to give away their mythic guilt. Gimi men exclude women from "the solidarity of all the participants" in the primal crime and full participation in the rites of expiation on the grounds that motherhood and female reproductive physiology are a kind of moral lapse that women themselves *could* correct. Indeed, so intentional and performance-based do Gimi myths consider the derivation of difference between the sexes to be that to maintain it – and to 'keep women in their place' – they regularly reenact the mythic deeds which created the difference in the first place. Freud says that "[t]otemic religion arose from the filial sense of guilt, in an attempt to allay that feeling and to appease the father by deferred obedience to him" (Freud 1972 [1913]: 145). In the Gimi context, I suggest, "the burning sense of guilt" engendered by 'killing the father' in myth manifests itself in both sexes at puberty in features of anatomy and physiology that appear "suddenly" as defects.

The underlying premise of the exchange of "head" payments – the idea that *if only* a woman were a reliable partner, willing to reciprocate, she could be a donor like a man – is not just a way to blame women for their own exclusion, a way to demonstrate that every woman's wish is to remain locked in deadly fusion with her father and her child whom she often treats as one and the same. To make women guilty for what they *are*, as if they chose perversely to mensturate, breastfeed, and nurture wholly dependent beings, the myths and rites of initiation of *both* sexes assert that sexual difference is the outcome of *primordial deeds* regularly reenacted in the present. This fantasy seems to appeal to Gimi women as well as to men because, besides blaming women for their own misfortune and treating them as outcasts, it also promotes the idea that sexual identity is a transferable commodity subject to theft like a flute. For reasons that Freud alone seems to have grasped, women *contribute* to the fiction that sexual assignment is somehow temporary, inessential, and the result of women's own capriciousness and bad character. If women are entirely or largely to blame, their reasoning seems to be, then perhaps they can *undo* the 'bad choices' they themselves made. In the view of *both* Gimi sexes, to be female is a misfortune that arose in the mythic past and *can be* – if only women were less recalcitrant about letting go of their children – reversed in the ritual present. Beneath myths of protest and rites of defiance, Gimi women also agree with men that a woman is neither willing to give up her child nor capable of keeping it without disastrous results.

"In the Beginning Was The Deed"

"It has been stated and restated," says Lévi-Strauss, "that what makes *Totem and Taboo* unacceptable as an interpretation of incest and its origins, is … [that it] do[es] not correspond to any fact or group of facts occupying a given place in history" (Lévi-Strauss 1969 [1949]: 491).

What is more, treating *Totem and Taboo* as Freud's speculation about proto-historical fact begets the untenable corollary, labeled the "'Jungian' defect," that "the consequences of this event have had a persisting effect on the brain and behaviour of the human animal *by some process of genetic inheritance*" (Freeman 1970: 62, emphasis in original). There is no such thing as a "biologically inherited … archetypical mneme." As everyone knows, "culture is socially inherited and historically diffused" (La Barre 1958: 290). Even those who consider *Totem and Taboo* to be "the single most important insight into the nature of culture" lament Freud's "ambiguity in stating a timeless psychological process as if it were a single historical event" (*Ibid*: 291). How, then, is one to interpret the very last sentence of *Totem and Taboo* where Freud insists, citing Goethe, that "'in the beginning was the Deed'" (Freud 1972 [1913]: 161)?

The question is especially pertinent to the present analysis because I treat the myths of Gimi women and men, separately and together, as templates or 'blueprints' for the manufacture of ritual objects – brides, flutes, child payments – which I describe as material condensations of mythic scenarios whose exchange among men alters the catastrophic endings myths envisage. If the Gimi rites of passage and exchange recapitulate mythic imagery, then it would seem that fantasy *preceeds* reality, myth inspires rite, wish instigates deed. "Accordingly the mere hostile *impulse* against the father, the mere existence of a wishful *phantasy* of killing and devouring him, would have been enough to produce the moral reaction that created totemism and taboo" (Freud 1972 [1913]: 159–160, emphases in original). But Freud rejects this interpretation. To an uneasy Ernest Jones, Freud replied that in *The Interpretation of Dreams,* "'I described the wish to kill one's father, and now [in *Totem and Taboo*] I have been describing the actual killing; after all it's a big step from a wish to a deed'" (Jones 1953: 354 cited in Wallace 1980: 163).

Understandably, Freud's many critics focus on Chapter IV of *Totem and Taboo.* But the preceeding three Chapters are essential to understanding the last one and Freud's ultimate reference to Goethe on the primacy of "the Deed." His explanation of "the omnipotence of thoughts" in Chapter III begins with E. B. Tylor's famous definition of magic as "mistaking an ideal connection for a real one," meaning that "[r]elations which hold between the ideas of things are assumed to hold equally between the things themselves," which may sound like little more than 'wishing makes it so' (Freud 1972 [1913]: 79 citing Tylor 1971 [1891]: I: 116; *Ibid*: 85). "Things become less important than ideas of things: whatever is done to the latter will inevitably also occur to the former" – a proposition which also applies *ex post facto* (*Ibid*). Not only does "wishing" something make it happen as, say, an imitation of rain like spitting may make rain fall; but also when something happens, like rain falling, crops flourishing, or sun rising in the morning, it is due to human agency, a principle Freud illustrates by citing a few of James Frazer's countless examples of "sympathetic magic" (*Ibid:* 82–83 citing Frazer 1911: 201). Among all "actual events," Freud notes, referring again to Tylor and to Arthur Shopenhauer, observation of the death of another, "the survivors' position in relation to the dead," is the greatest provocation to "magical thinking" (*Ibid*: 87, 92). "Primitive man would thus be submitting to the supremacy of death with the same gesture with which he seemed to be denying it" (*Ibid*: 93).

For Freud, death is the *supreme reality* about which human beings are perfectly ambivalent, both accepting and rejecting it "with the same gesture." In the case of a small-scale, kinship-based society like the Gimi in late twentieth Century Highland Papua New Guinea and in societies of the so-called "elementary" type described by Lévi-Strauss and others, Freud's dictum translates into the proposition that, when it comes to death, there are no natural causes or arbitrary events: "the natural thing was the indefinite prolongation of life – immortality" (*Ibid*: 76). Not only killings in war (the signal achievement of male adulthood in the past) but also *the fact of death itself* inspires belief in human volition and responsibility – the notion of a primoridal *deed* – a *fait accompli* – because only something men and women *have already done* can account for present reality as the *retaliation*, an untenable state which men and women can *now undo* through elaborate ritual effort. No less than death, it seems to me, extrapolating from the Gimi, the anatomical distinction between the sexes and imperatives of human neoteny are "supreme realities" based in biology that inspire fear and denial and give rise to extravagant efforts to reverse or remedy them. Adapted to the Gimi, "the Deed" that Freud insists is first and foremost and that "stands at the outset of every philosophy" (*Ibid*: 87 citing Schopenhaur) may refer not only to death but also to anatomical differences between the sexes and human neoteny as biological facts people simultaneously accept and deny by treating them as deliberate past acts open to repair. Subjected to "the omnipotence of thoughts," as Freud defines it, and combined as elements of a single narrative or set of narratives, inevitable 'facts of life' may acquire the meaning of a primordial parricide or parent-slaughter which inspires everlasting remorse and attempts to atone.

Part II

"Eating the Head of the Child"

From the perspective of what I interpret to be the underlying agreement between Gimi women's and men's separate myths and ostensibly secret portions of initiation rites, Gimi kinship is a system designed to *undo motherhood*, a project of immense difficulty and complexity given its deep and convoluted roots formed during both the child's *and the mother's* conceptions, gestations and early lives. Gimi kinship operates on the premise that to liberate the child from its mother's deadly 'dyadic grip' requires that the mother herself be extricated from her own prehistoric entanglements – *her* dyadic links to her father, mother and brother established while she herself was a foetus occupying her mother's body represented as her "house" in myth and ritual. The Gimi kinship system works to promote each person's survival, development and well-being by extricating her as a unique individual from the morass into which *both she and her mother* were born.

Seen as conflicting narratives about the primal father's decapitation and eviction from mother, men's myths seem to circumscribe, condense and invert those of women. In rites of exchange, however, cannibal rituals of the past being a prime example, men give fuller expression to women's side of the story, using public deeds instead of secret words to step up their opposition and to dismantle women's alternative versions of the prehistoric past. The pair of unborn "Boys left at home alone" in women's myth of the Home Invaders are counterparts of the lone baby Boy in men's "secret" Flute myth. When the two narratives are 'read' together, or treated as pictograms and superimposed, women's story suggests that the

Boys in both myths are inside the womb during pregnancy and that the obstacle they encounter and "cannot see" is not a hairy Plug to be "looked down" upon inside a Flute, as men would have it, but rather the ravenous "heads" of a Giant Penis, split into Father and Firstborn Son, arriving from high above. The reason the Boy in men's Flute myth at first does not *see* the plug in his Sister's flute, women's myth suggests, is the same reason the Boys cannot *see* the faces of the two Invaders who come to "play around" with them while their Parents are gone. While the Parents are "away in the forest," lost in coital abandon – making sweet music – they leave their unborn Boys "at home alone" to confront the Giant Penis all by themselves. The Boys inside the womb cannot see the Invaders' faces when they arrive gaily singing and dancing up and down Mother's mountainsides because the other end of their body, their other "heads," are outside the womb and out of sight. Whereas the Boy in men's Flute myth tried to get rid of the Giant by pulling out the Plug in his Sister's Flute and ended up sacrificing his life, the two Boys in women's myth attempt to *negotiate* with the huge Invaders in desperation, offering up each and every morsel of marsupial meat as substitutes for their more delicious foetal selves (See Chap. 5).

Women's myths and rites *scroll back* to enlarge the frame of men's Flute myth and take in not only the doorway of women's "flute house" where "tall grass" grows, but also the roof where the primal Father tears open a hole in the thatch and inserts his Giant Penis, exposing the presence men conceal inside the Flute Plug. To "steal" his Sister's Flute, women's myths show, the Boy has to go *back* inside his Sister/Mother and confront *head on* the "head" of their Father's Penis. The intrauterine encounter is 'homosexual' – foetal head to *glans penis*, open fontanelle to ejaculating urethra – and it is exciting and painful: mucous fills the Boys' "noses" and tears fall from their eyes. Inside the womb, father's seminal fluid is the boys' only nourishment. But, eventually, the repeated head-to-head encounters enrage the Giant Father and his identical grown-up Firstborn: the Two 'reinvade' the mountain valley between the Daughter/Sister's thighs to *re*claim what they lost there in the first place, returning to "play around" with the trapped Boys with gay abandon whenever they please. Left unattended and alone, the Boys try to entice the Home Invaders with 'other meat' lest, on their next incursion, the Pair devour the Boys instead, repossessing what is already theirs.

Women's myths depict the primal Father-inside-Mother taking back the ones he made: the Old Man disguised as the Widow in 'Eros and Psyche' murders the heroine's baby Brother by tossing a hot stone into his wide open "first mouth." But the heroine rescues her dead Brother, who is also her "firstborn," and runs away with him inside her net bag to find a Husband "who will pay my brideprice" – a man who will *engage in exchange instead of murder*. While women's myths condemn the Mother's Father as a relentless killer and a cannibal, they also provide the scenario for compromise through rites of exchange: 'wild meat' for Boys' lives. Men's Flute myth *cuts the heroine out of the frame*. In men's 'close-up,' the only females on the scene *are* the scene of the action, the plugged-up Sister inside her house/Mother. The murdered Brother is his own hero, a curious baby – adventurous but blind – who dares to re-enter his Sister, unplug her Flute and steal it at the cost of his life. The baby Brother *removes himself* from his Sister by eating her maidenhead – putting his mouth on what women's myth reveals to be his Father's penis – and acquiring "female pubic hair" on his face as the mark of his revolutionary cannibal deed.

Women's myth reveals that the one the Boy robbed was *not* his older, more aware Sister but rather the Old Man lurking unseen beneath her skirts who murdered the Boy in jealous fury. The baby Brother the Father killed while his "first mouth" was wide open, and whose corpse is wrapped in barkcloth like a pair of flutes that his Sister transports over mountains in search of a real Husband, *is* the Father's severed head. Men's Flute myth portrays the Boy's disastrous encounter inside the First Woman *as if she were all alone*. Their Father's severed "head" is disguised as his Sister's bloodied "plug of pubic hair;" and as the fur-covered chunks of marsupial meat men stuff into the "vaginas" of the flutes they hide inside the bride's net bag. To make his Sister fit for another man, the Boy-hero of men's Flute myth slays her "first husband" *in utero* and is killed in revenge, exiting her body as menstrual blood. Opening his Sister to a 'second husband' was a suicide mission, men's myth proclaims, leaving men no choice but to rescue adolescent sons from their mothers and bring them back to life in the seclusion of men's houses. According to men's propaganda, the Boy Flute-thief ends up *as* his Sister's "firstborn" Child whom men confiscate *'after the fact,'* after the mother's crime has already been committed. Men seize their sons and seclude them inside the "men's house," bringing them back to life through "secret" rites of rebirth which women must never witness lest they effortlessly repossess what they once kept hidden for themselves alone.

When the initiated and gorgeously-decorated "red birds" emerge from seclusion newly reborn as young men created by men, the program of rescue from their mothers continues its lifelong public phase in the exchange of "head" payments. Since mothers are supposedly the whole problem, the exchanges designed to liberate the boys not only exclude the women themselves as principal transactors but also, paradoxically, follow the scenarios of women's narratives. In the past, sometimes on pain of death, men excluded women from men's houses and rites of initiation. But, according to women's songs, spells, ritual theatre and separate myths and initiation rites, men's remedies also require more individualized and sustained measures directed *not only* against the boys' own mothers but also against the mothers' fathers and brothers who are the living heirs of the mythic Father whom men *camouflage as part of women's bodies and whose separate existence women expose*. It is Gimi women who – by exposing men's 'cover-up' and bringing the primal Father and his identically-voracious Firstborn Son into the light of day, so to speak – create the ritual agenda men follow in order to stop the Giant from *too-easily reclaiming* the progeny he creates as identical offshoots of his limitless Self. Women's revelations about the Father's hidden presence paradoxically help to determine men's organization of the exchanges that exclude them. Exchanges of "head" payments reciprocally transfer to a woman's 'second husband' – the main beneficiary of her brother's mythic parricide – the task of supplying *replacement* "heads" that both rescue the Giant's children from his gaping maw and, in doing so, make good the sordid affair between primal Father and Son.

Unlike the Sister in men's myth or any woman, in men's view, the female inititate's or bride's real or close classificatory fathers and brothers are 'open for business': unlike a mother, men can be pursuaded to accept *substitutes* for a child and thus 'undo' its primordial death as menstrual blood. In the rites of exchange, the mother's husband offers her brother 'other meat' that is nearly as delicious as the baby Boy the Old Man killed in myth, replacements that will induce him (in the persons of his ritual counterparts) to let *his daughter's child go – no longer wish to devour it* – because the child, or rather the "head" payments that consistently replace it, no longer originate inside the father, are no longer parts of himself that he lost during *his daughter's* conception and forever wishes to recoup. With "head" payments – gifts of cooked marsupials or pork and other valuables like marsupial furs and Bird of Paradise plumages and, nowadays, PNG bank notes (all of which I compare to Freud's totem animal!) – as proper inducements, the mother's father and brother will let the child go so it can escape into the world outside the Mother/Sister/Daughter whose "house" Father no longer inhabits as his only place of residence.

Despite all the "heads" his ritual counterparts accept and eat, however, the Father/Moon's relentless monthly visits reveal that he still wants to repossess his every Daughter's every Child. Because of his rapacious greed, the Daughter's 'second husband' has to supply 'other meat' over and over again (especially at the conclusion of rites of passage) throughout a son's life and until the marriage of a daughter. The rules of sister exchange marriage help to level the playing field by creating *reciprocal* interest between brothers-in-law, sparing each one from having to plead in desperation like the trapped Boys in women's myth of the Home Invaders. By making each man the mother's brother of the other's children, the marriage rules give *two* Fathers, or rather their ritual counterparts, incentive to accept "head" payments in lieu of cursing the children and condemning them to death (See Chap. 2).

A Return Visit with the Boys Left at Home Alone

To 'undo motherhood,' and replace the mother with her brother as 'male mother' to her children, Gimi men do more than merely disparage everything female and exclude women as full partners with men in the rites of exchange. Men manufacture "head" payments as facsimiles of key episodes in women's myths and rites about the primal Father's murder and dismemberment – something men's own myths euphemize or avoid altogether. By circulating among themselves material objects that encapsulate episodes in women's myths, men subvert women's narratives, blame women entirely for the Father's murder and confiscate their children as the essential remedy women themselves 'refuse' to perform.

In women's myth of the Home Invaders, "the boys at home alone" offer the two Invaders each and every one of a marsupial's delectable limbs and organs as substitutes for their own (see Chap. 7, p. 177). The boys' offers of "head" payments leave the Invaders unimpressed, still angry and hungry for the boys themselves. But when a pair of brothers-in-law *reciprocally* recapitulate women's myth in the exchange of "head" payments, they compel the Invaders' living counterparts, the mother's father and brother, to accept replacements and spare the boys retroactively, as it were. Through the exchange of "head" payments, male affines follow women's mythic agenda in order to reverse or forestall the dénouement. Rather than lie in wait with his Wife to murder the two Invaders, the Husband's and Boys' Father's ritual counterparts come to terms with the Invaders' ritual heirs who are his wife's father and brother. The relationships altered by men's ritual appropriation of women's myths and corresponding 'adaptations' of their own Flute myth may be summarized as follows:

> *The Mother's Brother – Sister's Husband* During his own prehistory, as a small Boy drawn irresistably by the music of Flutes, the mother's brother went *back* inside his Sister/Mother to "eat the head" of their Father's penis, *unaware* that, as a small Boy crawling on all fours, he could *no longer* feed upon it as he had done during gestation. His re-entry into his Sister enraged their Father who ate him back up: the Old Man tossed a hot stone down his wide-open "first mouth" and turned him into dead meat. *In utero*, inside his Sister's "flute house," the mother's brother *became* what "came back to eat him," namely, the Giant's severed head, his Sister's "firstborn," the dead blood that leaks between her thighs and whose traces remain to this day inside his nose and penis requiring him to undergo regular purges in men's "secret" blood-letting rites.
>
> When the mother's brother "eats the head" of his sister's child as part of a public exchange with his sister's husband, he rids his body of her menstrual blood because the new food, supplied by her 'second husband' replaces what he ate inside his Sister/Mother during his own gestation – the "head"

of their Father's penis. According to the procreative/digestive mode of reproduction, the more "head" payments the mother's brother accepts, i.e., the more *substitutes* for his Sister's hairy maidenhead /menstrual blood/*own dead self* he consumes *in ritual*, the more he 'excretes' what he originally ate/ate him inside his Sister *in myth*. The more often a man "eats the head" of his sister's child during rites of exchange, the more he rids himself of the Father's blood he ate/became inside his Sister, and the closer he gets to becoming a man remade by other men in the world outside the First Woman's body.

Accepting "head" payments from his sister's 'second' husband, consuming *a substitute* for the "head" of his own Father's penis, compels him to 'let go' of the original and quit the place where he ate it – his Sister's body, his Father's "house." By "eating the head" of his sister's child in rites of exchange, the mother's brother eats a piece of a different Father, one who never inhabited his Sister and therefore has no wish to devour him. By "eating the head" of his sister's child – accepting 'other food' in place of *his* Father – the mother's brother, and the part of him who is still his sister's "firstborn," become the offspring of another Father, the father of his sister's second husband who fed him 'other meat.' After "eating the head of his sister's child," a man and his sister's child are 'no longer' severed pieces of their own Father and, therefore, no longer 'dead'.

When brothers-in-law exchange "head" payments, each man ingests substitute meat – the "head" of a *different* Father – and lets go of the "head" of his own Father, who is *himself*, the dead baby wrapped in bark cloth his Sister transported inside her net bag and presented to her 'second husband.' His sister's 'second husband' – the donor of "head" payments – ousts the "first husband" *and* his "firstborn," not by lying in wait to murder them together with his Wild Wife after a hunting expedition to kill marsupials in the forest, but rather by coming to terms inside the settlement with his wife's brother (heir to the second 'Home Invader'), providing him with 'other meat' that induces him to quit the premises of the Wife/Sister and 'rederives' her child from the donors of "head" payments.

The Sister/Mother/Wife "Head" payments which empty the mother's brother of his sister's menstrual blood and 'bring him back to life' likewise empty his sister of *him* – the dead issue of their Father, the Moon, her "firstborn"

> incarnated in her menstrual blood. The sister, too, is thus progressively purged of Moon's blood by the successive births of children on whose behalf her husband makes "head" payments to her father and brother. But the sister/wife's gradual 'purification' through the two men's continuing exchanges of "head" payments on behalf of each of her children is also the gradual cancellation of her motherhood and installation of her brother as 'male mother' to her children.

Because "head" payments have a mythic agenda, they are owed in perpetuity. The husband's debt to his wife's brother is virtually unamortizable because he has to *substantiate* the original contribution – the ejaculations, the 'lost heads' – that brought each child into being. "Heads" must be returned to the mythic impregnator-father/firstborn brother in the amount they were eaten by the "boys left home alone" – boys whom the husband now wishes to alienate from his wife's father and brother, two sadistic interlopers who keep coming back to "play around" with his boys. To possess the boys as his own, their mother's husband has to offer "head" payments to *match* the many acts of intercourse required to put a child inside his wife 'the first time' – while she herself was unborn and fed on the head of her father's penis – and deposit his own substance instead.

Children are made once *in utero* by the mother's father *as the mother's brother* and again *ex utero* between men of different patrilineages or clans who, having already exchanged sisters in marriage, continue to exchange "head" payments in order to alienate their sisters' children. Over time, and according to a procreative/digestive mode of reproduction, "head" payments establish the donor's parthenogenetic and incestuous tie to his own children. Men 'bypass' their wives/sisters in order retroactively to [re-]create children outside the mother's body as persons men can exchange in marriage, organize into warrior cohorts and manipulate in the wider society. Through the exchange of "head" payments, men produce sons and daughters who are *no longer* unseparate from their original Parent/s because their mothers' fathers and brothers have "eaten their heads" instead.

Gimi Men 'Package' Women's Narratives of Incest and Murder as Objects of Exchange

When the men of two Gimi patriclans or patrilineages exchange wives followed by lifetimes of reciprocally-rendered goods and services (including bamboo flutes revealed to sons in male initiation rites and "head" payments of whole cooked pigs and marsupials, maruspial furs, Bird of Paradise and parrot plumages and nowadays PNG bank notes), they exchange myths of origin in the attempt to supplant the incests – and implacable rage – into which each partner in the exchange was originally conceived: 'The saga packaged in the gift I offer you is *my* story. But when you eat/play/wear/consume/copulate with it you make my story part of you: since my story is no longer entirely mine, it is no longer incestuous and no longer the source of unending fury. When the mother's father and brother – living surrogates for the Giant Penis/Moon/primordial Father and his "firstborn" portrayed in women's myths and theatrical performances – accept the "head of the child," which is a replacement for the child's very life, they also separate *themselves* from their own mythic counterparts.

Gimi objects of exchange arrest the myths' main events and achieve the pivotal outcome by expelling the primal Father from Mother's body, a pair so perfectly combined they appear to be a single object. Ritual exchanges of 'replacement meat' cut the primal Fathers down to size and convert their "heads" into totemic feasts, converting myths of incest and cannibalism into a template for kinship, which is designed *first of all to divide* children from their mothers and allow them to engage in new kinds of non-dyadic relations.

In the exchange of sisters, a Gimi man gives away the part of the mythic Father he hated and killed and that *only his sister insists on keeping*, identifying with, and making a part of her body. And he receives a 'severed part of the Father' – that is, another man's sister – who looks very much like the one he "ate" and on whose account he acquired a beard, but who is *not her* and, therefore, he did not cause to menstruate and does not hate: 'The saga packaged in the sister I offer you is my crime; but when you marry her, you make her/my story part of you. When my story is no longer all mine, it is no longer a crime …' To resolve their own ambivance toward the primal father, Gimi men concoct a relentless slander against their sisters – identifying them entirely with the hated Father of myth – the parts of him that are cut-off, spoiled, disposable, and guilty, too, because Sisters were co-conspirators, motivated for reasons of their own to kill the Father who raped them.

As a bride, a Gimi woman serves as the moving vehicle of her brother's mythic guilt. Unlike her brother, a woman will never be able to divest herself of her participation in their father's demise because she will never be a *donor* of "head" payments. Women protest men's propaganda but are also complicit, accepting the underlying premise of exchange that women are to blame for their own exclusion: that if only a mother were somehow willing to let go of the piece of the Father she stole, the "head" she helped to sever, she could be a donor like a man.

Note

1. Because of their intimate connection, Gimi myths and rites are often discussed together. Mythic figures and artifacts are capitalized to distinguish them from their ritual counterparts. But pronouns that refer to mythic figures appear in lower case. Big Man and Big Woman, individuals recognized as important persons and leaders in the community, are also capitalized.

References

Bamberger, Joan. 1974. The Myth of Matriarchy: Why Men Rule in Primitive Society. In *Women, Culture and Society*, ed. M.Z. Rosaldo and Louise Lamphere. Stanford: Stanford University Press.

Frazer, Sir James George. 1911. *The Magic Art* (2 vols.) *The Golden Bough*. 3rd ed. Part 1. London.

———. 1963 [1922]. *The Golden Bough: A Study of Magic and Religion*. Abridged edition. New York: Macmillan.

Freeman, Derek. 1970. Totem and Taboo: A Reappraisal. In *Man and His Culture: Psychoanalytic Anthropology After Totem and Taboo*, ed. Werner Muensterberger. New York: Taplinger Publishing Co.

Freud. 1972 [1913]. *Totem and Taboo.* Trans. James Strachey [1950]. London: Routledge and Kegan Paul.

Gillison, Gillian. 2016. Whatever Happened to the Mother? A New Look at the Old Problem of the Mother's Brother in Three New Guinea Societies: Gimi, Daribi and Iatmul. *Oceania* 86 (I): 2–24.

Jones, Ernest. 1953. *The Life and Work of Sigmund Freud.* 3 vols. New York: Basic Books.

La Barre, Weston. 1958. The Influence of Freud on Anthropology. *The American Imago* 15 (3): 275–328.

Levi-Strauss, Claude. 1969 [1949]. *The Elementary Structures of Kinship.* Boston: Beacon Press.

The Oxford Universal Dictionary. 1955. Revised and edited by C.T. Onions. 3rd ed. Oxford: The Clarendon Press.

Spiro, Melford. 1968. Virgin Birth, Parthenogenesis, and Physiological Parernity. An Essay on Cultural Interpretation. *Man, n.s* 3: 242–261.

Tylor, Sir Edward Burnett. 1891[1871]. *Primitive Culture.* 3rd ed. 2 vols. London.

Wallace, Edwin R. 1980. The Primal Parricide. *Bulletin of the History of Medicine* 54: 153–165.

Note on Appendices I and II: Shared Features of the Myths of Gimi Women and Men

Gimi myths are collective inventions of sophisticated adults perfected over generations but they convey the attitude of an iconic *individual,* male or female, from whose perspective and understanding of their predicament at a particular moment in life everything in the myth unfolds. In the same way that a dream is the production of a single dreamer, everything in a Gimi myth—the characters, events, artifacts, and settings—reveals the world-view of a prototypical hero or heroine who is the counterpart of the person undergoing a "life crisis" or rite of passage: an adolescent enduring the ordeals of initiation, say, or a bride being sent off in marriage and arriving in the home of the groom.

Gimi myths occur in the primordial past. Like the myths and rites of many peoples, those of the Gimi conflate the beginning of time and the world with the conception and birth of the first human being, a convention that transforms a woman's body and the bloody terrain "between her thighs" into a mythic cosmos. The stories of both Gimi sexes use the imagery of domestic architecture, forest landscape, items of material culture and wilderness plants and creatures to enlarge to immense proportion an intrauterine world. Women's and men's houses, garden shelters, hunting lodges, net bags, digging sticks, bows and arrows, traps for marsupials and cassowaries, mountain ridges and mountain tops, valleys,

G. Gillison, *She Speaks Her Anger: Myths and Conversations of Gimi Women*, Culture, Mind, and Society, https://doi.org/10.1007/978-3-030-49352-3

rivers, caves, giant trees, liana vines, wild yams and other edible wildlife, decorative red flowers and leaves, tall grasses, turkey nests, birds, snakes, frogs, grubs and bats all portray or furnish the primordial universe inside and near the exit of the First Woman's body where the entire world as we know it began.

Gimi myths portray a primordial era that was bloody and traumatic both as illustration of things that no longer exist on account of the hero's or heroine's world-shattering deeds; and as object lesson or template for collective rites of passage that may achieve the same transformation today. Importantly, the villains and evil exploits pictured in Gimi myths do not describe actual Gimi women and men or their behaviours.

Appendix I
Gimi Women's Myths: Stories of the Wild Woman

hoEEbada or *hoEEEdada*, literally "thus speaks the wild woman" and "thus spoke the wild woman," introduce and conclude most women's narratives.

The following partial list of women's narratives is in alphabetical order. Page numbers indicate where the text of all or part of a myth or its discussion begins.

The Dream Man Chap. 4 p. 127, 131; Chap. 8 p. 248

Characters	Objects and Utensils	Setting
Marsupial Hunter-Husband	Marsupial Traps	High Forest
Wild-Woman Wife	Bloody Rope of Liana Vine	Treetop House
Dream Mother	Arrow's Butt End	Mountain Top
Dream Man	Burial Platform	Tall Tree
Dream Children		Base of the Tree
		Settlement

G. Gillison, *She Speaks Her Anger: Myths and Conversations of Gimi Women*, Culture, Mind, and Society, https://doi.org/10.1007/978-3-030-49352-3

'Eros and Psyche' Chap. 6 p. 213; Chap. 7 p. 229; Chap. 8 p. 248, 266

Characters	Objects and Utensils	Setting
Adolescent Heroine	Banana-Plant Omen	Forest Stream
Widowed Mother	Women's Mourning Regalia	Mountainous Forest
Infant Brother	Woman's Digging Stick	Mother's House
Ogre Father/Wild Man	Wild Man's Murdering Stick	Garden Shelter
Heroine's Little Dog	Broken Bamboo Water Container	
Husband-to-be	Hot Stone	
All Birds that Fly	Woman's Net Bag	
	Hollowed Tree Trunk used for Burial	

The Giant Penis Chap. 1 p. 12, 23; Chap. 3 p. 117; Chap. 4 p. 134, 145; Chap. 5 p. 170, 177; Chap. 6 p. 225; Chap. 7 p. 237

Characters	Objects and Utensils	Setting
Adolescent Heroine/First Woman	Rope of Liana Vine	Forest
Giant Penis/Marsupial Hunter	Giant Penis' Net Bag	Mother's House
Hunting Dog	Heroine's Axe or Knife	
Marsupial Prey		

The Home Invaders Chap. 5 p. 177; Chap. 8 p. 264, 268

Characters	Objects and Utensils	Setting
Two Boys Left at Home Alone	Marsupial Parts and Organs	Facing Mountainsides
Parents on Hunting Expedition	"Head" Payments	Mountain Valley
Pair of Giant Home Invaders	Woman's Digging Stick	Woman's House/ Mother's House
	Man's Bamboo Spear	

The Rape of the Python Chap. 4 p. 138, 153; Chap. 5 p. 169

Characters	Objects and Utensils	Setting
Cassowary Hunter	Cassowary Trap	Mountain Forest
Adolescent Heroine	Two Leaves of Wild Taro	Mother's House
Giant Cassowary	Man's Eyeballs in Bamboo Tube	Forest Hunting Lodge
Python	Python's Severed Head	
Cassowary Hunter's Wife		
Heroine's Mother's Brother		

The Torrent Lark Chap. 6 p. 201

Characters	Objects and Utensils	Setting
Beautiful Heroine	Pencil-thin Bamboo Tube	Forest Hunting Lodge
Heroine's Mother	Marsupial Feces	Forest Tree
Ring-Tailed Possum	Woman's Net Bag	Taro Garden
Ogre Father/Wild Man	Oven made from Hollowed Tree Stump	Lower Reaches of the River
Murdered Firstborn Child	Heated Stones for Oven	River's Source in High Mountains
Torrent Lark	Child's Body Decorations	
	Red Pandanus Oil	
	Red and Black Leaves	

The Wild Woman and the Phallic Tree Chap. 3 p. 83

Characters	Objects and Utensils	Setting
Tree-Man Trickster	Bow and Arrows	Forest
Wild Woman-Marsupial	Woman's Net Bag	Settlement
Firstborn Child	Wild Foods	Men's House

Appendix II Gimi Men's Myths: Stories of the First Woman or Two Women and a Hybrid Men's Tale

The following partial list of men's narratives is in alphabetical order. Page numbers indicate where the text of all or part of a myth or its discussion begins.

The Theft of the Flute Chap. 1 p. 9; Chap. 4 p. 133, 138, 152; Chap. 7 p. 237; Chap. 8 p. 247

Characters	Objects and Utensils	Setting
The First Woman Her Baby Brother	Sacred Bamboo Flute Plug of Female Pubic Hair	Doorway of Woman's House Interior of Woman's House

The Theft of the Flute Part II: The First Woman Closes Herself Up Again Chap. 6 p. 224; Chap. 7 p. 236; Chap. 8 p. 253

Characters	Objects and Utensils	Setting
Small Boy First Woman	Very Long Man's Net Bag Small Stone	Tree Top in High Forest Stagnant Pool

G. Gillison, *She Speaks Her Anger: Myths and Conversations of Gimi Women*, Culture, Mind, and Society, https://doi.org/10.1007/978-3-030-49352-3

A Boy Falls in Love with a Wild Woman Chap. 3 p. 115

Characters	Objects and Utensils	Setting
Beautiful Wild Woman Her "Innocent" Fiancé	Bamboo Tubes Stuffed with Wedding Pork Bride's Decorations	Interior of Woman's Pig House Men's House

Index[1]

[1] Note: Page numbers followed by 'n' refers to notes

G. Gillison, *She Speaks Her Anger: Myths and Conversations of Gimi Women*, Culture, Mind, and Society, https://doi.org/10.1007/978-3-030-49352-3

The manufacturer's authorised representative in the EU is Springer
Nature Customer Service Centre GmbH, Europaplatz 3, 69115 Heidelberg,
Germany. If you have any concerns regarding our products, please
contact ProductSafety@springernature.com

Printed and bound by CPI Group (UK) Ltd, Croydon, CR0 4YY
30/09/2026
02225646-0004